THE BEST OF
*Oriental*
COOKING

# THE BEST OF
# Oriental
# COOKING

General Editor: JENI WRIGHT

CHANCELLOR
PRESS

**General Editor:** Jeni Wright

**Authors:**

Sri Owen

Patricia Herbert

Ornsiri Selby-Lowndes

Gloria Zimmerman

Bach Ngo

Deh-ta Hsiung

Jan Leeming

**Consultants:**

Gloria Zimmerman

Kitty Sham

First published in 1980 by
Octopus Books Limited
part of Reed International Books
under the title *The Encyclopedia of Asian Cooking*

This abridged edition published in 1992 by
Chancellor Press
Michelin House
81 Fulham Road
London SW3 6RB

ISBN 1 85152 182 8

Printed in Hong Kong

# Contents

**Notes**

Standard spoon measurements are used in all recipes:
1 tablespoon = one 15 ml spoon
1 teaspoon = one 5 ml spoon
All spoon measures are level.

Fresh herbs are used unless otherwise stated. If unobtainable substitute a bouquet garni of the equivalent dried herbs, or use dried herbs instead but halve the quantities stated.

Quantities are given in both metric and imperial measures. For each recipe, follow either set of measures but not a mixture of both because they are not interchangeable.

# Malaysia, Singapore and Indonesia

## Sri Owen

This area comprises such a variety of races, landscapes and cultures that a common tradition of cooking and eating seems unlikely. However, there is a certain unity among the recipes of the region. Many dishes also show how this South-East Asian cuisine has been affected by travellers and immigrants; there is evidence of Indian, Chinese, Dutch and even British influence but all dishes are essentially local in origin and flavour; in the Indonesian word – asli.

There are other common factors. The Malay Peninsula and the islands share a tropical monsoon climate and large areas are extremely fertile. The South China Sea contains plenty of fish and seafood. It is also fairly easy to navigate, which has encouraged goods and culinary ideas, including spices and recipes, to circulate freely around the islands. The staple food is rice, which is harvested with appropriate ceremony from the flooded fields or sawah which make a mosaic of the contours of every hillside. Rice is the mainstay of South-East Asian cooking. Spices are also important, especially cumin, galingale, lemon grass, ginger, cloves, tamarind, cinnamon and turmeric. These are the spices which first brought Europeans to the Indies. Some of them have been familiar in the Western kitchens ever since, others remain exotic or little used, but today nearly all of them can be obtained here quite easily.

## Cooking Techniques and Utensils

Broadly speaking, people cook in the same way throughout the area. Charcoal stoves are used to provide the intense heat needed for rapid frying or grilling (broiling). Ovens are almost unknown, although for convenience some of the recipes in this chapter have been adapted for oven-cooking.

Meat and vegetables are usually cut into small pieces before cooking, either to enable them to be cooked very quickly, or to increase the absorption of spice and sauce flavourings during slow-simmering. Another reason for this is probably because in the past all solid food had to be eaten gracefully with the fingers of the right hand alone.

Almost all the essential utensils needed for Indonesian and Malaysian cooking can be found in any kitchen anywhere in the world. There are three special items, however, that are worth buying if Indonesian and Malaysian dishes are to be cooked often. The first is a wajan, a round-bottomed frying pan (skillet), which is more generally known by its Chinese name of wok. It sits comfortably on a charcoal stove or gas ring and is ideally shaped to spread heat evenly while stir-frying – which is as important in Indonesian cooking as it is in Chinese. It is also easy to clean. A wajan is however unsuitable for cooking on an electric hotplate so a wide flat-bottomed heavy pan, such as a Spanish paella dish, should be used instead.

The second item is a rice steamer, which is a very useful piece of equipment if rice is to be cooked often because it practically guarantees perfectly cooked rice every time. The rice is first boiled in an ordinary pan, then transferred to the steamer when it has absorbed all the water and cooked for a further 10 minutes. Leftover rice can be reheated in the steamer.

The third item, which is perhaps the most important is an ulek-ulek (pestle) and a cobek (mortar), made of wood or stone. Many of the recipes in this chapter require garlic, chillis and other ingredients to be pounded to a paste and, although this can be achieved in an electric blender, there is always the risk that the resulting paste will be too watery. A conventional mortar and pestle is satisfactory, but there is nothing quite like the genuine ulek-ulek and cobek.

## Ingredients

Apart from rice and spices, many other specialist ingredients are widely used throughout the Indonesian-Malaysian world. Coconut palms grow everywhere and the coconut flesh and oil are added to many meat dishes and sweets. Santen,* made by pressing the natural oils out of the flesh of the coconut and mixing them in water, is used constantly. It imparts a distinctive but delicate flavour to dishes, and acts as a thickening agent.

Another ingredient widely used is the pungent, dark-coloured shrimp paste which the Indonesians call terasi,* but which is elsewhere known as blacan or balachan. It has a very strong flavour and should therefore be used in tiny quantities.

Three different chillis give Indonesian food its hot reputation; lombok hijau* (green), lombok merah* (red) and lombok rawit.* Florists often sell lombok rawit as decorative houseplants, but they are, in fact, the hottest of all chillis. It is true that Indonesians are accustomed to eating hot peppers and find it hard to go without them, but this does not mean that all Indonesian food has to be hot; any of the recipes given here can equally well be made with little or no chilli. The quantity of chilli given is in any case small and will do no more than give the dish a slight kick, which should not offend even the most sensitive of mouths! It is the seeds of the chilli which are the hottest part, and these can be discarded, if preferred. Boiled rice or a few slices of raw cucumber will cool the mouth quickly if too much chilli has been eaten – far more quickly than water.

## Serving

Although an everyday family meal may simply consist of rice, served with one or two dishes of vegetables and possibly a little meat or fish, even the most minor social occasion in Indonesia, Malaysia or Singapore calls for plenty of good food. Any celebration is likely to be accompanied by an elaborate array of side dishes, relishes, sauces, *Serundeng* (see page 12), *Krupuk* (see page 12) and huge amounts of rice. The Dutch in the islands adapted the custom for their own use and called it *rijsttafel*, or rice table. There are no separate courses at a meal of this kind, but the sweet usually appears some time towards the end of the meal. All the main dishes are served together and everyone helps themselves.

Almost all the dishes in this chapter can be eaten simply with a fork. A spoon is useful when eating dishes which have a sauce, or large quantities of rice. Chopsticks are not used for Indonesian or Malaysian food; they are however, used for dishes of Chinese origin, such as the noodle dishes from Singapore.

China tea – without milk or sugar – is a good drink to take with food of this kind, although cold lager or a full-bodied wine may alternatively be served.

## Spelling and pronunciation

The Indonesian and Malaysian national languages are already very similar, and are likely to grow closer still. Within the last decade or so, the spelling of both languages has been standardized, and the revised spelling is used in this chapter. The letter *j* is now pronounced as *j* in the English word 'judge'. The letter *c* is pronounced as *ch* as in the English 'church'. *Cobek* is therefore pronounced *cho-bek* with a very short final *k*, and *kencur* is *k'n-choor*. Apart from these exceptions, Indonesian and Malaysian words can be pronounced roughly as they are spelt.

## Origins

Many of the dishes described in this chapter will be familiar to anyone who has been to South-East Asia, or has eaten his way through the menu in an Indonesian or Malaysian restaurant! Others I have recalled from my early life in Sumatra and Java, or have collected from members of my family and friends. The country of origin of a recipe is given wherever I have felt this was justified. If no origin is given, the dish belongs about equally to Singapore, Malaysia and Indonesia.

# Soto Ayam
## Spiced Chicken Soup

### METRIC/IMPERIAL

1.5 litres/2½ pints water
1 small chicken, quartered
4 Dublin Bay (king) prawns, cleaned, deveined and halved
salt
freshly ground black pepper
2 kemiri,* chopped
4 shallots, peeled and chopped
2 garlic cloves, peeled and chopped
1 teaspoon ground ginger
pinch of turmeric powder
pinch of chilli powder
vegetable oil for frying
1 tablespoon light soy sauce
75 g/3 oz bean sprouts, cleaned
1 potato, peeled and sliced into very thin rounds

**To garnish:**
few lemon slices
coriander leaves*

### AMERICAN

6¼ cups water
1 small chicken, quartered
4 jumbo shrimp, cleaned, deveined and halved
salt
freshly ground black pepper
2 kemiri,* chopped
4 shallots, peeled and chopped
2 garlic cloves, peeled and chopped
1 teaspoon ginger powder
pinch of turmeric powder
pinch of chili powder
vegetable oil for frying
1 tablespoon light soy sauce
1¼ cups bean sprouts, cleaned
1 potato, peeled and sliced into very thin rounds

**To garnish:**
few lemon slices
coriander leaves*

### METHOD

Bring the water to the boil in a large pan. Add the chicken, prawns (shrimp) and salt and pepper to taste, then cover and simmer for 40 minutes.

Strain and reserves 1.2 litres/2 pints/ 5 cups of the cooking liquid. Shred the meat from the chicken. Peel the prawns (shrimp) and discard the heads, then cut each one into 4 or 5 pieces.

Put the kemiri, shallots and garlic in a *cobek* or mortar and pound to a very smooth paste. Add the ginger, turmeric and chilli powder and mix well.

Heat 2 tablespoons oil in a wok or deep frying pan (deep-fat fryer), add the spice paste and fry for a few seconds. Stir in 300 ml/½ pint/1¼ cups of the reserved

cooking liquid, the soy sauce, chicken and prawns (shrimp). Simmer for 10 minutes, then add the remaining cooking liquid and simmer for a further 10 minutes. Add the bean sprouts, taste and adjust the seasoning, then continue cooking for 3 minutes.

Meanwhile, heat a little oil in a frying pan (skillet), add the potato slices and fry until crisp on both sides.

Divide the potato slices equally between 4 to 6 warmed soup bowls. Ladle the soup into the bowls, then garnish with the lemon slices and coriander. Serve hot.

SERVES 4 to 6

# Laksa Lemak
## Prawn (Shrimp) and Vermicelli Soup
### Singapore

This soup is traditionally garnished with *Sambal Bajak* (see page 34), but since this is hot and spicy, you may prefer to serve it in a separate bowl so that guests can help themselves according to taste.

### METRIC/IMPERIAL

600 ml/1 pint water
100 g/4 oz pork fillet or chicken breast meat
salt
freshly ground black pepper
175 g/6 oz laksa*
1½ tablespoons vegetable oil
5 shallots, peeled and finely sliced
4 spring onions, cut into 1 cm/½ inch lengths
2 garlic cloves, peeled and crushed
1 teaspoon ground ginger
1 teaspoon coriander powder
½ teaspoon turmeric powder
175 g/6 oz peeled frozen prawns
300 ml/½ pint thick santen*
2 blocks yellow tahu,* cut into thick strips
75 g/3 oz bean sprouts, cleaned
1-2 teaspoons Sambal Bajak (see page 34) to garnish (optional)

### AMERICAN

2½ cups water
¼ lb pork loin or chicken breast meat
salt
freshly ground black pepper
6 oz laksa*
1½ tablespoons vegetable oil
5 shallots, peeled and finely sliced
4 scallions, cut into ½ inch lengths
2 garlic cloves, peeled and crushed
1 teaspoon ginger powder
1 teaspoon coriander powder
½ teaspoon turmeric powder
1 cup shelled frozen shrimp
1¼ cups thick santen*
2 blocks yellow tahu,* cut into thick strips
2 cups bean sprouts, cleaned
1-2 teaspoons Sambal Bajak (see page 34) to garnish (optional)

### METHOD

Bring the water to the boil in a large pan. Add the pork or chicken and salt and pepper to taste. Cover and simmer for 40 minutes.

Strain and reserve the cooking liquid. Cut the meat into small cubes.

Put the laksa in a pan and cover with boiling water. Cover and leave to stand for 5 minutes. Drain thoroughly.

Heat the oil in a wok or deep frying pan (deep-fat fryer), add the shallots and fry for 1 minute, then add the spring onions (scallions), garlic and spices. Fry for 30 seconds, stirring constantly, then add the meat and prawns (shrimp). Stir-fry for 1 minute, then add the reserved cooking liquid and simmer for 25 minutes.

Add the laksa and santen and bring very slowly to the boil, stirring gently to prevent the santen from curdling. Add the tahu and bean sprouts and simmer for 5 to 8 minutes, stirring occasionally.

Pour into a warmed soup tureen, then garnish with the Sambal Bajak, if using. Serve hot.
SERVES 4 to 6

Soto Ayam; Laksa Lemak; Mie Bakso

# Mie Bakso

## Noodle Soup with Meatballs

Indonesia

*Bakso* or *baso*, is a cake or ball made of meat, fish, prawns (shrimp) or bean curd, or a combination of these. In this recipe, the *Bakso* is made with beef. If liked, you can make the meatballs in advance to avoid preparing and cooking just before serving.

### METRIC/IMPERIAL

**Soup:**

*100 g/4 oz egg noodles*
*salt*
*2 tablespoons vegetable oil*
*3 shallots, peeled and finely sliced*
*2 garlic cloves, peeled and finely sliced*
*pinch of ground ginger*
*1 tablespoon light soy sauce*
*1.5 litres/2½ pints beef stock*
*4 spring onions, cut into thin rounds*
*2 carrots, peeled and cut into thin rounds*
*50 g/2 oz mange tout peas, topped and tailed*
*3 Chinese cabbage leaves*
*freshly ground black pepper*

**Meatballs:**

*225 g/8 oz lean beef*
*3 tablespoons cornflour*
*1 egg white*
*2 teaspoons sea salt*

### AMERICAN

**Soup:**

*¼ lb egg noodles*
*salt*
*2 tablespoons vegetable oil*
*3 shallots, peeled and finely sliced*
*2 garlic cloves, peeled and finely sliced*
*pinch of ginger powder*
*1 tablespoon light soy sauce*
*6¼ cups beef stock*
*4 scallions, cut into thin rounds*
*2 carrots, peeled and cut into thin rounds*
*15–18 snow peas, topped and tailed*
*3 stalks bok choy*
*freshly ground black pepper*

**Meatballs:**

*½ lb lean beef*
*3 tablespoons cornstarch*
*1 egg white*
*2 teaspoons coarse salt*

### METHOD

Bring a large pan of water to the boil. Add the noodles and ½ teaspoon salt and boil for 5 minutes. Drain, rinse under cold running water, then drain and set aside.

To make the meatballs: Work the beef through the fine blade of a mincer (grinder) several times, then chop with a heavy knife until it is almost a paste. Transfer to a bowl, add the cornflour (cornstarch), egg white and salt and pepper to taste. Mix well, then shape into small balls, about the size of marbles. Drop them one by one into a bowl containing 600 ml/1 pint/2½ cups water and the coarse sea salt.

Bring 600 ml/1 pint/2½ cups water to the boil in a large pan. Add a pinch of salt, then remove the meatballs from the salted water with a slotted spoon and drop them one at a time into the boiling water. Boil for 5 to 8 minutes, then drain and set aside.

Just before serving, heat the oil in a large pan. Add the shallots and garlic and fry for 1 minute, stirring constantly. Add the ginger, soy sauce, stock, spring onions (scallions) and carrots. Simmer for 5 minutes, then add the mange tout (snow peas) and cabbage (bok choy). Taste and adjust the seasoning, then simmer for a further 3 to 4 minutes.

Add the noodles and meatballs, increase the heat and cook for a further 1 minute. Serve immediately.

SERVES 6 to 8

## Sayur Lodeh Jakarta
### Creamy Vegetable Soup

Indonesia

This soup becomes a rich vegetable stew if more vegetables are added and the quantity of water decreased. It can then be served as one of the side dishes at a *rijsttafel.**

#### METRIC/IMPERIAL

1 medium aubergine, sliced
salt
4 kemiri,* chopped
4 shallots, peeled and chopped
1 slice terasi*
2 garlic cloves, peeled and chopped
    (optional)
1 red or green chilli, chopped
    (optional)
25 g/1 oz ebi*
1.2 litres/2 pints water
2 teaspoons coriander powder
pinch of sereh powder*
2 daun jeruk purut*
½ teaspoon brown sugar
50 g/2 oz French or runner beans,
    topped, tailed and cut into
    2.5 cm/1 inch lengths
50 g/2 oz white cabbage or cauliflower
    florets, shredded or finely chopped
50 g/2 oz bamboo shoot, finely sliced
50 g/2 oz watercress, stalks discarded
    (optional)
50 g/2 oz creamed coconut*

#### AMERICAN

1 medium eggplant, sliced
salt
4 kemiri,* chopped
4 shallots, peeled and chopped
1 slice terasi*
2 garlic cloves, peeled and chopped
    (optional)
1 red or green chili, chopped
    (optional)
⅓ cup ebi*
5 cups water
2 teaspoons coriander powder
pinch of sereh powder*
2 daun jeruk purut*
½ teaspoon brown sugar
15 string beans, topped, tailed and cut
    into 1 inch lengths
¾ cup shredded cabbage or 1 large
    cauliflower floret, finely chopped
½ cup bamboo shoot, finely sliced
½ bunch watercress, stalks discarded
    (optional)
¼ cup thick santen*

#### METHOD

Sprinkle the aubergine (eggplant) slices with salt, leave to stand for 30 minutes, then rinse under cold running water.

Meanwhile, put the kemiri in a *cobek* or mortar with the shallots, terasi, garlic and chilli, if using. Pound to a very smooth paste, then transfer to a small pan. Add the ebi and 120 ml/4 fl oz/½ cup water and boil for 2 to 3 minutes.

Strain the liquid into a clean pan. Add the remaining water, coriander, sereh, daun jeruk purut and sugar. Bring to the boil, then add the vegetables except the watercress. Simmer for 5 minutes.

Add the watercress, if using, and the creamed coconut (santen) and simmer until the coconut has dissolved, stirring constantly. Taste and adjust the seasoning, then pour into a warmed soup tureen. Serve hot.
SERVES 4

## Soto Madura
### Spicy Beef Soup

Indonesia

This is a rich, meaty soup which can be served as a starter, or with other dishes as part of a main course.

#### METRIC/IMPERIAL

1.5 litres/2½ pints water
450 g/1 lb boned brisket of beef,
    trimmed
salt
freshly ground black pepper
75 g/3 oz peeled frozen prawns
4 kemiri*
6 shallots, peeled
3 garlic cloves, peeled
2 tablespoons corn oil
1 teaspoon ground ginger
1 teaspoon turmeric powder
½ teaspoon chilli powder (optional)
**To garnish:**
1 tablespoon chopped coriander
    leaves*
1 tablespoon chopped onion, fried
4 lemon slices

## AMERICAN

6¼ cups water
1 lb boneless brisket of beef, trimmed
salt
freshly ground black pepper
2 medium frozen shrimp, shelled
4 kemiri*
6 shallots, peeled
3 garlic cloves, peeled
2 tablespoons corn oil
1 teaspoon ginger powder
1 teaspoon turmeric powder
½ teaspoon chili powder (optional)
**To garnish:**
1 tablespoon chopped coriander
   leaves*
1 tablespoon chopped onion, fried
4 lemon slices

## METHOD

Bring the water to the boil in a large pan. Add the beef with a little salt and pepper, then cover and simmer for 40 minutes.

Strain and reserve the cooking liquid. Cut the beef into small cubes, discarding any fat and gristle.

Mince (grind) together the prawns (shrimp), kemiri, 3 shallots and the garlic. Heat 1 tablespoon of the oil in a pan, add the minced (ground) mixture and fry for 1 minute. Stir in the ginger, turmeric and half the reserved cooking liquid. Cover and simmer for 15 minutes.

Meanwhile, finely chop the remaining shallots. Heat the remaining oil in a large pan, add the shallots and fry until golden brown. Add the beef, 2 tablespoons of the reserved cooking liquid, a little salt and the chilli powder, if using. Cover and simmer for 2 minutes.

Strain the prawn (shrimp) and kemiri liquid into the beef mixture, then add the remaining reserved cooking liquid. Bring to the boil, then lower the heat, cover and simmer for 40 to 50 minutes.

Taste and adjust the seasoning, then pour into a warmed soup tureen. Garnish with the coriander, onion and lemon slices. Serve hot.
SERVES 6

# Rempeyek Kacang
## Savoury Peanut Brittle

These little peanut snacks are delicious at any time of day, but they go particularly well with pre-dinner drinks. It is advisable to use very fine rice powder* to make them – ordinary rice flour does not give the best results. If stored in an airtight container, Rempeyek will keep for at least two weeks.

## METRIC/IMPERIAL

2 kemiri,* chopped
1 garlic clove, peeled and chopped
2 teaspoons coriander powder
1 teaspoon salt
100 g/4 oz rice powder*
250 ml/8 fl oz water
175 g/6 oz whole shelled peanuts,
   halved if large
300 ml/½ pint vegetable oil

## AMERICAN

2 kemiri,* chopped
1 garlic clove, peeled and chopped
2 teaspoons coriander powder
1 teaspoon salt
1 cup rice powder*
1 cup water
1 cup whole shelled peanuts, halved if
   large
1¼ cups vegetable oil

## METHOD

Put the kemiri and garlic in a *cobek* or mortar and pound to a very smooth paste. Add the coriander and salt and stir well, then mix in the rice powder and water to make a smooth, liquid batter. Stir in the peanuts.

Heat 5 tablespoons of the oil in a non-stick frying pan (skillet). Place spoonfuls of the batter in the pan. Fry each one for 1 minute, then remove from the pan with a slotted spoon and drain on kitchen paper towels. Repeat until all the batter is used up, adding more oil to the pan as necessary. Stir the uncooked batter from time to time, adding a little water if it becomes dry while standing.

Pour the remaining oil into a wok or deep-fryer. Add any remaining oil from the pan and heat to 180°C/350°F. Add about 8 rempeyek to the pan and fry for about 1 minute until golden brown, turning them several times during frying. Drain and leave until cold before serving.
MAKES 50 to 55

# Pergedel Jagung
## Corn Fritters

These can be served as a snack on their own, or as part of a meal with other vegetables.

## METRIC/IMPERIAL

6 corn on the cob, or 1 × 326 g/11½ oz
   can sweetcorn, drained
75 g/3 oz peeled prawns (optional)
4 shallots, peeled
2 garlic cloves, peeled (optional)
1 red chilli, or ½ teaspoon chilli powder
1 teaspoon coriander powder
salt
1 large egg, beaten
vegetable oil for shallow-frying

## AMERICAN

6 corn on the cob, or 1 × 12 oz can corn
   kernels, drained
2 medium shrimp, shelled (optional)
4 shallots, peeled
2 garlic cloves, peeled (optional)
1 red chilli, or ½ teaspoon chili powder
1 teaspoon coriander powder
salt
1 large egg, beaten
vegetable oil for shallow-frying

## METHOD

If you are using corn on the cob, grate the kernels off the cobs. Mince (grind) the prawns (shrimp), shallots, garlic and red chilli, if using. Mix with the corn, then add the coriander and salt to taste. Add the egg and beat thoroughly.

Heat 5 tablespoons oil in a frying pan (skillet), then drop a heaped tablespoonful of the mixture into the pan. Flatten with a fork, then repeat this process until there are 5 or 6 fritters in the pan. Fry for about 2½ minutes, then turn over and cook the other side. Remove from the pan with a slotted spoon and drain on kitchen paper towels. Repeat until all the mixture is used, adding more oil to the pan as necessary. Serve hot or cold.
SERVES 4

Rempeyek Kacang

## Serundeng

### Roast Grated Coconut with Peanuts

Indonesia

Serundeng is an Indonesian side dish which has both a delicious taste and texture. Serve guests with a very small quantity as a little goes a long way. If stored in an airtight container, Serundeng will keep for several weeks.

#### METRIC/IMPERIAL

7 tablespoons vegetable oil
75 g/3 oz whole shelled peanuts
3 kemiri,* chopped
3 shallots, peeled and chopped
2 garlic cloves, peeled and chopped
1 slice terasi*
2 teaspoons coriander powder
pinch of cumin powder
pinch of laos powder*
175 g/6 oz desiccated coconut
1 teaspoon brown sugar
2 tablespoons tamarind water*
1 salam leaf*
salt
150 ml/¼ pint water

12

#### AMERICAN

7 tablespoons vegetable oil
½ cup whole shelled peanuts
3 kemiri,* chopped
3 shallots, peeled and chopped
2 garlic cloves, peeled and chopped
1 slice terasi*
2 teaspoons coriander powder
pinch of cumin powder
pinch of laos powder*
1 cup shredded coconut
1 teaspoon brown sugar
2 tablespoons tamarind water*
1 salam leaf*
salt
⅔ cup water

#### METHOD

Heat 5 tablespoons of the oil in a small frying pan (skillet), add the peanuts and fry for about 5 minutes until just brown, shaking the pan constantly. Remove from the pan and leave to cool. Put the kemiri, shallots, garlic and terasi in a *cobek* or mortar and pound to a smooth paste. Stir in the coriander, cumin and laos.

Heat the remaining oil in a wok or deep frying pan (deep-fat fryer). Add the spice paste and fry for 1 minute, stirring constantly. Stir in the coconut, then the sugar, tamarind water, salam leaf and salt to taste. Stir-fry for a few minutes, then add the water and simmer until the water is completely absorbed. Cover and cook gently for 50 minutes to 1 hour until golden brown, stirring frequently.

Add the peanuts, then remove from the heat and cool before serving.
SERVES 4
*Illustrated on page 62.*

## Krupuk

### Shrimp Crackers (Crisps)

Krupuk, or Krupuk Udang, are sold in Chinese shops and supermarkets, and sometimes in delicatessens. They are uncooked and look like thin, flat, pink tongues, about 10 cm/4 inches long. When cooked, they are light and crisp and similar to the shrimp slices served in Chinese restaurants, although they are larger, brighter pink and, in most people's opinion, have more flavour. The Chinese name for them is *kapeng*.

#### METHOD

To cook shrimp crackers: Heat about 300 ml/½ pint/1¼ cups vegetable oil in a wok or deep frying pan (deep-fat fryer). Drop the crackers into the pan, one at a time; they will immediately swell to several times their original size. Try to press the crackers reasonably flat with a fish slice during the first 1 to 2 seconds of frying, while they are still soft, otherwise they will buckle and twist and not cook properly. Fry for a few seconds further, then remove from the pan and drain off the excess oil. Leave to cool, then serve immediately, or store in an airtight container and eat within 24 hours. Serve with drinks or as part of a meal.

**Preparing Martabak**

# Martabak

## Stuffed Savoury Pancakes (Crêpes)

### Indonesia/Singapore

Strictly speaking, Martabak are not pancakes (crêpes) at all, but quick-fried envelopes of very thin dough, stuffed with minced (ground) meat and spices. They are very popular as snacks to be eaten in the open air; you can buy them at Indonesian market stalls or from street vendors who will make them especially for you, absolutely fresh and with ingredients to suite your taste.

If you are making them at home, they can accompany a meal, or be served with drinks beforehand, or they can be eaten as a snack at any time of day. Cold Martabak are excellent as part of a packed lunch.

This recipe gives instructions for making your own dough, but if preferred you can buy packets of *wun tun* (wonton skins)* from Chinese supermarkets and use them for the casing instead – 100 g/ 4 oz/¼ package is the right quantity for this amount of filling.

METRIC/IMPERIAL

**Dough:**
275 g/10 oz plain flour
salt
2 eggs
water to mix

**Filling:**
1 tablespoon olive oil
1–2 large onions, peeled and finely
    sliced
2 garlic cloves, peeled and crushed
1 teaspoon coriander powder
½ teaspoon cumin powder
½ teaspoon ground ginger
½ teaspoon chilli powder
½ teaspoon turmeric powder
1 teaspoon sereh powder*
salt
450 g/1 lb cooked lamb or beef,
    minced

**To finish:**
2–3 eggs, according to taste
50 g/2 oz spring onions, chopped
25 g/1 oz coriander leaves,* chopped
vegetable oil for shallow-frying

AMERICAN

**Dough:**
2½ cups all-purpose flour
salt
2 eggs
water to mix

**Filling:**
1 tablespoon olive oil
1–2 large onions, peeled and finely
    sliced
2 garlic cloves, peeled and crushed
1 teaspoon coriander powder
½ teaspoon cumin powder
½ teaspoon ginger powder
½ teaspoon chili powder
½ teaspoon turmeric powder
1 teaspoon sereh powder*
salt
1 lb cooked lamb or beef, ground

**To finish:**
2–3 eggs, according to taste
5 medium scallions, chopped
¾ cup chopped coriander leaves*
vegetable oil for shallow-frying

METHOD

To make the dough: Sift the flour and salt into a bowl, break in the eggs and mix well. Knead thoroughly, adding enough water to make a smooth, firm dough.

Roll the dough into a ball on a board lightly sprinkled with cornflour (cornstarch). Flatten the ball with a rolling pin and very carefully pull it out into the thinnest possible sheet. Cut the dough into 7.5 cm/3 inch squares, then chill in the refrigerator until required.

To make the filling: Heat the olive oil in a wok or deep frying pan (deep-fat fryer), add the onions and garlic and fry gently until soft. Add the spices and salt and fry for 30 seconds, stirring constantly. Add the meat, stir well and fry for 1 to 2 minutes, stirring constantly. Leave to cool for 30 minutes to 1 hour.

To finish: Break the eggs into the filling. Add the spring onions (scallions) and coriander and stir well. Place a few squares of dough on a board, lightly sprinkled with cornflour (cornstarch). Place a heaped tablespoon of filling on each square and put another square on top, then press the edges of the dough together firmly to seal.

Heat 5 tablespoons oil in a frying pan (skillet). When the oil is very hot, add the martabak and press down with a fish slice for a few seconds. Fry for about 1 minute on each side, turning them once only. Remove from the pan with a slotted spoon and drain on kitchen paper towels. Repeat with the remaining ingredients, adding more oil to the pan as required. Serve hot or cold, cut into triangles if preferred.

SERVES 6 to 8

**Note:** When cooked, the martabak should be flat and evenly filled with meat; the casing should be quite crisp around the edges, but soft in the centre.

## Rempah-Rempah

### Prawn (Shrimp) and Bean Sprout Fritters

Malaysia

These are normally made without prawns (shrimp), but their addition certainly makes the fritters tastier. Serve as a side dish with a rice meal, or as a snack with drinks.

#### METRIC/IMPERIAL

100 g/4 oz peeled prawns, chopped or minced
225 g/8 oz bean sprouts
4 spring onions, thinly sliced
2 shallots, peeled and finely sliced
2 garlic cloves, peeled and crushed
2 tablespoons chopped coriander leaves* (optional)
2 tablespoons coarsely grated white coconut flesh (optional)
50 g/2 oz rice flour* or self-raising flour
1 teaspoon baking powder
1 teaspoon coriander powder
1 teaspoon ground ginger
½ teaspoon chilli powder
3 tablespoons water
1 egg, beaten
salt
freshly ground black pepper
vegetable oil for deep-frying
lemon slices to garnish

#### AMERICAN

3 medium shrimp, shelled and chopped or ground
½ lb bean sprouts
4 scallions, thinly sliced
2 shallots, peeled and finely sliced
2 garlic cloves, peeled and crushed
2 tablespoons chopped coriander leaves* (optional)
2 tablespoons coarsely grated white coconut flesh (optional)
½ cup rice flour* or self-rising flour
1 teaspoon baking powder
1 teaspoon coriander powder
1 teaspoon ginger powder
½ teaspoon chili powder
3 tablespoons water
1 egg, beaten
salt
freshly ground black pepper
vegetable oil for deep-frying
lemon slices to garnish

#### METHOD

Put all the ingredients for the fritters in a bowl and mix well. Form the mixture into small balls about the size of walnuts, or flatten them into burger shapes.

Heat the oil in a wok or deep-fryer and fry the rempah-rempah for 1½ to 2 minutes until golden brown. Remove from the pan with a slotted spoon and drain on kitchen paper towels. Transfer to a serving dish and garnish with lemon slices. Serve hot or cold.

SERVES 6 to 8 as a side dish

## Sambal Goreng Udang dan Telur

### Prawns (Shrimp) and Eggs in Spicy Coconut Sauce

Indonesia

#### METRIC/IMPERIAL

575 g/1¼ lb Dublin Bay (king) prawns, peeled
5 kemiri,* chopped
3 red chillis, seeded and chopped, or 2 teaspoons sambal ulek*
1 small onion, peeled and chopped
2 garlic cloves, peeled and chopped
1 slice terasi*
2 teaspoons coriander powder
1 teaspoon ground ginger
½ teaspoon sereh powder*
pinch of laos powder*
2 tablespoons vegetable oil
3 ripe tomatoes, skinned, seeded and chopped
salt
1 salam leaf*
2 daun jeruk purut* (optional)
150 ml/¼ pint water
150 ml/¼ pint very thick santen*
4 hard-boiled eggs, shelled and halved
75 g/3 oz mange tout peas, topped and tailed

**To garnish:**
1 cooked, unpeeled Dublin Bay (king) prawn
lemon twist

### AMERICAN

1¼ lb jumbo shrimp, shelled
5 kemiri,* chopped
3 red chilis, seeded and chopped, or
    2 teaspoons sambal ulek*
1 small onion, peeled and chopped
2 garlic cloves, peeled and chopped
1 slice terasi*
2 teaspoons coriander powder
1 teaspoon ginger powder
½ teaspoon sereh powder*
pinch of laos powder*
2 tablespoons vegetable oil
3 ripe tomatoes, skinned, seeded
and chopped
salt
1 salam leaf*
2 daun jeruk purut* (optional)
⅔ cup water
⅔ cup very thick santen*
4 hard-cooked eggs, shelled and
    halved
22–25 snow peas, topped and tailed
**To garnish:**
1 cooked, unshelled jumbo shrimp
lemon twist

### METHOD

Discard the heads from the prawns (shrimp), then cut each one in half.

Put the kemiri, chillis or sambal ulek, onion, garlic and terasi in a *cobek* or mortar and pound to a very smooth paste. Add the spices and mix well.

Heat the oil in a pan, add the spice paste and fry for 1 minute, stirring constantly. Add the prawns (shrimp), tomatoes and salt to taste. Stir, then cover and simmer gently for 2 minutes.

Stir in the salam leaf, daun jeruk purut, if using, and water, then increase the heat and boil, uncovered, for 5 minutes.

Lower the heat, add the santen and eggs, and simmer for 8 minutes, stirring frequently. Add the mange tout (snow peas) and simmer for 3 minutes until they are quite tender and the sauce is thick. Taste and adjust the seasoning, then transfer to a serving dish and garnish with the prawn (shrimp) and lemon twist. Serve hot, with *Serundeng* (see page 12).
SERVES 4

# Gerinting Udang
## Spiced Fried Prawns (Shrimp)
### Singapore

This dish should really be made with freshly boiled prawns (shrimp), but it is still delicious with precooked prawns (shrimp) from the fishmonger. Serve as a side dish with rice, or as a snack.

### METRIC/IMPERIAL

450 g/1 lb peeled prawns
2 tablespoons tamarind water*
pinch of turmeric powder
½ teaspoon ground ginger
2 shallots, peeled and sliced
2 garlic cloves, peeled and crushed
1 tablespoon light soy sauce
150 ml/¼ pint vegetable oil
**Batter:**
7 tablespoons rice powder* or plain
    flour
5 tablespoons water
salt
freshly ground black pepper
1 small egg, beaten

### AMERICAN

1 lb shelled shrimp
2 tablespoons tamarind water*
pinch of turmeric powder
½ teaspoon ginger powder
2 shallots, peeled and sliced
2 garlic cloves, peeled and crushed
1 tablespoon light soy sauce
⅔ cup vegetable oil
**Batter:**
½ cup rice powder* or all-purpose
    flour
⅓ cup water
salt
freshly ground black pepper
1 small egg, beaten

### METHOD

Discard the heads from the prawns (shrimp), but leave on the tails. Place in a bowl with the tamarind water, turmeric, ginger, shallots, garlic and soy sauce. Stir well, then leave to marinate for at least 30 minutes.

Meanwhile, make the batter. Put the rice powder or flour in a bowl, then gradually stir in the water. Add salt and pepper to taste, then beat in the egg.

Drain the marinade from the prawns (shrimp) and shallots. Dip the prawns (shrimp) and shallots into the batter.

Heat the oil in a frying pan (skillet), then add the prawns (shrimp) and shallots, one at a time until the bottom of the pan is covered. Fry until golden brown and crisp, then turn over and fry the underside. Serve hot or cold.
SERVES 4

Gerinting Udang; Sambal Goreng
Udang dan Telur; Rempah-Rempah

# Bola-Bola Tahu
## Fried Prawn (Shrimp) and Bean Curd Balls
### Malaysia

#### METRIC/IMPERIAL

3 blocks tahu*
225 g/8 oz peeled prawns
2 garlic cloves, peeled and crushed
   (optional)
1 tablespoon cornflour
1 egg, beaten
salt
freshly ground black pepper
vegetable oil for deep-frying
**Sauce:**
3 large ripe tomatoes, chopped
2 shallots, peeled and sliced
1 garlic clove, peeled and crushed
150 ml/¼ pint water
1 tablespoon light soy sauce
2 teaspoons lemon juice or vinegar
2 teaspoons sugar
50 g/2 oz mange tout peas, topped and
   tailed (optional)
**To garnish:**
few fried onion rings
chopped coriander leaves*

#### AMERICAN

3 blocks tahu*
½ lb shelled shrimp
2 garlic cloves, peeled and crushed
   (optional)
1 tablespoon cornstarch
1 egg, beaten
salt
freshly ground black pepper
vegetable oil for deep-frying
**Sauce:**
3 large ripe tomatoes, chopped
2 shallots, peeled and sliced
1 garlic clove, peeled and crushed
⅔ cup water
1 tablespoon light soy sauce
2 teaspoons lemon juice or vinegar
2 teaspoons sugar
15–18 snow peas, topped and tailed
   (optional)
**To garnish:**
few fried onion rings
chopped coriander leaves*

#### METHOD

Put the tahu in a bowl and mash to a smooth paste. Mince (grind) the prawns (shrimp), then add to the tahu, together with the garlic if using, the cornflour (cornstarch), egg and salt and pepper to taste. Mix well, then form into small balls, about the size of walnuts.

Heat the oil in a wok or deep frying pan (deep-fat fryer) to 180°C/350°F. Add the prawn balls and deep-fry until golden brown. Remove from the pan with a slotted spoon and drain on kitchen paper towels.

Meanwhile, make the sauce. Put the tomatoes, shallots, garlic and water in a pan. Bring to the boil, and boil for 5 minutes. Strain the mixture into a clean pan, then add the remaining sauce ingredients, with salt and pepper to taste. Return to the heat and simmer for 3 minutes.

Add the prawn balls to the sauce and simmer for about 1 minute until heated through, stirring gently. Garnish with onion rings and coriander and serve immediately.
SERVES 4

# Kepiting Pedas
## Crab with Chilli
### Singapore

This dish is better without the soft meat from the shell of the crab, so reserve this for another dish if you are using whole crabs. In Singapore, the crab is eaten with the fingers, but a fork can be used to help extract the crabmeat from its shell.

#### METRIC/IMPERIAL

2 medium crabs, boiled, or 8 large
   crab claws
3 tablespoons vegetable oil
1 tablespoon lemon juice
salt
**Sauce:**
5 red chillis, seeded and chopped
1 onion, peeled and chopped
2 garlic cloves, peeled and chopped
1 teaspoon ground ginger
2 tablespoons vegetable oil
2 ripe tomatoes, skinned, seeded and
   chopped, or 2 teaspoons tomato
   purée
1 teaspoon sugar
1 tablespoon light soy sauce
3 tablespoons water

AMERICAN

2 medium crabs, boiled, or 8 large
   crab claws
3 tablespoons vegetable oil
1 tablespoon lemon juice
salt
**Sauce:**
5 red chilis, seeded and chopped
1 onion, peeled and chopped
2 garlic cloves, peeled and chopped
1 teaspoon ginger powder
2 tablespoons vegetable oil
2 ripe tomatoes, skinned, seeded and
   chopped, or 2 teaspoons tomato
   paste
1 teaspoon sugar
1 tablespoon light soy sauce
3 tablespoons water

METHOD

Clean the crabs thoroughly, then cut
each body into 2 or 4 pieces. Chop the
claws into 2 or 3 pieces if they are very
large.

Heat the oil in a frying pan (skillet), add
the crab pieces and fry for 5 minutes,
stirring constantly. Add the lemon juice
and salt to taste, then remove from the
heat and keep hot.

To make the sauce: Put the chillis,
onion and garlic in a *cobek* or mortar and
pound to a very smooth paste. Add the
ginger and stir well to mix.

Heat the oil in a wok or deep frying pan
(deep-fat fryer). Add the spice paste and
fry for 1 minute, stirring constantly. Add
the tomatoes, sugar and soy sauce and
stir-fry for 2 minutes, then stir in the
water. Add salt if necessary and simmer
for a further 1 minute.

Add the crab and stir to coat each
piece in the sauce. Serve hot.
SERVES 4

**Kepiting Pedas; Bola-Bola Tahu; Sambal
Sotong**

# Goreng Sotong
## Fried Squid
## Singapore

The secret of this dish is the marinade,
which needs at least 2 hours to be effect-
ive – preferably longer. Serve Goreng
Sotong as a side dish with rice, or by itself
as a starter.

METRIC/IMPERIAL

750 g/1½ lb squid
4 tablespoons tamarind water*
½ teaspoon turmeric powder
1 teaspoon ground ginger
pinch of chilli powder
4 shallots, peeled and sliced
3 garlic cloves, peeled and crushed
½ teaspoon salt
1 teaspoon dark soy sauce (optional)
vegetable oil for deep-frying

AMERICAN

1½ lb squid
¼ cup tamarind water*
½ teaspoon turmeric powder
1 teaspoon ginger powder
pinch of chili powder
4 shallots, peeled and sliced
3 garlic cloves, peeled and crushed
½ teaspoon salt
1 teaspoon dark soy sauce (optional)
vegetable oil for deep-frying

METHOD

Clean the squid, discarding the ink sac
and head. Chop the tentacles into
2.5 cm/1 inch lengths, then slice the
squid into thin rings.

Put the squid in a bowl with the remaining ingredients. Leave to marinate for at
least 2 hours.

Drain the squid and discard the marinade. Heat the oil in a wok or deep frying
pan (deep-fat fryer) to 180°C/350°F.
Deep-fry the squid for 5 to 6 minutes,
stirring occasionally. Remove from the
pan with a slotted spoon and drain on
kitchen paper towels. Serve hot.
SERVES 4

# Sambal Sotong
## Squid in Red Chilli Sauce
## Singapore

Despite its name, this is a main dish, not a
relish. The chillis give a good red colour,
but if you find they make it too hot, use
paprika or sweet red peppers instead.

METRIC/IMPERIAL

1 kg/2 lb squid
1 tablespoon white vinegar
750 ml/1¼ pints water
5 kemiri,* chopped
6 large red chillis, seeded and
   chopped
6 shallots, peeled and chopped
1 slice terasi* (optional)
2 teaspoons ground ginger
pinch of cumin powder
pinch of turmeric powder
pinch of sereh powder*
2 tablespoons vegetable oil
3 tablespoons tamarind water*
1 teaspoon brown sugar
salt

AMERICAN

2 lb squid
1 tablespoon white vinegar
3 cups water
5 kemiri,* chopped
6 large red chilis, seeded and
   chopped
6 shallots, peeled and chopped
1 slice terasi* (optional)
2 teaspoons ginger powder
pinch of cumin powder
pinch of turmeric powder
pinch of sereh powder*
2 tablespoons vegetable oil
3 tablespoons tamarind water*
1 teaspoon brown sugar
salt

METHOD

Clean the squid, discarding the ink sac
and head. Chop the tentacles into 1 cm/
½ inch lengths, then cut the squid into
small squares. Mix the vinegar with
600 ml/1 pint/2½ cups of the water, then use
to rinse the squid. Drain immediately.

Put the kemiri, chillis, shallots and
terasi in a *cobek* or mortar and pound to
a very smooth paste. Add the spices and
mix well.

Heat the oil in a pan, add the spice
paste and fry for 1 minute, stirring constantly. Add the squid and tamarind water
and fry for a further 3 minutes. Stir in the
sugar, salt and remaining water and
simmer for 5 to 6 minutes, stirring
frequently. Serve hot.
SERVES 4 to 6

## Pais Ikan
### Aromatic Baked Fish
Indonesia

There are variations of this dish all over Indonesia, and it has many different names. This version is from Sunda, in West Java. If preferred, the *santen** can be omitted, in which case the spice mixture (*bumbu**) should be scraped off the fish after baking, and the fish grilled (broiled) simply with oil or butter.

### METRIC/IMPERIAL

1.5 kg/3–3½ lb conger eel, or 2 large
   mackerel, cleaned
salt
10 shallots, peeled and finely sliced
4 garlic cloves, peeled and finely
   sliced
1 cm/½ inch piece of fresh root
   ginger,* peeled and cut into thin
   strips
4 sereh stalks,* cut into thin rounds or
   1½ teaspoons sereh powder*
3 green chillis, seeded and cut into
   thin rounds, or 1 teaspoon chilli
   powder
1½ teaspoons turmeric powder
3 daun jeruk purut*
3 tablespoons chopped mint
3 whole cloves
pinch of grated nutmeg
pinch of cumin powder
pinch of laos powder*
2 teaspoons brown sugar
1 tablespoon dark soy sauce
juice of 1 small lime or ½ lemon
300 ml/½ pint thick santen*
1 tablespoon olive oil or melted butter

### AMERICAN

3–3½ lb conger eel, or 2 large
   mackerel, cleaned
salt
10 shallots, peeled and finely sliced
4 garlic cloves, peeled and finely
   sliced
½ inch slice of fresh ginger root,*
   peeled and cut into thin strips
4 sereh stalks,* cut into thin rounds, or
   1½ teaspoons sereh powder*
3 green chilis, seeded and cut into thin
   rounds, or 1 teaspoon chili powder
1½ teaspoons turmeric powder
3 daun jeruk purut*
3 tablespoons chopped mint
3 whole cloves
pinch of grated nutmeg
pinch of cumin powder
pinch of laos powder*
2 teaspoons brown sugar
1 tablespoon dark soy sauce
juice of 1 small lime or ½ lemon
1¼ cups thick santen*
1 tablespoon olive oil or melted butter

### METHOD

If using conger eel, rub it with a little salt. Make several shallow cuts on each side, spacing them fairly wide apart. If using mackerel, discard the heads, score the skin and rub with a little salt.

Put the remaining ingredients, except the santen and oil or butter, in a bowl. Mix well, then rub all over the fish. Wrap in foil and cook in a preheated moderate oven (180°C/350°F, Gas Mark 4) for 45 minutes.

Remove the foil from the fish, then scrape the spice mixture into a small pan. Add the santen, bring to the boil, then lower the heat and simmer until the mixture is quite thick.

Put the fish in a shallow flameproof dish. Strain the spice and santen mixture over the top, then add the oil or butter. Grill (broil) under a preheated hot grill (broiler), turning the fish once, until golden brown on both sides. Serve hot or cold.
SERVES 4

## Pangek Ikan
### Spiced Poached Trout
Indonesia

This way of cooking river fish is well known in West Sumatra. *Paku** or *pakis* – young fern shoots (fiddleheads) – are used to add an alluring, quite indefinable flavour to the dish. In Indonesia, large quantities of fish are cooked at the same time in a deep earthenware pot and the fish are removed from the pot as and when required. It is possible to keep the dish in the refrigerator for as long as 1 week, but the whole dish must be reheated before serving – even if you wish to serve only part of it.

### METRIC/IMPERIAL

8 small river trout, cleaned
salt
8 kemiri,* chopped
4 red chillis, chopped, or 1 tablespoon
   sambal ulek*
8 shallots, peeled and chopped
4 garlic cloves, peeled and chopped
2 teaspoons ground ginger
1 teaspoon turmeric powder
½ teaspoon laos powder*
750 ml/1¼ pints very thick santen*
7 tablespoons tamarind water*
575 g/1¼ lb paku*
2 salam leaves*
40 g/1½ oz mint sprigs

### AMERICAN

8 small river trout, cleaned
salt
8 kemiri,* chopped
4 red chilis, chopped, or 1 tablespoon
   sambal ulek*
8 shallots, peeled and chopped
4 garlic cloves, peeled and chopped
2 teaspoons ginger powder
1 teaspoon turmeric powder
½ teaspoon laos powder*
3 cups very thick santen*
7 tablespoons tamarind water*
1¼ lb fiddlehead ferns*
2 salam leaves*
¾ cup mint sprigs

**Pangek Ikan; Pais Ikan**

## Ikan Bakar
### Grilled (Broiled) Fish
Indonesia

Both freshwater and sea fish can be cooked in this way – the secret is simply that the fish must be absolutely fresh. For optimum flavour, cook the fish over a charcoal barbecue.

METRIC/IMPERIAL

4 fresh rainbow trout or mackerel, cleaned
juice of 1 lime, or 1 tablespoon white vinegar
2 garlic cloves, peeled and crushed
salt
**Sauce:**
2 tomatoes, skinned
2 red chillis
1 slice terasi*
2 shallots, peeled
1 teaspoon dark soy sauce (optional)

AMERICAN

4 fresh rainbow trout or mackerel, cleaned
juice of 1 lime, or 1 tablespoon white vinegar
2 garlic cloves, peeled and crushed
salt
**Sauce:**
2 tomatoes, skinned
2 red chilis
1 slice terasi*
2 shallots, peeled
1 teaspoon dark soy sauce (optional)

METHOD

Make several shallow cuts on both sides of the fish, then rub with the lime juice or vinegar, the garlic and salt. Leave to stand for 30 minutes.

Grill (broil) the fish under a preheated hot grill (broiler) for 10 to 15 minutes until cooked through, turning them over once during cooking. Transfer to a baking (cookie) sheet lined with foil, arranging them side by side in a single layer.

To make the sauce: Put the tomatoes, chillis, terasi and shallots under the grill (broiler) for 2 minutes. Transfer the chillis, terasi and shallots to a cobek or mortar and pound to a paste.

Put the paste in a pan with the tomatoes and soy sauce, if using. Heat gently for 1 minute, breaking the tomatoes down with a wooden spoon.

Pour the sauce over the fish, then return to the hot grill (broiler) and grill (broil) for 1 minute. Serve immediately.
SERVES 4

METHOD

Rub the fish with salt. Put the kemiri, chillis, if using, shallots and garlic in a cobek or mortar and pound to a very smooth paste. Add the spices, santen, tamarind water and 1 teaspoon salt and mix well.

Line a flameproof casserole with a layer of paku (fiddleheads). Arrange a single layer of trout on top, then cover with more paku (fiddleheads). Repeat these layers until all the trout and paku (fiddleheads) have been used, finishing with a layer of paku (fiddleheads).

Arrange the salam leaves and mint on top, then pour over the spice mixture. Cover with a tight-fitting lid and simmer gently for 1 hour Serve hot.
SERVES 4

## Ayam Goreng Jawa
### Fried Chicken Javanese-style
Indonesia

Before frying chicken, the Javanese boil it first, either in water or *santen** with plenty of spices.

METRIC/IMPERIAL

1 chicken, weighing 1.5 kg/3–3½ lb, cut into serving pieces
5 shallots, peeled and finely sliced
4 garlic cloves, peeled and finely sliced
2 teaspoons coriander powder
½ teaspoon cumin powder
pinch of sereh powder*
pinch of laos powder*
pinch of grated nutmeg
1 small cinnamon stick (optional)
1 bay leaf
1 teaspoon brown sugar (optional)
salt
900 ml/1½ pints water
vegetable oil for deep-frying

AMERICAN

1 chicken, weighing 3–3½ lb, cut into serving pieces
5 shallots, peeled and finely sliced
4 garlic cloves, peeled and finely sliced
2 teaspoons coriander powder
½ teaspoon cumin powder
pinch of sereh powder*
pinch of laos powder*
pinch of grated nutmeg
1 small cinnamon stick (optional)
1 bay leaf
1 teaspoon brown sugar (optional)
salt
3¾ cups water
vegetable oil for deep-frying

METHOD

Put all the ingredients in a heavy pan. Bring to the boil, then lower the heat, cover and simmer for about 1 hour until the chicken is tender and almost all the stock has been absorbed, turning occasionally during cooking.

Remove the chicken from the pan and leave to cool. Heat the oil in a deep-fat fryer to 180°C/350°F. Add the chicken and deep-fry for about 10 minutes until golden brown. Remove from the pan with a slotted spoon and drain on kitchen paper towels. Serve hot.
SERVES 4

## Ayam Panggang Kecap
### Roast and Grilled (Broiled) Chicken with Soy Sauce
Malaysia

METRIC/IMPERIAL

1 chicken, weighing 1.5 kg/3–3½ lb
salt
2 tablespoons dark soy sauce
2 shallots, peeled and finely sliced
2 garlic cloves, peeled and crushed
½ teaspoon chilli powder
juice of ½ lemon or lime
2 teaspoons sesame seed oil*
oil for basting (optional)

AMERICAN

1 chicken, weighing 3–3½ lb
salt
2 tablespoons dark soy sauce
2 shallots, peeled and finely sliced
2 garlic cloves, peeled and crushed
½ teaspoon chili powder
juice of ½ lemon or lime
2 teaspoons sesame seed oil*
oil for basting (optional)

METHOD

Rub the chicken with salt, then roast in a preheated moderately hot oven (190°C/375°F, Gas Mark 5) for 45 minutes or until golden brown. Leave to cool.

Cut the chicken into 4 pieces, then beat the flesh to loosen the fibres. Mix together the remaining ingredients and rub over the chicken. Cover and leave to marinate for 1 hour, turning the chicken pieces occasionally.

Just before serving, reheat the chicken under the grill (broiler), brushing it first with oil, if liked. Serve hot.
SERVES 4

## Kelia Ayam
### Indonesian Chicken Curry
Indonesia

This dish can be cooked in advance and reheated just before serving.

METRIC/IMPERIAL

8 shallots, peeled and chopped
2 garlic cloves, peeled and chopped
4 kemiri,* chopped
2 tablespoons water
600 ml/1 pint thick santen*
1 teaspoon ground ginger
1 teaspoon chilli powder
1 teaspoon turmeric powder
1 salam leaf*
salt
1 chicken, weighing 1.5 kg/3–3½ lb, cut into serving pieces

AMERICAN

8 shallots, peeled and chopped
2 garlic cloves, peeled and chopped
4 kemiri,* chopped
2 tablespoons water
2½ cups thick santen*
1 teaspoon ginger powder
1 teaspoon chili powder
1 teaspoon turmeric powder
1 salam leaf*
salt
1 chicken, weighing 3–3½ lb, cut into serving pieces

METHOD

Place the shallots, garlic, kemiri and water in an electric blender and work until smooth. Transfer the liquid to a wok or deep frying pan (deep-fat fryer) and add the santen, spices, salam leaf, salt and chicken. Simmer for 1 to 1½ hours until the sauce is thick, then taste and add more salt if necessary. Serve hot.
SERVES 4

# Saté Ayam

## Chicken Saté

This is one of the easiest and most versatile kinds of saté* to prepare, as well as being one of the most popular. It is equally good served with rice, eaten as a snack with drinks, or as a starter with cucumber salad and *Lontong* (see page 33). Use bamboo skewers if available.

If you have a charcoal barbecue, use this for cooking saté*; otherwise an ordinary gas or electric stove will give satisfactory results.

Saté Ayam can either be served on its own or with the sauces for *Saté Kambing* (see page 26). If serving without sauce, double the marinade quantities and brush over the meat during grilling (broiling).

Ayam Goreng Jawa; Kelia Ayam; Ayam Panggang Kecap

METRIC/IMPERIAL

1 kg/2 lb boned chicken, skinned
  (preferably from breast and thigh)
1 tablespoon dark soy sauce
2 shallots, peeled and finely sliced
1 garlic clove, peeled and crushed
pinch of chilli powder (optional)
1 tablespoon lemon juice (optional)

AMERICAN

2 lb boned chicken, skinned
  (preferably from breast and thigh)
1 tablespoon dark soy sauce
2 shallots, peeled and finely sliced
1 garlic clove, peeled and crushed
pinch of chili powder (optional)
1 tablespoon lemon juice (optional)

METHOD

Cut the chicken into 2.5 cm/1 inch cubes. Mix together the remaining ingredients in a bowl. Add the chicken and stir to coat thoroughly, then cover and leave to marinate for at least 1 hour.

Divide the chicken pieces equally between 4 skewers and grill (broil) for 5 to 8 minutes, turning frequently. Serve hot.
SERVES 4
*Illustrated on page 33.*

21

# Babi Kecap
## Pork in Soy Sauce
Singapore

### METRIC/IMPERIAL

*4 garlic cloves, peeled*
*2 tablespoons plain flour*
*1 tablespoon light soy sauce*
*750 g/1½ lb pork fillet, cut into cubes*
*75 g/3 oz Chinese dried mushrooms,\**
*  soaked in warm water for 30*
*  minutes, or 100 g/4 oz button*
*  mushrooms, sliced*
*7 tablespoons vegetable oil or melted*
*  pork fat*
*1 teaspoon ground ginger*
*5 spring onions, thinly sliced*
*freshly ground black pepper*
*3 tablespoons dark soy sauce*
*1 teaspoon white vinegar*
*2 tablespoons rice wine\* (optional)*

### AMERICAN

*4 garlic cloves, peeled*
*2 tablespoons all-purpose flour*
*1 tablespoon light soy sauce*
*1½ lb pork loin, cut into cubes*
*3 oz Chinese dried mushrooms,\**
*  soaked in warm water for 30 minutes,*
*  or 1 cup sliced button mushrooms*
*7 tablespoons vegetable oil or melted*
*  pork fat*
*1 teaspoon ginger powder*
*5 scallions, thinly sliced*
*freshly ground black pepper*
*3 tablespoons dark soy sauce*
*1 teaspoon white vinegar*
*2 tablespoons rice wine\* (optional)*

### METHOD

Crush 2 garlic cloves and mix with the flour and light soy sauce. Coat the pork with this mixture, then leave to stand for at least 30 minutes. Meanwhile, drain the Chinese mushrooms, if used, then discard the hard stalks and cut each mushroom cap into 4 pieces.

Heat the oil or fat in a wok or deep frying pan (deep-fat fryer). Add half the meat and fry for 6 to 8 minutes until browned on all sides, turning frequently. Fry the remaining meat in the same way. Remove from the pan with a slotted spoon and drain on kitchen paper towels.

Pour off all but 2 to 3 tablespoons oil from the pan, then add the mushrooms and fry for 3 minutes. Slice the remaining garlic and add to the pan with the ginger. Stir, then add the meat, spring onions (scallions), pepper, soy sauce and vinegar. Stir-fry for 2 minutes, then add the rice wine, if using. Serve hot, with accompaniments, such as *Tumis Buncis* (see page 29).
SERVES 4

# Bebek Hijau
## Duck in Green Chilli Sauce
Indonesia

This dish improves if it is prepared 24 hours before required so the fat can be skimmed off. If a milder sauce is preferred, use green peppers instead of chillis.

### METRIC/IMPERIAL

*10 green chillis, seeded and chopped*
*8 kemiri,\* chopped*
*3 tablespoons coconut oil or peanut oil*
*10 shallots, peeled and finely sliced*
*4 garlic cloves, peeled and finely sliced*
*2 teaspoons ground ginger*
*½ teaspoon turmeric powder*
*pinch of laos powder\**
*1 sereh stalk,\* bruised, or ½ teaspoon*
*  sereh powder\**
*1 duck, weighing 1.75 kg/4–4¼ lb,*
*  skinned and cut into 8 pieces*
*3 tablespoons tamarind water\**
*1 daun kunyit\* (optional)*
*3 daun jeruk purut\* (optional)*
*1 bay leaf*
*salt*
*freshly ground black pepper*
*300 ml/½ pint water*
*2 tablespoons snipped chives*

### AMERICAN

*10 green chilis, seeded and chopped*
*8 kemiri,\* chopped*
*3 tablespoons coconut oil or peanut oil*
*10 shallots, peeled and finely sliced*
*4 garlic cloves, peeled and finely sliced*
*2 teaspoons ginger powder*
*½ teaspoon turmeric powder*
*pinch of laos powder\**
*1 sereh stalk,\* bruised or ½ teaspoon*
*  sereh powder\**
*1 duck, weighing 4–4¼ lb, skinned and*
*  cut into 8 pieces*
*3 tablespoons tamarind water\**
*1 daun kunyit\* (optional)*
*3 daun jeruk purut\* (optional)*
*1 bay leaf*
*salt*
*freshly ground black pepper*
*1¼ cups water*
*2 tablespoons snipped chives*

### METHOD

Put the chillis and kemiri in a *cobek* or mortar and pound to a very smooth paste.

Heat the oil in a pan, add the shallots and garlic and fry gently until lightly browned. Add the chilli and kemiri paste, stir-fry for 1 minute, then stir in the spices and sereh. Add the remaining ingredients, except the water and chives. Stir well, then cover and simmer gently for 45 minutes.

Remove the lid, increase the heat and boil for 10 minutes, stirring occasionally. Add the water and chives and cook for 15 minutes.

Discard the sereh stalk, if used, daun kunyit, daun jeruk purut and bay leaf. Correct the seasoning. Leave to cool, then chill in the refrigerator overnight.

Skim off the fat, reheat and serve hot with rice and accompaniments, such as *Oseng-Oseng Wortel dan Bloemkool* (see page 27).
SERVES 4

# Saté Babi
## Pork Saté
Singapore

There are endless *saté\** variations, using different meat and marinade ingredients.

Try to include a little fat with each piece of meat, or the *saté\** will become dry when cooked. For optimum flavour, use a charcoal barbecue for cooking. Use bamboo skewers if available.

### METRIC/IMPERIAL

*750 g/1½ lb pork fillet*
*2 tablespoons light soy sauce*
*2 garlic cloves, peeled and crushed*
*2 shallots, peeled and chopped*
*2 teaspoons five spice powder\**
*1 tablespoon clear honey*
*freshly ground black pepper*

### AMERICAN

*1½ lb pork loin*
*2 tablespoons light soy sauce*
*2 garlic cloves, peeled and crushed*
*2 shallots, peeled and chopped*
*2 teaspoons five spice powder\**
*1 tablespoon honey*
*freshly ground black pepper*

### METHOD

Cut the pork into 2.5 cm/1 inch cubes, then slice each cube in half so that the chunks of meat are quite thin. Put the pork in a bowl with the remaining ingredients and mix well. Leave to marinate for 2 to 3 hours.

Divide the pork pieces equally between 4 kebab skewers, then place the skewers on a wire rack. Put the rack on a baking (cookie) sheet and roast in a preheated moderate oven (180°C/350°F, Gas Mark 4) for 30 minutes. Transfer to a preheated hot grill (broiler) and grill (broil) for 5 to 8 minutes, turning frequently. Serve immediately.
SERVES 4
*Illustrated on page 33.*

**Bebek Hijau, served with Nasi Putih (see page 32) and Oseng-Oseng Wortel dan Bloemkool (see page 27); Babi Kecap, served with Tumis Buncis (see page 29)**

## Rendang Padang

### A Traditional Sumatran Beef Dish

Indonesia

#### METRIC/IMPERIAL

*1.5 kg/3–3½ lb brisket of beef or chuck
  steak, cut into large chunks*
*1.75 litres/3 pints thick santen\**
*10 shallots, peeled and sliced*
*4 garlic cloves, peeled and crushed*
*2 teaspoons ground ginger*
*4 teaspoons chilli powder, or 2
  tablespoons sambal ulek\**
*1 teaspoon laos powder\**
*1½ teaspoons turmeric powder*
*2 salam leaves\**
*1 daun kunyit\* (optional)*
*salt*

#### AMERICAN

*3–3½ lb brisket or chuck steak, cut into
  large chunks*
*7½ cups thick santen\**
*10 shallots, peeled and sliced*
*4 garlic cloves, peeled and crushed*
*2 teaspoons ginger powder*
*4 teaspoons chili powder, or 2
  tablespoons sambal ulek\**
*1 teaspoon laos powder\**
*1½ teaspoons turmeric powder*
*2 salam leaves\**
*1 daun kunyit\* (optional)*
*salt*

#### METHOD

Put all the ingredients in a wok or deep frying pan (deep-fat fryer). Simmer, uncovered, for 1 to 1½ hours or until the sauce becomes very thick, stirring occasionally.

Taste and add more salt if necessary, then simmer for a further 1½ hours until the meat becomes dark brown and has absorbed almost all the liquid in the pan, stirring frequently. Serve hot or cold, with rice and accompaniments, such as *Urap* (see page 29).

SERVES 8 to 10

## Dendeng Pedas

### Fried Steak with Chilli

Indonesia

In Indonesia, *dendeng* is thinly sliced meat which is coated in spices, then dried in the sun. The slices are coated with crushed red chillis, which make the meat *pedas* – chilli-hot. *Dendeng* should be tender and brittle as a result of its exposure to many hours of hot sunshine. It is sold ready to cook in packets in Indonesian shops and markets, but outside Indonesia a good Dendeng Pedas can be made using this recipe.

#### METRIC/IMPERIAL

*575 g/1¼ lb rump steak or topside of
  beef*
*2 teaspoons coriander powder*
*2 tablespoons tamarind water\**
*1 teaspoon brown sugar*
*salt*
*freshly ground black pepper*
*8 red chillis, seeded and chopped*
*4 shallots, peeled and chopped*
*2 garlic cloves, peeled and chopped*
*6 tablespoons vegetable oil*
*1 teaspoon lemon juice*

#### AMERICAN

*1¼ lb New York sirloin, hip or top
  round steak*
*2 teaspoons coriander powder*
*2 tablespoons tamarind water\**
*1 teaspoon brown sugar*
*salt*
*freshly ground black pepper*
*8 red chilis, seeded and chopped*
*4 shallots, peeled and chopped*
*2 garlic cloves, peeled and chopped*
*6 tablespoons vegetable oil*
*1 teaspoon lemon juice*

#### METHOD

Slice the meat thinly across the grain, then cut the slices into 5 cm/2 inch squares. Arrange in a single layer on a plate and sprinkle with the coriander, tamarind water, sugar, and salt and pepper to taste.

Press each piece with your hands so that the spices are thoroughly absorbed into the meat, then spread the slices out on the plate again. Leave to stand for 2 to 3 hours (in the sun if possible).

Put the chillis, shallots and garlic in a *cobek* or mortar and pound until broken, but not reduced to a paste.

Heat the oil in a heavy frying pan (skillet). Add the meat and fry until evenly browned and cooked through. Remove from the pan with a slotted spoon and keep hot.

Add the pounded mixture to the oil remaining in the pan and fry for 2 to 3 minutes, stirring constantly. Return the meat to the pan and stir to coat with the spice mixture. Add the lemon juice and salt to taste and stir well. Serve hot, with rice and accompaniments, such as *Acar Kuning* (see page 30), *Serundeng* (see page 12), *Krupuk* (see page 12) and *Sambal* (see page 35).

SERVES 4

*Illustrated on page 30.*

Kambing Korma (above); Rendang Padang, served with Urap (see page 29) and Nasi Putih (see page 32)

# Kambing Korma
## Lamb Curry
Malaysia

### METRIC/IMPERIAL

4 shallots, peeled
3 garlic cloves, peeled
6 kemiri*
450 ml/¾ pint thick santen*
575 g/1¼ lb boned leg of lamb, cut into small cubes
salt
3 tablespoons vegetable oil
1 small onion, peeled and finely sliced
1½ teaspoons coriander powder
½ teaspoon cumin powder
1 teaspoon ground ginger
pinch of laos powder*
4 whole cloves
2.5 cm/1 inch piece of cinnamon stick
3 whole cardamoms
1 salam leaf*
1 sereh stalk,* bruised, or ½ teaspoon sereh powder*
3 tablespoons tamarind water*
½ teaspoon freshly ground white pepper

### AMERICAN

4 shallots, peeled
3 garlic cloves, peeled
6 kemiri*
2 cups thick santen*
1¼ lb boneless leg of lamb, cut into small cubes
salt
3 tablespoons vegetable oil
1 small onion, peeled and finely sliced
1½ teaspoons coriander powder
½ teaspoon cumin powder
1 teaspoon ginger powder
pinch of laos powder*
4 whole cloves
1 inch piece of cinnamon stick
3 whole cardamoms
1 salam leaf*
1 sereh stalk,* bruised, or ½ teaspoon sereh powder*
3 tablespoons tamarind water*
½ teaspoon freshly ground white pepper

### METHOD

Mince (grind) the shallots, garlic and kemiri, then transfer to an electric blender, add 2 tablespoons santen and work to a smooth paste.

Put the mixture in a bowl, add the lamb and a little salt and mix well. Leave to marinate for 30 minutes.

Heat the oil in a pan, add the onion and fry gently until soft. Add the spices, salam leaf and sereh. Stir-fry for a few seconds, then add the meat and marinade and fry for 2 minutes. Add the tamarind water, salt and pepper. Cover and cook gently for 15 minutes, stirring every 5 minutes to prevent burning. Stir in the remaining santen and simmer for 40 minutes or until the meat is tender and the sauce is quite thick.

Discard the salam leaf, sereh stalk, if using, cloves, cinnamon stick and cardamoms. Taste and adjust the seasoning. Serve hot.
SERVES 4

# Gulé Kambing
## Aromatic Lamb Stew
Indonesia

This is a very liquid stew, which can be served as a spicy, meaty soup.

### METRIC/IMPERIAL

4 kemiri,* chopped
1 small onion, peeled and chopped
3 garlic cloves, peeled and chopped
2 teaspoons coriander powder
1 teaspoon ground ginger
½ teaspoon turmeric powder
pinch of white pepper
pinch of cayenne pepper
pinch of chilli powder
pinch of laos powder*
2 tablespoons vegetable oil
1 kg/2¼ lb boned leg or shoulder of
   lamb, cut into small cubes
1 teaspoon brown sugar
4 tablespoons tamarind water*
salt
1 sereh stalk,* bruised
1 small cinnamon stick
3 whole cloves
1 salam leaf*
450 ml/¾ pint water
450 ml/¾ pint thick santen*

### AMERICAN

4 kemiri,* chopped
1 small onion, peeled and chopped
3 garlic cloves, peeled and chopped
2 teaspoons coriander powder
1 teaspoon ginger powder
½ teaspoon turmeric powder
pinch of white pepper
pinch of cayenne pepper
pinch of chili powder
pinch of laos powder*
2 tablespoons vegetable oil
2–2¼ lb boneless leg or shoulder of
   lamb, cut into small cubes
1 teaspoon brown sugar
¼ cup tamarind water*
salt
1 sereh stalk,* bruised
1 small cinnamon stick
3 whole cloves
1 salam leaf*
2 cups water
2 cups thick santen*

### METHOD

Put the kemiri, onion and garlic in a cobek or mortar and pound to a very smooth paste. Add the spices and mix well.

Heat the oil in a pan, add the spice paste and fry for 1 minute, stirring constantly. Add the lamb and stir-fry for 1 to 2 minutes, then stir in the sugar, tamarind water and salt to taste. Cover and simmer for 4 minutes.

Add the remaining ingredients except the santen. Cover and simmer for a further 20 minutes. Add the santen and a little salt if necessary, then cover and simmer for 20 to 25 minutes, stirring occasionally.

Discard the sereh, cinnamon, cloves and salam leaf. Pour into a warmed soup tureen. Serve hot, with rice and accompaniments, such as Urap (see page 29).
SERVES 6 to 8

# Saté Kambing

## Lamb Saté

Make sure that some fat is included with the meat or the saté* will be dry. Use bamboo skewers if available.

As with all satés,* a charcoal barbecue should ideally be used for cooking, but an ordinary gas or electric stove will give satisfactory results.

This recipe gives two sauces – either or both may be served with saté* – in separate bowls so that guests can help themselves. Saté Kambing is particularly good served with Lontong (see page 33).

### METRIC/IMPERIAL

1 kg/2–2¼ lb boned leg or shoulder of
   lamb, cut into small cubes
**Marinade:**
2 tablespoons dark soy sauce
2 tablespoons tamarind water*
4 shallots, peeled and finely chopped
3 garlic cloves, peeled and crushed
½ teaspoon chilli powder
1 teaspoon ground ginger
½ teaspoon coriander powder
1 teaspoon brown sugar
**Peanut sauce:**
5 tablespoons vegetable oil
100 g/4 oz whole shelled peanuts
3 shallots, peeled and chopped
1 garlic clove, peeled and chopped
1 slice terasi*
pinch of chilli powder
salt
1 tablespoon peanut oil
300 ml/½ pint water
1 tablespoon tamarind water*
1 teaspoon brown sugar
**Chilli sauce:**
3 tablespoons dark soy sauce
2 shallots, peeled and finely sliced
1 garlic clove, peeled and crushed
1 green chilli, finely chopped, or
   ¼ teaspoon chilli powder
juice of ½ lemon
1 teaspoon olive oil (optional)
½ teaspoon brown sugar

### AMERICAN

2–2¼ lb boneless leg or shoulder of
   lamb, cut into small cubes
**Marinade:**
2 tablespoons dark soy sauce
2 tablespoons tamarind water*
4 shallots, peeled and finely chopped
3 garlic cloves, peeled and crushed
½ teaspoon chili powder
1 teaspoon ginger powder
½ teaspoon coriander powder
1 teaspoon brown sugar
**Peanut sauce:**
⅓ cup vegetable oil
½ cup whole shelled peanuts
3 shallots, peeled and chopped
1 garlic clove, peeled and chopped
1 slice terasi*
pinch of chili powder
salt
1 tablespoon peanut oil
1¼ cups water
1 tablespoon tamarind water*
1 teaspoon brown sugar
**Chili sauce:**
3 tablespoons dark soy sauce
2 shallots, peeled and finely sliced
1 garlic clove, peeled and crushed
1 green chili, finely chopped, or
   ¼ teaspoon chili powder
juice of ½ lemon
1 teaspoon olive oil (optional)
½ teaspoon brown sugar

### METHOD

Put the lamb in a bowl with the marinade ingredients. Stir well, then leave to marinate for at least 2 hours, preferably overnight.

Divide the lamb cubes equally between 6 skewers. Grill (broil) for 5 to 8 minutes, turning frequently.

To make the peanut sauce: Heat the vegetable oil in a small frying pan (skillet), add the peanuts and fry for about 5 minutes until just brown, shaking the pan constantly. Remove from the pan and leave to cool, then work to a powder in an electric grinder, or using a cobek or mortar.

Put the shallots, garlic and terasi in a cobek or mortar and pound to a very smooth paste. Add the chilli powder and salt to taste and mix well.

Heat the peanut oil in a pan, add the spice paste and fry gently for a few seconds, stirring constantly. Add the water and bring to the boil, then add the ground peanuts, tamarind water and sugar. Stir, then taste and add more salt if necessary. Continue boiling until the sauce is thick, stirring constantly.

To make the chilli sauce: Put all the ingredients in a bowl and mix well.
SERVES 6
Illustrated on page 33.

# Oseng-Oseng Wortel dan Bloemkool

## Sauté of Carrots and Cauliflower

Indonesia

### METRIC/IMPERIAL

*6 carrots, peeled and sliced diagonally*
*175 g/6 oz cauliflower florets*
*2 tablespoons vegetable oil or melted*
 *butter*
*1 garlic clove, peeled and crushed*
*1 slice terasi,\* crushed (optional)*
*4 spring onions, chopped into*
 *1 cm/½ inch lengths*
*1 tablespoon light soy sauce*
*pinch of chilli powder*
*pinch of ground ginger*
*salt*

### AMERICAN

*6 carrots, peeled and sliced diagonally*
*3 large cauliflower florets*
*2 tablespoons vegetable oil or melted*
 *butter*
*1 garlic clove, peeled and crushed*
*1 slice terasi,\* crushed (optional)*
*4 scallions, cut into ½ inch lengths*
*1 tablespoon light soy sauce*
*pinch of chili powder*
*pinch of ginger powder*
*salt*

### METHOD

Add the carrots and cauliflower to a pan of boiling water. Boil for 3 minutes, then drain.

Heat the oil or butter in a wok or deep frying pan (deep-fat fryer). Add the garlic and terasi and fry for a few seconds. Stir in the spring onions (scallions) and soy sauce, then add the carrots and cauliflower. Add the remaining ingredients and cook for 2 minutes, stirring constantly. Serve hot.

SERVES 4

*Illustrated on page 23.*

Gulé Kambing, served with Urap (see page 29) and Nasi Putih (see page 32)

27

# Gado-Gado

## Cooked Mixed Salad with Peanut Dressing

Like *saté*,* you will find Gado-Gado wherever you go in Malaysia, Singapore or Indonesia. For those who are fond of peanut sauce, this is an ideal dish to have by itself for a light lunch, or serve at any meal with rice and meat.

### METRIC/IMPERIAL

**Sauce:**
*vegetable oil for deep-frying*
*100 g/4 oz whole shelled peanuts*
*1 slice terasi**
*2 shallots, peeled and chopped*
*1 garlic clove, peeled and chopped (optional)*
*salt*
*½ teaspoon chilli powder or sambal ulek**
*½ teaspoon brown sugar*
*400 ml/14 fl oz water*
*25 g/1 oz creamed coconut* (optional)*
*1 tablespoon lemon juice*

**Salad:**
*75 g/3 oz cabbage, shredded*
*2 medium carrots, peeled and sliced*
*75 g/3 oz cauliflower florets*
*75 g/3 oz French or runner beans, topped, tailed and sliced*
*100 g/4 oz bean sprouts*
*1 medium potato, peeled and sliced*
*¼ cucumber, sliced*

**To garnish:**
*1–2 hard-boiled eggs, shelled and sliced*
*Krupuk, broken into pieces (see page 12)*
*few fried onion slices*
*1 lettuce*

### AMERICAN

**Sauce:**
*vegetable oil for deep-frying*
*½ cup whole shelled peanuts*
*1 slice terasi**
*2 shallots, peeled and chopped*
*1 garlic clove, peeled and chopped (optional)*
*salt*
*½ teaspoon chili powder or sambal ulek**
*½ teaspoon brown sugar*
*1¾ cups water*
*2 tablespoons thick santen* (optional)*
*1 tablespoon lemon juice*

**Salad:**
*1 cup shredded cabbage*
*2 medium carrots, peeled and sliced*
*2 small cauliflower florets*
*20–24 string beans, topped, tailed and sliced*
*2 cups bean sprouts*
*1 medium potato, peeled and sliced*
*¼ cucumber, sliced*

**To garnish:**
*1–2 hard-cooked eggs, shelled and sliced*
*Krupuk, broken into pieces (see page 12)*
*few fried onion slices*
*1 head of lettuce*

### METHOD

To make the sauce: Heat the oil in a wok or deep frying pan (deep-fat fryer) and fry the peanuts for 5 to 6 minutes. Drain thoroughly on kitchen paper towels. Allow to cool, then work to a fine powder in an electric grinder, or with a pestle and mortar.

Put the terasi, shallots and garlic, if using, in a *cobek* or mortar. Pound to a very smooth paste, then add a little salt. Heat 1 tablespoon vegetable oil in a pan, add the paste and fry for 1 minute, stirring constantly. Add the chilli powder or sambal ulek, sugar and water, bring to the boil, then add the ground peanuts. Stir well, then simmer until thick, stirring occasionally. Add the creamed coconut (santen) if using, and stir until dissolved. Keep hot.

28

Gado-Gado; Urap; Tumis Buncis

## Urap
### Cooked Salad with Coconut Dressing
Indonesia

For this salad, you can vary the combination of vegetables as you wish. Do not overcook them or they will lose their crispness and flavour.

METRIC/IMPERIAL

*1 slice terasi,\* grilled*
*2 garlic cloves, peeled and chopped*
*1 shallot, peeled and chopped*
*½ teaspoon chilli powder*
*1 teaspoon brown sugar*
*1 tablespoon tamarind water\**
*salt*
*100 g/4 oz grated white coconut flesh*
*100 g/4 oz cabbage, shredded*
*100 g/4 oz French or runner beans, topped and tailed*
*2 medium carrots, peeled and sliced*
*100 g/4 oz bean sprouts*
**To garnish:**
*few watercress sprigs*
*few cucumber slices*

AMERICAN

*1 slice terasi,\* broiled*
*2 garlic cloves, peeled and chopped*
*1 shallot, peeled and chopped*
*½ teaspoon chili powder*
*1 teaspoon brown sugar*
*1 tablespoon tamarind water\**
*salt*
*2 cups grated white coconut flesh*
*1½ cups shredded cabbage*
*¼ lb string beans, topped and tailed*
*2 medium carrots, peeled and sliced*
*2 cups bean sprouts*
**To garnish:**
*few watercress sprigs*
*few cucumber slices*

METHOD

Put the terasi, garlic and shallot in a *cobek* or mortar and pound to a very smooth paste. Add the chilli powder, sugar, tamarind water and salt and mix well. Combine with the coconut.

Cook the cabbage, beans, carrots and bean sprouts separately in boiling water for 3 to 5 minutes; they should still be crisp. Drain thoroughly.

Just before serving, toss the vegetables in the coconut mixture and pile the salad into a serving bowl. Garnish with watercress and cucumber slices. Serve warm.

SERVES 4

## Tumis Buncis
### Spiced French Beans
Indonesia

METRIC/IMPERIAL

*2 tablespoons vegetable oil*
*3 shallots, peeled and finely sliced*
*1 garlic clove, peeled and crushed (optional)*
*1 teaspoon ground ginger*
*pinch of chilli powder*
*pinch of grated nutmeg*
*450 g/1 lb French beans, topped, tailed and halved*
*salt*
*freshly ground black pepper*
*6 tablespoons strong-flavoured chicken stock, or 1 chicken stock cube dissolved in 6 tablespoons water*

AMERICAN

*2 tablespoons vegetable oil*
*3 shallots, peeled and finely sliced*
*1 garlic clove, peeled and crushed (optional)*
*1 teaspoon ginger powder*
*pinch of chili powder*
*pinch of grated nutmeg*
*1 lb string beans, topped, tailed and halved*
*salt*
*freshly ground black pepper*
*6 tablespoons strong-flavored chicken stock, or 1 chicken bouillon cube dissolved in 6 tablespoons water*

METHOD

Heat the oil in a pan, add the shallots and garlic and fry gently for 1 minute. Stir in the remaining ingredients, except the stock, and cook for 2 minutes.

Stir in the stock, cover and simmer gently for 5 minutes. Remove the lid and cook for a further 2 to 3 minutes, stirring constantly. Correct the seasoning. Serve hot.

SERVES 4

---

Cook the cabbage, carrots, cauliflower, beans, bean sprouts and potato separately in boiling water for 3 to 5 minutes; they should still be crisp. Drain thoroughly.

Arrange the vegetables on a large serving dish; place the cabbage on the dish first, then the carrots, cauliflower, beans and bean sprouts. Arrange the cucumber and potato slices around the edge, then garnish with the egg slices, krupuk and fried onion. Garnish the edge of the dish with lettuce leaves.

Stir the lemon juice into the sauce, then, either pour over the vegetables, or hand separately. Serve warm.

SERVES 6 to 8

# Acar Kuning
## Cooked Vegetable Salad

### METRIC/IMPERIAL

175 g/6 oz French beans, topped and
   tailed
175 g/6 oz carrots, peeled
1 cucumber, peeled
3 kemiri,* chopped
2 shallots, peeled and chopped
1 garlic clove, peeled and chopped
½ teaspoon turmeric powder
½ teaspoon ground ginger
pinch of chilli powder
2 tablespoons vegetable oil
10 pickling onions, peeled
4 tablespoons white vinegar
250 ml/8 fl oz water
175 g/6 oz cauliflower florets
1 red chilli, cored, seeded and cut into
   strips
1 green pepper, cored, seeded and
   cut into strips
2 teaspoons brown sugar
1 teaspoon dry mustard
salt

### AMERICAN

1½ cups string beans, topped and tailed
3 medium carrots, peeled
1 cucumber, peeled
3 kemiri,* chopped
2 shallots, peeled and chopped
1 garlic clove, peeled and chopped
½ teaspoon turmeric powder
½ teaspoon ginger powder
pinch of chili powder
2 tablespoons vegetable oil
10 small white onions, peeled
¼ cup white vinegar
1 cup water
3 large cauliflower florets
1 red chili, cored, seeded and cut into
   strips
1 green pepper, cored, seeded and
   cut into strips
2 teaspoons brown sugar
1 teaspoon dry mustard
salt

## METHOD

Cut each bean into 3 or 4 pieces, then cut the carrots into pieces about the same size. Cut the cucumber in half lengthways, scoop out the seeds and discard, then cut the flesh into pieces the same size as the carrots and beans.

Put the kemiri, shallots and garlic in a *cobek* or mortar and pound to a very smooth paste. Add the spices, and stir well.

Heat the oil in a pan, add the spice paste and fry for 1 minute, stirring constantly. Add the onions, stir-fry for a few seconds, then add the vinegar and a little of the water. Cover and cook for 2 minutes, then stir in the carrots and beans Cover and cook for 3 minutes, then add the cauliflower and peppers.

Add the remaining water, cover and cook for a further 6 minutes. Add the sugar, mustard and cucumber, stir, then cover and cook for 2 minutes. Remove the lid and cook for 2 to 3 minutes, stirring constantly. Taste and add salt if necessary. Serve hot or cold.
SERVES 4

# Gulai Pakis
## Vegetable Curry
Indonesia/Malaysia

*Paku,\** or *Pakis* – young fern shoots or fiddleheads – are gathered in the woods and along the river banks in Malaysia and Indonesia. If they are unobtainable, use curly kale instead.

### METRIC/IMPERIAL

6 kemiri,* chopped
6 shallots, peeled and chopped
3 garlic cloves, peeled and chopped
2 red chillis, seeded and chopped, or
  ½ teaspoon chilli powder
2 teaspoons ground ginger
1 teaspoon turmeric powder
pinch of laos powder*
pinch of sereh powder*
salt
450 ml/¾ pint thick santen*
4 tablespoons tamarind water,* or ½
  under-ripe mango, peeled and
  chopped
3 sprigs mint or sweet basil
575 g/1¼ lb paku* or young curly kale,
  cut into 5 cm/2 inch lengths

### AMERICAN

6 kemiri,* chopped
6 shallots, peeled and chopped
3 garlic cloves, peeled and chopped
2 red chilis, seeded and chopped, or
  ½ teaspoon chili powder
2 teaspoons ginger powder
1 teaspoon turmeric powder
pinch of laos powder*
pinch of sereh powder*
salt
2 cups thick santen*
¼ cup tamarind water,* or ½ under-ripe
  mango, peeled and chopped
3 sprigs mint or sweet basil
1¼ lb fiddlehead ferns* or young kale,
  cut into 2 inch lengths

### METHOD

Put the kemiri, shallots, garlic and chillis, if using, in a *cobek* or mortar and pound to a very smooth paste. Add the spices, including the chilli powder if using, salt, santen, tamarind water or mango, and mint or basil; mix well.

Transfer this mixture to a pan, bring to the boil and boil for 5 minutes. Add the paku or kale, cover and simmer for 10 to 15 minutes. Remove the lid, increase the heat and boil to reduce the sauce. Taste and add more salt if necessary. Serve hot.
SERVES 4

**Dendang Pedas (see page 24), served with Krupuk (see page 12), Serundeng (see page 12), Sambal (see page 35) and Acar Kuning (see page 30)**

# Sayur Lemak
## Vegetable Stew
Malaysia

### METRIC/IMPERIAL

½ small marrow, peeled
2 medium potatoes, peeled and
  quartered
3 shallots, peeled and thinly sliced
1 garlic clove, peeled and thinly sliced
1 green chilli, seeded and thinly sliced
7 tablespoons water
1 teaspoon turmeric powder
1 teaspoon ground ginger
1 sereh stalk,* bruised
salt
450 ml/¾ pint beef or chicken stock
100 g/4 oz cabbage, coarsely shredded
50 g/2 oz creamed coconut*

### AMERICAN

½ small summer squash, peeled
2 medium potatoes, peeled and
  quartered
3 shallots, peeled and thinly sliced
1 garlic clove, peeled and thinly sliced
1 green chili, seeded and thinly sliced
7 tablespoons water
1 teaspoon turmeric powder
1 teaspoon ginger powder
1 sereh stalk,* bruised
salt
2 cups beef or chicken stock
1½ cups coarsely shredded cabbage
¼ cup thick santen*

### METHOD

Cut the marrow (squash) into chunks about the same size as the potato quarters, discarding the seeds.

Put the shallots in a pan with the garlic, chilli, water, turmeric, ginger, sereh and a little salt. Bring to the boil and boil for 2 minutes, then add the potatoes and half the stock.

Cover and simmer for 4 minutes, then add the cabbage, marrow (squash) and remaining stock. Simmer for 6 minutes, then add the creamed coconut (santen) and stir until dissolved. Taste and adjust the seasoning. Serve hot.
SERVES 4

# Nasi Putih
## Boiled White Rice

For cooking rice, choose a saucepan with a thick, heavy base. During the final stage of cooking, a thin layer of rice will stick to the bottom of the pan, unless you invest in a rice steamer.

A rice steamer is simply a pan with holes in it, which is placed inside a pan of boiling water. The rice is first boiled in an ordinary pan as described below, then transferred to the steamer, when it has absorbed all the water. Leftover rice can be kept in a steamer for up to 24 hours after boiling, then reheated by gentle steaming.

### METRIC/IMPERIAL

*350 g/12 oz long-grain rice*
*600 ml/1 pint water*

### AMERICAN

*1½ cups long-grain rice*
*2½ cups water*

### METHOD

Wash the rice thoroughly under cold running water. Drain, then place in a pan with the water; do not add salt. Bring to the boil, stirring once or twice, then lower the heat and simmer, uncovered, until all the water has been absorbed into the rice. Stir once, then lower the heat and cover the pan with a tight-fitting lid – it should be as near airtight as possible. Cook very gently for 10 minutes. Serve hot.

SERVES 4 to 6

# Nasi Goreng
## Fried Rice

The ingredients in this basic recipe can be varied according to taste and availability. Fried rice may be served as an alternative to *Nasi Putih*, or as a satisfying meal in itself – if suitably garnished. It is usually eaten with meat or fish and vegetables and is particularly popular served with baked or grilled (broiled) fish, or any kind of *saté**

The chillis or chilli powder in this recipe give the rice a good red colour, but they do make it hot – substitute paprika if you prefer milder rice.

On a restaurant menu, *Nasi Goreng Istimewa* usually indicates that the rice is well-garnished and topped with a fried egg.

### METRIC/IMPERIAL

*275 g/10 oz long-grain rice*
*450 ml/¾ pint water*
*2 tablespoons vegetable oil, clarified butter or pork fat*
*4 shallots, peeled and thinly sliced*
*2 red chillis, seeded and thinly sliced, or 2 teaspoons sambal ulek**
*50 g/2 oz pork, beef or bacon, chopped*
*1 tablespoon light soy sauce*
*1 teaspoon tomato ketchup or tomato purée (optional)*
*salt*

**To garnish:**
*few fried onion slices*
*1 plain omelet made with 1 egg, cut into strips*
*few coriander leaves* or parsley sprigs*
*few cucumber slices*

### AMERICAN

*1¼ cups long-grain rice*
*2 cups water*
*2 tablespoons vegetable oil, clarified butter or pork fat*
*4 shallots, peeled and thinly sliced*
*2 red chilis, seeded and thinly sliced, or 2 teaspoons sambal ulek**
*¼ cup chopped pork, beef or bacon, firmly packed*
*1 tablespoon light soy sauce*
*1 teaspoon tomato ketchup or tomato paste (optional)*
*salt*

**To garnish:**
*few fried onion slices*
*1 plain omelet, made with 1 egg, cut into strips*
*few coriander leaves* or parsley sprigs*
*few cucumber slices*

### METHOD

At least 2 hours before the dish is required, wash the rice thoroughly, then cook in the water as for *Nasi Putih*.

Heat the oil in a wok or deep frying pan (deep-fat fryer), add the shallots and chillis, if using, and fry for 1 to 2 minutes. Add the meat or bacon and fry for 3 minutes, stirring constantly, then add the rice, soy sauce, tomato ketchup or purée (paste) and sambal ulek, if using. Fry, stirring, for 5 to 8 minutes, then taste and add salt if necessary.

Transfer to a warmed serving dish and garnish with the onion, omelet, coriander or parsley and cucumber. Serve immediately.

SERVES 4

# Nasi Kuning
## Savoury Yellow Rice

This is a brightly coloured dish which is often served at feasts and celebrations. It can be served simply as an alternative to *Nasi Putih*, or garnished with the same ingredients as *Nasi Goreng*.

### METRIC/IMPERIAL

*350 g/12 oz long-grain rice*
*2 tablespoons vegetable oil or clarified butter*
*1 teaspoon turmeric powder*
*600 ml/1 pint chicken stock*
*1 teaspoon coriander powder*
*½ teaspoon cumin powder*
*1 cinnamon stick*
*1 whole clove*
*1 salam leaf**

### AMERICAN

*1½ cups long-grain rice*
*2 tablespoons vegetable oil or clarified butter*
*1 teaspoon turmeric powder*
*2½ cups chicken stock*
*1 teaspoon coriander powder*
*½ teaspoon cumin powder*
*1 cinnamon stick*
*1 whole clove*
*1 salam leaf**

### METHOD

Soak the rice in cold water for 1 hour, wash thoroughly under cold running water, then drain.

Heat the oil or butter in a pan, add the rice and fry for 2 minutes. Stir in the turmeric and fry for 2 minutes, then add the remaining ingredients and boil until the rice has absorbed all the liquid. Continue cooking for 10 minutes as for *Nasi Putih*, either in a rice steamer or pan with a tight-fitting lid. Serve hot.

SERVES 4 to 6

# Nasi Lemak
## White Rice in Santen

In Indonesia this kind of rice is called *Nasi Uduk* or *Nasi Gurih*.

### METRIC/IMPERIAL

*350 g/12 oz long-grain rice*
*600 ml/1 pint santen**
*½ teaspoon salt*

### AMERICAN

*1½ cups long-grain rice*
*2½ cups santen**
*½ teaspoon salt*

**Saté Ayam (see page 21); Saté Babi (see page 22); Saté Kambing (see page 26); served with Lontong**

## METHOD

Wash and cook the rice as for *Nasi Putih*, boiling it with the santen and salt instead of the water; stir several times during boiling. When all the santen has been absorbed by the rice, continue cooking for 10 minutes as for *Nasi Putih*, either in a rice steamer or pan with a tight-fitting lid. Serve hot.

SERVES 4 to 6

# Lontong

## Compressed Boiled Rice

### Indonesia

Traditionally, people in Java eat lontong as part of their celebration of the Muslim New Year; but it is a popular way of cooking rice at any time all over Indonesia.

The grains of rice are compressed by prolonged boiling inside a casing or packet. In the tropics, this casing is usually a banana leaf; another variation, called *ketupat*, is made in a similar way in a casing woven from palm fronds.

Plastic freeze-and-boil bags make a perfectly satisfactory substitute, or boil-in-the-bag rice can be used with equally good results. Lontong must be served cold, therefore the cooking needs to begin at least 8 hours before the meal is to be eaten.

## METRIC/IMPERIAL

*350 g/12 oz long-grain rice, or
3 × 100 g/4 oz packets boil-in-the-bag rice
water
pinch of salt*

## AMERICAN

*1½ cups long-grain rice
water
pinch of salt*

## METHOD

If using long-grain rice, divide the rice equally between 3 freeze-and-boil bags (approx 20 cm/8 inches square). Close the bags by sewing a seam 14 cm/5½ inches from the bottom to make rectangular packets, each about one third full of rice. Pierce a few very small holes in each bag.

Put the bags of rice into a large saucepan of boiling water, making sure that the rice is completely submerged. Add the salt and simmer for 1¼ hours, topping up with more boiling water as necessary to ensure that the rice is always covered. The rice is ready when compressed into a firm mass. Remove from the pan and leave to cool for at least 6 hours. Strip off the bags and slice the lontong into chunks. Serve cold.

SERVES 4 to 6

# Sambal Bajak

## Hot Relish

Indonesia

This sambal will keep for a long time, and is one of the most popular of the hot relishes.

### METRIC/IMPERIAL

20 red chillis, seeded and chopped
10 shallots, peeled and chopped
2 garlic cloves, peeled and chopped
5 kemiri,* chopped
1 slice terasi*
2 tablespoons vegetable oil
1 teaspoon ground ginger
1 teaspoon brown sugar
3 tablespoons tamarind water*
salt
150 ml/¼ pint thick santen*

### AMERICAN

20 red chilis, seeded and chopped
10 shallots, peeled and chopped
2 garlic cloves, peeled and chopped
5 kemiri,* chopped
1 slice terasi*
2 tablespoons vegetable oil
1 teaspoon ginger powder
1 teaspoon brown sugar
3 tablespoons tamarind water*
salt
⅔ cup thick santen*

### METHOD

Put the chillis, shallots, garlic, kemiri and terasi in a *cobek* or mortar and pound to a very smooth paste.

Heat the oil in a pan, add the paste and fry for 2 minutes. Add the ginger, sugar, tamarind water and salt to taste, stir well, then add the santen. Simmer for about 15 minutes until the sambal is thick and oily, stirring occasionally. Stir-fry for a further 2 to 3 minutes, then serve hot or cold.
SERVES 4

# Sambal Kelapa
## Coconut Relish

This sambal should be eaten on the day it is made.

### METRIC/IMPERIAL

*1 slice terasi,\* fried or grilled*
*2 garlic cloves, peeled and chopped*
*3–5 lombok rawit,\* chopped*
*1 small piece gula Jawa\**
*1 tablespoon tamarind water\**
*7 tablespoons freshly grated white coconut flesh*
*salt*

### AMERICAN

*1 slice terasi,\* fried or broiled*
*2 garlic cloves, peeled and chopped*
*3–5 lombok rawit,\* chopped*
*1 small piece gula Jawa\**
*1 tablespoon tamarind water\**
*7 tablespoons freshly grated white coconut flesh*
*salt*

### METHOD

Put the terasi, garlic, lombok rawit and gula Jawa in a *cobek* or mortar and pound to a very smooth paste. Add the remaining ingredients, with salt to taste, and mix well. Serve cold.
SERVES 4

# Sambal Terasi or Blacan
## Hot Relish

Indonesia/Malaysia

This sambal should be eaten on the day it is made.

### METRIC/IMPERIAL

*6–8 green or red chillis*
*1 shallot, peeled and chopped*
*1 garlic clove, peeled and chopped*
*1 slice terasi,\* grilled*
*½ teaspoon brown sugar*
*2 teaspoons lemon juice*
*salt*

### AMERICAN

*6–8 green or red chilis*
*1 shallot, peeled and chopped*
*1 garlic clove, peeled and chopped*
*1 slice terasi,\* broiled*
*½ teaspoon brown sugar*
*2 teaspoons lemon juice*
*salt*

### METHOD

Cook the chillis in boiling water for 6 to 8 minutes, then drain. Discard the seeds and chop the flesh, then pound in a *cobek* or mortar, with the shallot, garlic and terasi. Add the sugar, lemon juice and salt to taste. Mix well. Serve cold.
SERVES 4

# Pisang Goreng
## Fried Bananas

Do not use over-ripe bananas for this accompaniment dish.

### METRIC/IMPERIAL

*75 g/3 oz rice flour\**
*25 g/1 oz butter, melted*
*175 ml/6 fl oz santen\**
*pinch of salt*
*4 medium bananas*
*3 tablespoons clarified butter*

### AMERICAN

*¾ cup rice flour\**
*2 tablespoons melted butter*
*¾ cup santen\**
*pinch of salt*
*4 medium bananas*
*3 tablespoons clarified butter*

### METHOD

Put the flour, melted butter, santen and salt in a bowl and stir well to make a smooth, liquid batter.

Peel the bananas and cut each one in half lengthways or slice into rounds. Roll the banana pieces in the batter until they are well coated. Heat the clarified butter in a large frying pan (skillet), add the banana pieces and fry until golden brown on all sides, turning frequently. Serve hot.
SERVES 4

**Sambal Kelapa; Sambal Bajak; Sambal Terasi**

# Agar-Agar Dengan Serikaya

## Seaweed Pudding

### METRIC/IMPERIAL

7 g/¼ oz agar-agar strands*
1.2 litres/2 pints water
75 g/3 oz caster sugar
**Serikaya:**
3 small eggs
50 g/2 oz gula Jawa*
salt
600 ml/1 pint thick santen*

### AMERICAN

30–35 agar-agar strands*
5 cups water
6 tablespoons superfine sugar
**Serikaya:**
3 small eggs
⅓ cup gula Jawa*
salt
2½ cups thick santen*

### METHOD

Soak the agar-agar in just enough cold water to cover for at least 2 hours, preferably overnight.

Drain the agar-agar then put in a large pan with the water. Add the sugar and simmer for a few minutes until the agar-agar and sugar have dissolved, stirring occasionally. Strain through a fine nylon sieve (strainer) or muslin (cheesecloth), then pour into a 1 litre/2 pint/5 cup mould. Leave to cool, then store in the refrigerator until required.

To make the serikaya: Put the eggs and gula Jawa in a bowl over a pan and whisk until thick and fluffy. Add the salt and santen and whisk thoroughly. Pour into a pudding basin (heatproof bowl). Place in a steamer or large pan, containing 2.5 cm/1 inch boiling water, and steam for 10 to 15 minutes until thick.

Turn the agar-agar out onto a serving plate. Serve accompanied by the hot·or cold serikaya.
SERVES 8 to 10

**Lepat Bugis; Rujak; Kue Dadar**

# Kue Dadar

## Coconut Pancakes (Crêpes)
Singapore

### METRIC/IMPERIAL

**Filling:**
175 g/6 oz gula Jawa*
300 ml/½ pint water
225 g/8 oz freshly grated white coconut flesh
pinch of ground cinnamon
pinch of grated nutmeg
pinch of salt
2 teaspoons lemon juice
**Pancakes:**
100 g/4 oz plain flour
1 egg, beaten
300 ml/½ pint milk
lard for shallow-frying

### AMERICAN

**Filling:**
1 cup gula Jawa*
1¼ cups water
4 cups freshly grated white coconut flesh
pinch of ground cinnamon
pinch of grated nutmeg
pinch of salt
2 teaspoons lemon juice
**Crêpes:**
1 cup all-purpose flour
1 egg, beaten
1¼ cups milk
lard for shallow-frying

## METHOD

To make the filling: Put the gula Jawa and water in a pan and heat gently until the sugar has dissolved. Add the remaining ingredients, except the lemon juice, and mix well. Simmer gently for a few minutes until the coconut has absorbed all the water, yet is still moist.

To make the pancakes (crêpes): Sift the flour and a pinch of salt into a bowl. Add the egg, then gradually beat in the milk to make a smooth batter.

Grease an 18 cm/7 inch frying pan (skillet) and place over moderate heat. Pour in just enough batter to cover the base thinly, tilting the pan to spread it. Cook for 1 minute, then turn the pancake (crêpe) and cook the other side. Repeat with the remaining batter, to make 8 pancakes (crêpes).

Add the lemon juice to the filling and divide equally between the pancakes (crêpes). Roll up and serve warm or cold.

SERVES 4 or 8

# Rujak
## Spiced Fruit Salad

*Kedondong* is a tropical fruit with firm, crisp flesh. If unobtainable, use crisp dessert apples instead. *Jeruk Bali* is a large citrus fruit with red flesh. It is only available in Asia; ugli fruit or Texas grapefruit may be used as a substitute in the West.

### METRIC/IMPERIAL

1 under-ripe mango
2 kedondong, or crisp dessert apples
½ fresh pineapple
½ teaspoon salt
½ jeruk Bali, or 1 ugli fruit or Texas
    grapefruit
¼ cucumber, peeled and sliced
**Bumbu:**
1 lombok rawit,* chopped, or pinch of
    chilli powder
1 slice terasi,* grilled (optional)
100 g/4 oz gula Jawa*
pinch of salt
1 tablespoon tamarind water*

### AMERICAN

1 under-ripe mango
2 kedondong or crisp dessert apples
½ fresh pineapple
½ teaspoon salt
½ jeruk Bali, or 1 ugli fruit or Texas
    grapefruit
¼ cucumber, peeled and sliced
**Bumbu:**
1 lombok rawit,* chopped, or pinch of
    chili powder
1 slice terasi,* broiled (optional)
⅔ cup gula Jawa*
pinch of salt
1 tablespoon tamarind water*

### METHOD

Wash, peel and slice the mango, kedondong or apples and pineapple, then place in a bowl. Add just enough cold water to cover and stir in the salt. Peel the jeruk Bali, or other fruit, and divide into segments.

To make the bumbu: Put the lombok rawit, terasi and gula Jawa in a *cobek* or mortar, and pound until smooth. Add the salt and tamarind water and stir well.

Drain the fruit and arrange in a serving bowl with the jeruk Bali, or other fruit, and cucumber. Pour the bumbu over the fruit and fold gently to mix.

SERVES 4 to 6

# Lepat Bugis
## Coconut Cream Cups
### Indonesia

In Malaysia and Indonesia, these cups are usually made from banana leaves (as illustrated). If fresh coconut is not available, desiccated (shredded) coconut may be substituted.

### METRIC/IMPERIAL

225 g/8 oz rice flour*
350 ml/12 fl oz santen*
pinch of salt
**Filling:**
75 g/3 oz brown sugar
250 ml/8 fl oz water
100 g/4 oz freshly grated white coconut
    flesh
1 tablespoon glutinous rice flour*
**Coconut cream:**
250 ml/8 fl oz very thick santen*
pinch of salt

### AMERICAN

2 cups rice flour*
1½ cups santen*
pinch of salt
**Filling:**
½ cup brown sugar, firmly packed
1 cup water
2 cups freshly grated white coconut
    flesh
1 tablespoon sweet rice flour*
**Coconut cream:**
1 cup very thick santen*
pinch of salt

### METHOD

Put the rice flour in a pan, pour in the santen and mix well. Add the salt and cook until the mixture begins to thicken, stirring occasionally. Cook for a further 5 minutes, stirring constantly, then remove from the heat.

To make the filling: Put the sugar and water in a pan and heat gently until dissolved. Stir in the coconut, then simmer for a few minutes until it has absorbed all the water. Stir in the glutinous (sweet) rice flour and cook for 2 minutes, stirring constantly.

To make the coconut cream: Put the santen and salt in a heavy pan and boil for 3 minutes, stirring constantly.

Spoon about 2 teaspoons of this cream into 8 ramekins or individual heatproof dishes. Put 1 tablespoon of the rice flour mixture on top, then spoon over the filling. Divide the remaining rice flour mixture between the dishes then top with the remaining coconut cream. Steam for 10 to 15 minutes, then serve hot or cold.

SERVES 4

# Burma

## Patricia Herbert

Burma is probably one of the least well-known of all Asian countries and many people have no idea what Burmese food is like. Burmese restaurants are few and far between – even, surprisingly, in Burma itself. There is really nothing mysterious or different about Burmese cooking, and the best way to sample the food is to learn to cook it yourself. Burmese food is distinctive, although it incorporates certain elements from the cooking of neighbouring India and China, and shares some common features with other South-East Asian cuisines.

The Burmese have taken their food seriously for a long time. In the thirteenth century, a certain King Narathihapate ruled Pagan, a great Buddhist city whose thousands of stone temples can still be seen today. This King's nickname was 'Eater of Three Hundred Curries', because, in the words of the Burmese chronicles: 'Whensoever the King partook of food, there must always be three hundred dishes, salted and spiced, sweet and sharp, bitter and hot, luscious and parching.'

A typical Burmese meal will include a wide range of tastes, each designed to balance, contrast or complement the others. A Burmese menu is quite different from a Western one. A soup is nearly always included; this is not taken separately as a first course, but served at the same time as the main dish and sipped at intervals throughout the meal. Soups are usually light and refreshing to the palate. Sharp or slightly sour tasting soup is particularly popular.

The main dish will usually be a curry of meat, fish or vegetables. In general Burmese curries are not overpoweringly hot; those who crave extra hotness will nonchalantly nibble fiery green chillies dipped in salt! With very few exceptions, a Burmese meal is considered incomplete without a huge bowl of white boiled rice. This is usually cooked without salt or oil as the main dish provides the seasoning. Sometimes *Coconut Rice* (see page 49) is served instead of plain boiled rice. Vegetables are also served with each meal, cooked or served raw and either dipped in a sharp shrimp or vinegar sauce, or assembled into a salad. Burmese salads are made from a wide range of exotic ingredients, including banana bud flowers, green mangoes and all sorts of strange leaves, but more ordinary ingredients like tomatoes and cucumbers are also used. Various condiments accompany the meal, one of the most popular being *Ngapi-gyaw* (see page 48).

Burmese people rarely eat desserts, but at the

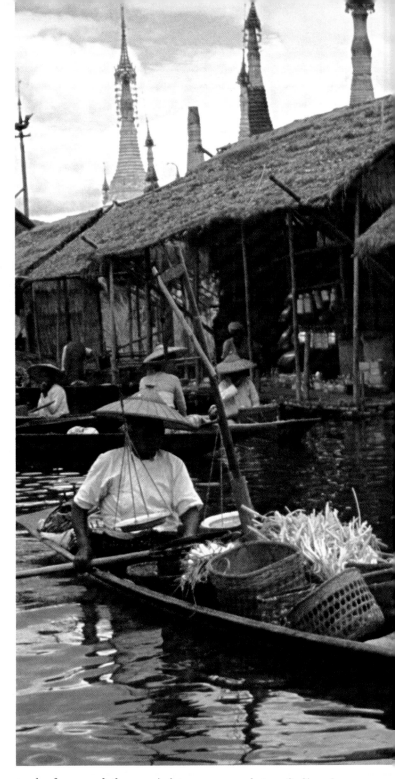

end of a meal they might serve a plate of sliced, fresh fruit. The Burmese have many recipes for delicious cake or pudding-type snacks called *món*, which they either make at home or, more frequently, buy from a roadside stall. Three recipes for Burmese *món* are given in this chapter – they are all easy to make and would make good desserts to finish a Burmese meal. Traditionally, wines and spirits are not served, but nowadays many people enjoy beer or wine with a Burmese meal.

One of Burma's most famous dishes, *U-nó Kauk-swè* (see page 44) is a one-course meal served without rice. Basically it consists of noodles and soup, with plenty of accompaniments mixed in at the time of eating. Families in Burma often cook this dish for large numbers on special occasions,

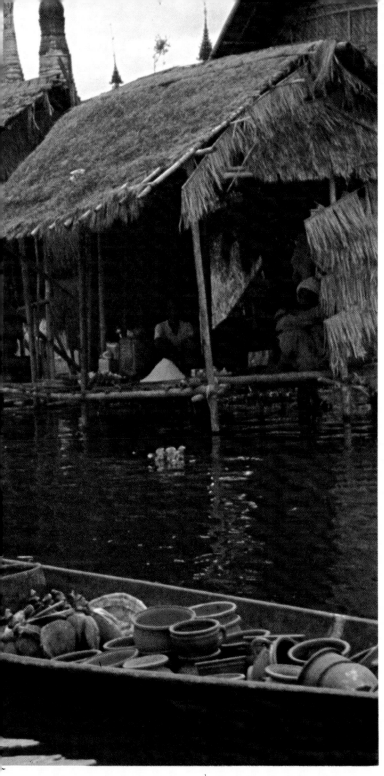

Burmese kitchen is a large stone mortar and pestle. Dawn breaks in Burma to the accompaniment of the pounding of pestle on mortar! The Burmese usually pound the onions, garlic, ginger and chillies that make up the basic flavouring of their curries. To simplify matters, the recipes in this chapter specify crushed garlic and chilli powder, but the onions and ginger should be pounded. In true Burmese style, you can of course, pound dried red chillies instead of using chilli powder. If you do not have a pestle and mortar, an electric grinder can be used instead.

### Ingredients

The Burmese use either peanut oil or sesame seed oil for cooking, but as these are quite heavy and rich for Western palates, corn, sunflower or vegetable oil can be used instead. Many Burmese dishes use salted shrimp paste, dried shrimps or shrimp sauce, and this is a feature shared with nearly all of the South-East Asian cuisines. Many Western people find shrimp paste a difficult taste to acquire and for this reason it is only included in the condiment *Ngapi-gyaw* (see page 48) for which it is essential. Dried shrimps and shrimp sauce impart a very pleasant flavour to soups and other dishes.

Another unusual Burmese ingredient is the fruit of the tamarind tree. This adds a sharpness to food which is more subtle than the taste of lemon or vinegar. Creamed coconut is added to certain special dishes; in Burma this is made by scraping the coconut flesh, then squeezing it in hot water to extract the cream and flavour.

### Serving

The Burmese usually sit at a round, low dining table for meals; the aim being to give a convivial atmosphere and to make sure that every dish is within reach. No ornaments or flowers are put on the table, as this would detract from the food. Each place on the table is laid with a plate and a soup bowl. A china soup spoon is provided for the soup, but the other dishes are usually eaten, very neatly and deftly, with the fingers, though the habit of eating with a fork and spoon is now becoming more widespread. The Burmese use small round serving dishes, except for one-course noodle dishes and the rice; these are put in large bowls in the centre of the table. The small dishes are constantly refilled and never allowed to become less than half full.

Burmese people like to keep their conversation to a minimum during a meal and concentrate on eating. In common with many Oriental cultures, it can be considered discourteous to the food to talk too much. Above all, the Burmese are a very tolerant people and they would be the first to say that you need not follow rigidly their way of serving the food. The main thing is to eat and enjoy it!

such as a baby's name giving day, or the day a son enters a monastery for his novitiate period. On these occasions, Buddhist monks are invited to the house to have a special meal and to recite prayers and blessings. Friends are invited too, but they will be fed a little later than the monks who eat first thing in the morning before returning to the monastery for the rest of the day. In Buddhist terms, it is an honour to feed monks and a way of earning merit which will ensure a better rebirth in one's next life.

### Cooking Utensils

Burmese cooking is usually over open wood fires or kerosene stoves. The cooking process is quite simple – usually a combination of frying and simmering – and no special cooking utensils are needed. However, an essential item in every

# Soup with Fresh Greens
## Hìn-nú-nwe Hìn-gyo

This is an everyday soup which is quick and very easy to make. The dried shrimps can be pounded at home or bought ready-powdered and the soup can be varied from day to day by adding different fresh green vegetables: water-cress, sorrel, spinach, cabbage, pea leaves or mustard leaves.

### METRIC/IMPERIAL

1.2 litres/2 pints water
1 medium onion, peeled and sliced
3 garlic cloves, peeled and sliced
3 tablespoons pounded dried shrimps*
½ teaspoon shrimp paste* (optional)
2 teaspoons soy sauce
1 teaspoon salt
225 g/8 oz fresh green leaves, washed

### AMERICAN

5 cups water
1 medium onion, peeled and sliced
3 garlic cloves, peeled and sliced
3 tablespoons pounded dried shrimps*
½ teaspoon shrimp paste* (optional)
2 teaspoons soy sauce
1 teaspoon salt
½ lb fresh green leaves, washed

### METHOD

Put the water, onion and garlic in a pan and bring to the boil. Lower the heat, then add the shrimps, shrimp paste, if using, soy sauce and salt. Stir well, then add the green leaves.

Boil for 5 minutes, taste and adjust the seasoning, then pour into a warmed soup tureen. Serve hot.
SERVES 4

# Clear Soup
## Hìn-gyo Yò-yò

This soup is usually served with rather oily dishes such as *Wet-thani* (see page 93). Its base is pork stock, made by boiling pork bones in water, but a stock made from a chicken or duck carcass can be used instead.

The soup can be made more substantial by adding cabbage, cauliflower, carrots, bean sprouts or noodles, and simmering the soup for 5 to 10 minutes longer than the time given below.

### METRIC/IMPERIAL

350 g/12 oz pork bones
5 peppercorns, crushed
3 garlic cloves, peeled and crushed
2 teaspoons soy sauce
1.5 litres/2½ pints water
salt
freshly ground black pepper
**To garnish:**
2 tablespoons finely chopped celery
  (optional)
3 tablespoons finely chopped spring
  onions, including green tops

### AMERICAN

¾ lb pork bones
5 peppercorns, crushed
3 garlic cloves, peeled and crushed
2 teaspoons soy sauce
6¼ cups water
salt
freshly ground black pepper
**To garnish:**
2 tablespoons finely chopped celery
  (optional)
3 tablespoons finely chopped scallions,
  including green tops

### METHOD

Put the pork bones, peppercorns, garlic, soy sauce and water in a large pan. Bring to the boil, then lower the heat and simmer for about 30 minutes.

Remove the bones from the soup with a slotted spoon. Add salt and pepper to taste, then transfer to a warmed soup tureen and sprinkle with the celery, if using, and spring onions (scallions). Serve hot.
SERVES 4

Radish and Fish Soup; Soup with Fresh
Greens; Clear Soup

# Radish and Fish Soup

## Mon-la-ú Hìn-gyo

This is a fairly rich soup, with a distinctive flavour which is imparted by the tamarind. It is usually made with long white radishes, but it can alternatively be made with spinach or sorrel leaves, or with sliced aubergine (eggplant) or okra.

### METRIC/IMPERIAL

225 g/8 oz filleted white fish (cod,
    haddock, etc.), cut into chunks
1 teaspoon salt
½ teaspoon turmeric powder
2 tablespoons vegetable oil
1 medium onion, peeled and pounded
3 garlic cloves, peeled and crushed
1 cm/½ inch piece of fresh root ginger,*
    peeled and pounded
½ teaspoon chilli powder
4 tomatoes, chopped
½ teaspoon shrimp paste* (optional)
1 tablespoon shrimp-flavoured soy
    sauce*
5 sprigs coriander leaves*
3 tablespoons dried tamarind pulp*
350 g/12 oz long white radish,*
    including green tops, peeled and
    thinly sliced

### AMERICAN

½ lb filleted white fish (cod, haddock,
    etc.), cut into chunks
1 teaspoon salt
½ teaspoon turmeric powder
2 tablespoons vegetable oil
1 medium onion, peeled and pounded
3 garlic cloves, peeled and crushed
½ inch piece of fresh ginger root,*
    peeled and pounded
½ teaspoon chili powder
4 tomatoes, chopped
½ teaspoon shrimp paste* (optional)
1 tablespoon shrimp-flavored soy
    sauce*
5 sprigs coriander leaves*
3 tablespoons dried tamarind pulp*
¾ lb long white radish,* including
    green tops, peeled and thinly sliced

### METHOD

Put the fish in a bowl and rub with the salt and turmeric. Set aside.

Heat the oil in a large pan. Mix together the onion, garlic, ginger and chilli powder. Add to the pan and fry gently until lightly coloured, then add the fish. Stir-fry for a few minutes, then add the tomatoes, shrimp paste, if using, soy sauce, 1.2 litres/2 pints/5 cups cold water and the coriander. Bring to the boil, then lower the heat and simmer for 15 minutes.

Meanwhile, put the tamarind in a bowl, pour over 6 tablespoons hot water, then knead to extract the flavour. Strain the liquid, discarding the tamarind pulp.

Add the tamarind liquid and radish to the pan and simmer for 15 minutes or until the radish is clear and tender. Taste and adjust the seasoning, then leave to stand for about 30 minutes to allow the full flavour to develop.

Reheat, then pour into a warmed soup tureen. Serve hot.
SERVES 4

# Prawn (Shrimp) Curry with Tomatoes

## Pazun Hìn

In Burma, large prawns (shrimp), are used to make this dish. If possible, try to use Dublin Bay or Pacific prawns (king shrimp), but if these are not obtainable, then ordinary prawns (shrimp) may be used instead.

### METRIC/IMPERIAL

575 g/1¼ lb peeled prawns
2 tablespoons shrimp-flavoured soy
 sauce*
½ teaspoon salt
½ teaspoon turmeric powder
4 tablespoons vegetable oil
1 large onion, peeled and pounded
4 garlic cloves, peeled and crushed
1 cm/½ inch piece of fresh root ginger,*
 peeled and pounded
½ teaspoon chilli powder
3 tomatoes, roughly chopped
2 tablespoons chopped coriander
 leaves*
4 tablespoons water
coriander leaves* to garnish

### AMERICAN

1¼ lb shelled shrimp
2 tablespoons shrimp-flavored soy
 sauce
½ teaspoon salt
½ teaspoon turmeric powder
¼ cup vegetable oil
1 large onion, peeled and pounded
4 garlic cloves, peeled and crushed
½ inch piece of fresh ginger root,*
 peeled and pounded
½ teaspoon chili powder
3 tomatoes, roughly chopped
2 tablespoons chopped coriander
 leaves*
¼ cup water
coriander leaves* to garnish

### METHOD

Put the prawns (shrimp) in a bowl with the soy sauce, salt and turmeric. Mix well, then set aside.

Heat the oil in a pan, add the onion, garlic, ginger and chilli powder and stir-fry until fragrant but not dry.

Add the prawns (shrimp), tomatoes and coriander, increase the heat slightly, then cover the pan and cook for 5 minutes. Stir in the water, lower the heat, cover and simmer for 10 to 15 minutes until the prawns are cooked and the water has been absorbed.

Transfer to a warmed serving dish and garnish with coriander leaves. Serve hot.
SERVES 4

# Spiced Fried Fish with Onions

## Ngà-gyaw

### METRIC/IMPERIAL

750 g/1½ lb white fish fillets (cod,
haddock, etc.), cut into 10 cm/4 inch
squares
½ teaspoon turmeric powder
1 tablespoon shrimp-flavoured soy
 sauce*
2 tablespoons dried tamarind pulp*
6 tablespoons hot water
7 tablespoons vegetable oil
2 medium onions, peeled and sliced
1½ teaspoons chilli powder

### AMERICAN

1½ lb white fish fillets (cod, haddock,
 etc.), cut into 4 inch squares
½ teaspoon turmeric powder
1 tablespoon shrimp-flavored soy
 sauce*
2 tablespoons dried tamarind pulp*
6 tablespoons hot water
7 tablespoons vegetable oil
2 medium onions, peeled and sliced
1½ teaspoons chili powder

### METHOD

Put the fish in a bowl and rub lightly with the turmeric and soy sauce. Set aside.

Put the tamarind in a bowl, cover with the hot water, then knead to extract the flavour. Strain the liquid, discarding the tamarind pulp.

Heat the oil in a large frying pan (skillet), add the onions and fry over brisk heat until golden and crisp. Remove from the pan with a slotted spoon and drain the onions on kitchen paper towels.

Pour off half the oil from the pan, then add the chilli powder. Increase the heat slightly, add the fish and fry quickly for 1 minute.

Add the tamarind liquid, cover and simmer for about 20 minutes until the fish is cooked and the liquid has almost all been absorbed. (If necessary, add a little more oil during cooking, to prevent sticking.)

Transfer to a warmed serving dish and sprinkle the fried onions over the fish. Serve hot.
SERVES 4

# Steamed Fish Parcels

## Ngà-baung-dok

In Burma, this subtly-flavoured dish is steamed in banana leaves (as illustrated), but in the West, foil may be substituted. If liked, spinach or lettuce may be used instead of the Chinese cabbage (bok choy) suggested here.

### METRIC/IMPERIAL

575 g/1¼ lb thick white fish fillets (cod,
 haddock, etc.), cut into
 7.5 × 3.5 cm/3 × 1½ inch pieces
2 teaspoons salt
½ teaspoon turmeric powder
3 small onions, peeled
2 garlic cloves, peeled and crushed
2.5 cm/1 inch piece of fresh root
 ginger,* peeled and pounded
½ teaspoon chilli powder
1 tablespoon rice flour*
50 g/2 oz creamed coconut,* roughly
 chopped
7 tablespoons boiling water
2 teaspoons vegetable oil
½ teaspoon powdered lemon grass*
10 Chinese cabbage leaves, washed
 and cut in half

## AMERICAN

1¼ lb thick white fish fillets (cod,
   haddock, etc.), cut into 3 × 1½ inch
   pieces
2 teaspoons salt
½ teaspoon turmeric powder
3 small onions, peeled
2 garlic cloves, peeled and crushed
1 inch piece of fresh ginger root,*
   peeled and pounded
½ teaspoon chili powder
1 tablespoon rice flour*
⅔ cup coconut milk*
2 teaspoons vegetable oil
½ teaspoon powdered lemon grass*
10 bok choy leaves, washed and cut
   in half

## METHOD

Put the fish in a bowl and rub lightly with
half the salt and turmeric. Set aside.

Thinly slice 1 onion, then pound the
remaining onions. Mix the pounded
onions to a paste with the remaining salt
and turmeric, the garlic, ginger, chilli
powder and rice flour.

If using creamed coconut, place in a
bowl, add the water and stir until the
coconut melts. Add (coconut milk) to the
onion paste with the oil, sliced onion and
the lemon grass. Mix well.

Cut ten 18 cm/7 inch squares of foil.
Place 1 piece of Chinese cabbage (bok
choy) on each foil square, then top with a
little of the paste mixture. Place a piece of
fish and a little more paste mixture on top
of this, then cover with another piece of
Chinese cabbage (bok choy). Fold the
foil, enclosing the filling, to form parcels.
Fold the edges together to seal.

Steam the parcels for 20 minutes or until
the fish is cooked through. Serve hot.
MAKES 10

# Burmese Chicken Curry

## Chet-thà Hsi-byan

This is a typical Burmese curry, cooked
in such a way that the 'oil returns' (hsi-
byan in Burmese) to the top of the dish at
the end of cooking. For the best flavour,
chop the chicken into small pieces across
the joints, as in Chinese cooking. As a
variation, omit the bay leaves and cinnamon and substitute 4 tomatoes,
roughly chopped, and ½ teaspoon powdered lemon grass.*

## METRIC/IMPERIAL

1 chicken, weighing 1.5 kg/3–3½ lb,
   chopped into pieces
2 tablespoons soy sauce
1 teaspoon salt
½ teaspoon turmeric powder
3 medium onions, peeled
4 garlic cloves, peeled
2.5 cm/1 inch piece of fresh root
   ginger,* peeled and pounded
1–2 teaspoons chilli powder, according
   to taste
5 tablespoons vegetable oil
3 bay leaves
1 piece of cinnamon stick

Prawn (Shrimp) Curry with Tomatoes;
Steamed Fish Parcels; Fried Spiced
Fish with Onions

## AMERICAN

1 chicken, weighing 3–3½ lb, chopped
   into pieces
2 tablespoons soy sauce
1 teaspoon salt
½ teaspoon turmeric powder
3 medium onions, peeled
4 garlic cloves, peeled
1 inch piece of fresh ginger root,*
   peeled and pounded
1–2 teaspoons chili powder, according
   to taste
⅓ cup vegetable oil
3 bay leaves
1 piece of cinnamon stick

## METHOD

Put the chicken in a bowl with the soy
sauce, salt and turmeric; mix well.

Pound 1 onion and 3 garlic cloves, mix
with the ginger and chilli powder, then
rub into the chicken.

Slice the remaining onions and garlic
thinly. Heat the oil in a large pan, add the
onions and garlic and fry gently for 5 to
10 minutes until soft and fragrant. Add
the chicken and any remaining pounded
mixture. Fry for 10 minutes until the
chicken is brown on all sides, stirring
occasionally.

Add the bay leaves and cinnamon and
enough water to just cover the chicken
(about 600 ml/1 pint/2½ cups). Increase the
heat and bring to the boil, then cover and
simmer for about 35 minutes until the oil
has risen to the surface, leaving a thick
curry sauce underneath. If there is too
much liquid towards the end of the cooking time, increase the heat and boil,
uncovered, until reduced and thickened.
Serve hot with plain boiled rice or
Coconut Rice (see page 49).
SERVES 4

# Chicken with Noodles and Coconut

## On-nó Kauk-swè

This is probably the most famous of all Burmese dishes: it is something of a feast, but it is not too difficult to prepare at home. Try to use the special split pea and lentil flours, as these give the dish its authentic Burmese flavour. Chick pea (garbanzos) flour may be substituted for the split pea flour, if this is more easily obtainable.

In Burma, the dish is served in wide soup bowls or plates – the noodles are placed in the bottom of the bowls, then a little of each of the accompaniments is sprinkled on top, followed by the hot chicken mixture. Each diner squeezes lemon juice over his serving just before eating.

### METRIC/IMPERIAL

1 chicken, weighing 1.5 kg/3–3½ lb, cut into large pieces
salt
½ teaspoon turmeric powder
3 litres/6 pints water
7 tablespoons vegetable oil
4 medium onions, peeled and pounded
4 garlic cloves, peeled and crushed
2.5 cm/1 inch piece of fresh root ginger,* peeled and pounded
2 teaspoons chilli powder
5 tablespoons split pea flour*
5 tablespoons lentil flour*
150 g/5 oz creamed coconut,* roughly chopped
1 kg/2 lb fresh or dried egg noodles

**To serve:**
6 tablespoons oil
12 garlic cloves, peeled and sliced crossways
3 hard-boiled eggs, shelled and quartered
2 onions, peeled and sliced
5 spring onions, including green tops, finely chopped
1 tablespoon chilli powder (optional)
2 lemons, quartered

### AMERICAN

1 chicken, weighing 3–3½ lb, cut into large pieces
salt
½ teaspoon turmeric powder
3 quarts water
7 tablespoons vegetable oil
4 medium onions, peeled and pounded
4 garlic cloves, peeled and crushed
1 inch piece of fresh ginger root,* peeled and pounded
2 teaspoons chili powder
5 tablespoons split pea flour*
5 tablespoons lentil flour*
1⅔ cups thick coconut milk*
2 lb fresh or dried egg noodles

**To serve:**
6 tablespoons oil
12 garlic cloves, peeled and sliced crossways
3 hard-cooked eggs, shelled and quartered
2 onions, peeled and sliced
5 scallions, including green tops, finely chopped
1 tablespoon chili powder (optional)
2 lemons, quartered

### METHOD

Rub the chicken with 1 tablespoon salt and the turmeric, then place in a very large pan. Add the water, bring to the boil, then lower the heat and simmer for about 25 minutes until the chicken is just cooked, but still firm. Remove the chicken from the pan; leave the cooking liquid to simmer gently over low heat.

Remove the skin and bones from the chicken and add them to the simmering cooking liquid. (For maximum flavour the chicken bones should be cracked, but this is not essential.) Cut the chicken meat into chunks.

Meanwhile, heat the oil in a large pan, add the onions, garlic, ginger and chilli powder and stir-fry for 5 minutes. Add the chicken meat and stir-fry for 5 to 10 minutes. Turn off the heat.

Mix the flours to a paste with about 200 ml/⅓ pint/1 cup cooking liquid and set aside. Strain the remaining cooking liquid into the pan containing the chicken meat.

Stir in the flour paste and bring to the boil. Lower the heat, add the creamed

Chicken with Noodles and Coconut

coconut (coconut milk) and simmer for about 20 minutes until the mixture has the consistency of thick pea soup, stirring frequently. If the mixture becomes too thick, add a little more water; if it is too thin, add a little more lentil flour paste. Turn off the heat, taste and adjust the seasoning, then cover the pan and set aside.

Cook the noodles in boiling salted water for about 7 minutes; drain and keep hot.

To serve: Heat the oil in a small frying pan (skillet), add a handful of the boiled noodles and fry over brisk heat until crisp. Remove from the pan with a slotted spoon and drain on kitchen paper towels, then place in a serving bowl.

Add the garlic to the pan, fry over brisk heat until golden and crisp, then transfer to a small serving bowl.

Reheat the chicken mixture, then pile into a warmed serving dish. Serve the remaining ingredients in separate small bowls as accompaniments to the chicken and noodles. Serve hot.

SERVES 6 to 8

# Red Pork
## Wet-thani

This dish is called 'Red or Golden Pork' because the oil in the dish is coloured by the chilli powder. The Burmese like to use fatty pork – either shoulder or belly – for this recipe, but if this is not to your taste, then pork fillet (tenderloin) may be used instead.

### METRIC/IMPERIAL

1 kg/2–2¼ lb boned pork, cut into
   2.5 cm/1 inch cubes
3 tablespoons soy sauce
1 teaspoon freshly ground black
   pepper
5 cm/2 inch piece of fresh root
   ginger,* peeled
3 medium onions, peeled and pounded
3 garlic cloves, peeled and crushed
200 ml/⅓ pint boiling water
1 teaspoon chilli powder
5 tablespoons vegetable oil

### AMERICAN

2–2¼ lb boneless pork, cut into 1 inch
   cubes
3 tablespoons soy sauce
1 teaspoon freshly ground black
   pepper
2 inch piece of fresh ginger root,*
   peeled
3 medium onions, peeled and pounded
3 garlic cloves, peeled and crushed
1 cup boiling water
1 teaspoon chili powder
⅓ cup vegetable oil

### METHOD

Put the pork in a bowl with 2 tablespoons soy sauce and the pepper; mix well.

Pound half the ginger, then mix with the onions and garlic. Stir in all but 1 tablespoon of the boiling water, then strain the mixture and retain both the liquid and the pounded ingredients.

Stir the chilli powder into the reserved boiling water. Cut the remaining ginger into thin strips. Heat the oil in a large heavy pan, add the ginger and fry until just sizzling, then add the pork and stir-fry until brown.

Add the liquid reserved from the pounded ingredients, cover the pan and simmer for about 10 minutes or until the liquid has almost all been absorbed. Add the chilli water, the remaining soy sauce and the reserved pounded mixture.

Cover and cook over low heat for about 40 minutes or until the pork is tender, stirring occasionally to prevent sticking. (If lean pork has been used, it may be necessary to add a little water during cooking.) Serve hot.

SERVES 4 to 6

# Beef Curry
## Amè-thà Hìn

The beef in this recipe needs to be marinated for at least 4 hours, preferably overnight. It is then cooked slowly with very little liquid, so it is best cooked in a heavy-based pan. Adjust the cooking time according to the quality of the meat.

### METRIC/IMPERIAL

1 kg/2–2¼ lb braising steak, cut into
   2.5 cm/1 inch cubes
1 tablespoon shrimp-flavoured soy
   sauce*
½ teaspoon turmeric powder
1 tablespoon malt vinegar
2 medium onions, peeled and pounded
4 garlic cloves, peeled and crushed
2.5 cm/1 inch piece of fresh root
   ginger,* peeled and pounded
1 teaspoon chilli powder
4 tablespoons vegetable oil
3 bay leaves
2 pieces of cinnamon stick
5 peppercorns
salt

### AMERICAN

2–2¼ lb chuck steak, cut into 1 inch
   cubes
1 tablespoon shrimp-flavored soy
   sauce*
½ teaspoon turmeric powder
1 tablespoon malt or cider vinegar
2 medium onions, peeled and pounded
4 garlic cloves, peeled and crushed
1 inch piece of fresh ginger root,*
   peeled and pounded
1 teaspoon chili powder
¼ cup vegetable oil
3 bay leaves
2 pieces of cinnamon stick
5 peppercorns
salt

### METHOD

Put the meat in a bowl with the soy sauce, turmeric and vinegar. Mix well, then leave to marinate for at least 4 hours, preferably overnight.

Mix together the onions, garlic, ginger and chilli powder. Heat the oil in a large heavy pan, add the pounded mixture and stir-fry for 10 minutes or until the mixture begins to brown.

Add the beef, bay leaves, cinnamon and peppercorns and enough water to half cover the beef. Cover and simmer over low heat for about 45 minutes or until the meat is tender; stir in a little water if necessary during cooking.

Taste and adjust the seasoning towards the end of the cooking time, adding a little salt according to taste. Serve hot.

SERVES 4 to 6

# Vegetable Curry
## Hìn-thì Hìn ywet Hìn-tamyò

The proportion of vegetables can be varied to suit individual tastes and availability.

### METRIC/IMPERIAL

3 medium potatoes, peeled and cut into
  3.5 cm/1½ inch cubes
1 medium aubergine, cut into
  2.5 cm/1 inch slices
4 carrots, peeled and diced
1 medium cauliflower, divided into
  florets
225 g/8 oz okra cut into 2.5 cm/1 inch
  lengths
4 tablespoons vegetable oil
1 medium onion, peeled and pounded
3 garlic cloves, peeled and crushed
1 cm/½ inch piece of fresh root ginger,*
  peeled and pounded
1 teaspoon chilli powder
½ teaspoon turmeric powder
75 g/3 oz dried salt fish,* roughly
  sliced (optional)
3 tomatoes, roughly chopped
3 tablespoons chopped coriander
  leaves*
1 fresh green chilli (optional)

### AMERICAN

3 medium potatoes, peeled and cut into
  1½ inch cubes
1 medium eggplant, cut into 1 inch
  slices
4 carrots, peeled and diced
1 medium cauliflower, divided into
  florets
½ lb okra, cut into 1 inch lengths
¼ cup vegetable oil
1 medium onion, peeled and pounded
3 garlic cloves, peeled and crushed
½ inch piece of fresh ginger root,*
  peeled and pounded
1 teaspoon chili powder
½ teaspoon turmeric powder
3 oz dried salt fish,* roughly sliced
  (optional)
3 tomatoes, roughly chopped
3 tablespoons chopped coriander
  leaves*
1 fresh green chili (optional)

### METHOD

Put the potatoes, aubergine (eggplant), carrots, cauliflower and okra in a bowl. Cover with cold water and set aside.

Heat the oil in a large pan, add the onion, garlic, ginger, chilli powder and turmeric and stir-fry until fragrant.

Add the salt fish, if using, stir-fry for 2 minutes, then stir in one third of the tomatoes and the coriander. Add the potatoes and just enough water to cover. (Add a little salt if salt fish is not used.) Bring to the boil, then lower the heat and simmer for 10 minutes.

Add the aubergine (eggplant) and carrots, simmer for 5 minutes, then add the cauliflower and a little more water, if necessary. Bring back to the boil, add the remaining tomatoes and the chilli, if using. Simmer for 5 minutes, then add the okra.

Lower the heat and simmer for 5 minutes or until the vegetables are cooked, but still firm, and most of the liquid has been absorbed. Discard the chilli, if used. Serve hot.

SERVES 4

**Vegetable Curry; Right: Ingredients for Assorted Vegetable Salad**

## Assorted Vegetable Salad

### Thanat-son-Thok

Although called a salad, the vegetables in this dish are blanched or quickly cooked first. The choice of vegetables can be varied according to taste and availability.

METRIC/IMPERIAL

4 carrots, scraped
salt
175 g/6 oz French beans, topped and
    tailed
100 g/4 oz okra
100 g/4 oz fresh bean sprouts
100 g/4 oz cauliflower florets
100 g/4 oz bamboo shoot (optional)
50 g/2 oz sesame seeds*
2 tablespoons vegetable oil
1 medium onion, peeled and sliced

AMERICAN

4 carrots, scraped
salt
1½ cups string beans, topped and tailed
1 cup okra
2 cups fresh bean sprouts
2 large cauliflower florets
1 cup bamboo shoot (optional)
5 tablespoons sesame seeds*
2 tablespoons vegetable oil
1 medium onion, peeled and sliced

METHOD

Cook the carrots in boiling salted water for about 7 minutes, then remove from the pan and leave to cool.

Cook the remaining vegetables separately in boiling salted water, allowing about 3 minutes for each vegetable – they should remain crunchy. Leave to cool.

Put the sesame seeds in a small, heavy frying pan (skillet) and fry over dry heat until 'toasted' golden brown, shaking the pan constantly. Remove from the pan and set aside.

Add the oil to the pan, heat gently, then add the onion. Fry over brisk heat until golden and crisp, then remove from the pan with a slotted spoon and drain on kitchen paper towels. Reserve 1 tablespoon of the oil.

Slice the carrots into thin matchstick strips. Slice the beans and okra diagonally into 1 cm/½ inch pieces. Arrange the vegetables in separate piles on a long serving dish.

Stir a pinch of salt into the reserved oil, drizzle over the vegetables, then sprinkle with the sesame seeds and fried onion. Serve cold or chilled.
SERVES 6 to 8

## Fried Aubergine (Eggplant)

### Hkayàn-thì Gyaw

This vegetable dish can be served as a side dish to a main meal of curry and rice, or eaten on its own. The aubergine (eggplant) can be baked in advance and the dish completed when required.

METRIC/IMPERIAL

1 large aubergine
2 tablespoons vegetable oil
1 medium onion, peeled and sliced
1 garlic clove, peeled and crushed
1 cm/½ inch piece of fresh root ginger,*
    peeled and pounded
½ teaspoon salt
2 spring onions, including green tops,
    finely chopped, to garnish

AMERICAN

1 large eggplant
2 tablespoons vegetable oil
1 medium onion, peeled and sliced
1 garlic clove, peeled and crushed
½ inch piece of fresh ginger root,*
    peeled and pounded
½ teaspoon salt
2 scallions, including green tops, finely
    chopped, to garnish

METHOD

Put the aubergine (eggplant) on a lightly oiled baking (cookie) sheet and bake in a preheated hot oven (220°C/425°F, Gas Mark 7) for about 1 hour or until soft to the touch, turning occasionally. Remove from the oven and leave to cool.

Heat the oil in a frying pan (skillet), add the onion and garlic and fry gently until beginning to brown.

Meanwhile, peel off the aubergine (eggplant) skin, scoop out the flesh and mash with a fork. Add to the pan with the ginger and salt, then stir-fry for 5 to 10 minutes.

Transfer to a warmed serving dish and garnish with the spring onions (scallions). Serve hot or cold.
SERVES 4

# Cucumber Salad
## Thanhat

This salad can also be made with carrots, cauliflower, runner (string) beans or fresh bean sprouts.

### METRIC/IMPERIAL

2 medium cucumbers, peeled, seeded
   and cut into 7.5 cm/3 inch long strips
3 tablespoons vinegar
1 teaspoon salt
6 tablespoons vegetable oil
2 medium onions, peeled and sliced
8 garlic cloves, peeled and sliced
½ teaspoon turmeric powder
1 teaspoon sugar
2 tablespoons sesame seeds*

### AMERICAN

2 medium cucumbers, peeled, seeded
   and cut into 3 inch long strips
3 tablespoons vinegar
1 teaspoon salt
6 tablespoons vegetable oil
2 medium onions, peeled and sliced
8 garlic cloves, peeled and sliced
½ teaspoon turmeric powder
1 teaspoon sugar
2 tablespoons sesame seeds*

### METHOD

Put the cucumber in a pan with 2 tablespoons of the vinegar and just enough water to cover. Bring to the boil, then lower the heat and simmer for about 4 minutes until the cucumber becomes transparent. Drain, sprinkle with ½ teaspoon salt, then leave to cool.

Heat the oil in a frying pan (skillet), add the onions and fry over brisk heat until golden and crisp. Remove from the pan with a slotted spoon and drain on kitchen paper towels. Add the garlic to the pan, fry until golden, then remove and drain.

Add the turmeric, sugar and remaining salt to the pan, stir, then add half the sesame seeds. Stir-fry for 1 to 2 minutes, remove from the heat and leave to cool in the pan.

Stir the remaining vinegar into the mixture in the pan, then add the cucumber and toss well. Drain off the excess oil and vinegar, then pile the cucumber into a pyramid shape on a serving plate. Sprinkle with the onion, garlic and remaining sesame seeds. Serve cold or chilled.
SERVES 4

# Tomato Salad
## Hkayàn-chin-thì Let-thok

This salad is best made with under-ripe tomatoes.

### METRIC/IMPERIAL

4 tablespoons vegetable oil
1 medium onion, peeled and sliced
4 medium tomatoes, thinly sliced
1 tablespoon pounded, roasted shelled
   peanuts (see page 81)
3 tablespoons chopped coriander
   leaves*
1 teaspoon shrimp-flavoured soy
   sauce*
juice of ½ lemon
coriander leaves* to garnish

### AMERICAN

¼ cup vegetable oil
1 medium onion, peeled and sliced
4 medium tomatoes, thinly sliced
1 tablespoon pounded, roasted shelled
   peanuts (see page 81)
3 tablespoons chopped coriander
   leaves*
1 teaspoon shrimp-flavored soy sauce*
juice of ½ lemon
coriander leaves* to garnish

### METHOD

Heat 3 tablespoons of the oil in a small frying pan (skillet), add the onion and fry over brisk heat until golden and crisp. Remove from the pan with a slotted spoon and drain on kitchen paper towels.

Put the tomatoes in a bowl, then add the peanuts, coriander, soy sauce and remaining oil and toss lightly to mix.

Arrange the tomato mixture on a serving plate, sprinkle with the lemon juice and top with the onion. Garnish with coriander. Serve cold or chilled.
SERVES 4

# Burmese Balachaung – Shrimp Condiment
## Ngapi-gyaw

Every household in Burma has its own special recipe for making this spicy shrimp condiment, which is eaten as an accompaniment to most meals. It may also be eaten as an unusual sandwich filling. A word of warning – Ngapi-gyaw smells strongly during cooking! It will keep for up to 6 months in a screw-top jar in the refrigerator.

### METRIC/IMPERIAL

1 tablespoon dried tamarind pulp*
   (optional)
200 ml/⅓ pint vegetable oil
1 medium onion, peeled and sliced
8 garlic cloves, peeled and sliced
   crossways
2.5 cm/1 inch piece of fresh root
   ginger,* peeled and sliced into
   strips
1 teaspoon chilli powder
1 teaspoon turmeric powder
200 g/7 oz dried shrimps,* pounded
2 teaspoons shrimp paste*

### AMERICAN

1 tablespoon dried tamarind pulp*
   (optional)
1 cup vegetable oil
1 medium onion, peeled and sliced
8 garlic cloves, peeled and sliced
   crossways
1 inch piece of fresh ginger root,*
   peeled and sliced into strips
1 teaspoon chili powder
1 teaspoon turmeric powder
2⅓ cups dried pounded shrimp*
2 teaspoons shrimp paste*

If using tamarind, place in a bowl, cover with 3 tablespoons hot water, then knead to extract the flavour. Strain the liquid, discarding the tamarind pulp.

Heat the oil in a wok or deep frying pan (deep-fat fryer), then fry the onion, garlic and ginger separately over brisk heat until golden and crisp. Remove from the pan with a slotted spoon and drain on kitchen paper towels.

Add the chilli powder to the pan and fry for 30 seconds, then add the turmeric and shrimps. Stir-fry until the shrimps are crisp and have absorbed most of the oil, then remove from the pan and drain off any excess oil.

Add the shrimp paste to the pan with the tamarind liquid, if using. Fry over low heat for about 3 minutes, stirring constantly to prevent burning. Return the shrimps to the pan, mix quickly together, then remove from the heat and stir in the onions, garlic and ginger. Allow to cool.

Serve cold in individual dishes, as an accompaniment.
MAKES 450 g/1 lb

# Coconut Rice

## Òn Htamìn

Coconut rice makes a pleasant change from plain boiled rice as an accompaniment to a main course. It goes particularly well with *Burmese Chicken Curry* (see page 43). For a variation, add 1 piece of cinnamon stick, 1 bay leaf, 2 cloves and 2 whole cardamoms – these will give the rice a delicious, slightly spicy flavour.

METRIC/IMPERIAL

*450 g/1 lb long-grain rice, washed thoroughly.*
*75 g/3 oz creamed coconut,\* roughly chopped*
*1 medium onion, peeled and quartered*
*½ teaspoon salt*
*1 teaspoon vegetable oil*

AMERICAN

*2¼ cups long-grain rice, washed thoroughly*
*6 tablespoons thick coconut milk\**
*1 medium onion, peeled and quartered*
*½ teaspoon salt*
*1 teaspoon vegetable oil*

METHOD

Measure the rice into cups, then transfer to a large pan. Measure 2 cups water for every cup of rice and add to the pan.

Add the remaining ingredients and bring to the boil over high heat. Cover the pan, lower the heat to a minimum and cook for about 20 minutes, until the rice is tender. Remove the lid and stir the rice once – the liquid should have been absorbed completely and the rice grains should be fluffy. Serve hot.
SERVES 6

**Tomato Salad; Cucumber Salad**

# Seaweed Jelly

### Kyauk-kyàw

This is a very firm jelly with an unusual coconut flavour. It sets in two layers – a creamy layer on top, with a cloudy layer underneath.

METRIC/IMPERIAL

25 g/1 oz dried agar-agar*
100 g/4 oz creamed coconut,* roughly chopped
225 g/8 oz granulated sugar

AMERICAN

1 oz dried agar-agar*
½ cup thick coconut milk*
1 cup granulated sugar

METHOD

Put the agar-agar in a bowl, add just enough cold water to cover and leave to soak for 2 to 3 hours.

Strain the agar-agar, discarding the water, then measure the agar-agar. For each measure of agar-agar, use double the amount of fresh water. (25 g/1 oz soaked agar-agar should fill a 600 ml/1 pint/2 cup measure, so the required amount of water will be about 1.2 litres/2 pints/5 cups.)

Put one quarter of the creamed coconut (coconut milk) in a small bowl. If using creamed coconut, bring 7 table-spoons of the measured water to the boil, pour over the coconut and stir until melted. Set aside.

Put the remaining creamed coconut (coconut milk) in a pan with the agar-agar and sugar. Bring the remaining water to the boil, add to the pan and simmer gently for about 10 minutes, until the mixture is smooth, stirring occasionally.

Pour the mixture into a shallow square dish. Leave to cool slightly, then pour over the reserved coconut. Leave in a cool place for about 1 hour until set, then cut into diamond shapes and arrange on a serving plate.
SERVES 6 to 8

# Tapioca Pudding

### Tha-gu Món

In Burma, palm sugar is used in this pudding; soft dark brown sugar can be used instead.

METRIC/IMPERIAL

225 g/8 oz tapioca
225 g/8 oz soft dark brown sugar
½ teaspoon salt
900 ml/1½ pints water
100 g/4 oz desiccated or freshly grated coconut
2 teaspoons caster sugar

AMERICAN

1⅓ cups tapioca
1 cup dark brown sugar, firmly packed
½ teaspoon salt
3¾ cups water
1⅓ cups shredded or freshly grated coconut
2 teaspoons superfine sugar

METHOD

Put the tapioca, brown sugar, salt and water in a pan and bring to the boil. Lower the heat and simmer for about 10 minutes until the tapioca becomes soft and transparent and the mixture is thick, stirring constantly.

Remove from the heat, pour into a greased shallow dish and leave until cold.

Scoop out the mixture in tablespoon-fuls, then roll in the coconut and caster (superfine) sugar. Arrange on a serving plate.
SERVES 6 to 8

Tapioca Pudding; Sesame Semolina
Pudding; Seaweed Jelly

# Sesame Semolina Pudding

## Sanwìn-makìn

The secret of the flavour of this pudding
is the dry cooking of the semolina.

### METRIC/IMPERIAL

*225 g/8 oz semolina*
*225 g/8 oz soft dark brown or*
  *demerara sugar*
*½ teaspoon salt*
*175 g/6 oz creamed coconut,\* roughly*
  *chopped*
*1.2 litres/2 pints boiling water*
*50 g/2 oz butter or margarine*
*2 teaspoons vegetable oil*
*2 medium eggs, beaten*
*75 g/3 oz seedless raisins*
*4 tablespoons sesame seeds\* or poppy*
  *seeds*

### AMERICAN

*1⅓ cups semolina*
*1 cup dark brown sugar, firmly packed*
*½ teaspoon salt*
*¾ cup thick coconut milk\**
*5 cups boiling water*
*¼ cup butter or margarine*
*2 teaspoons vegetable oil*
*2 medium eggs, beaten*
*½ cup seedless raisins*
*4 tablespoons sesame seeds\* or poppy*
  *seeds*

### METHOD

Put the semolina in a large heavy pan and
cook over low heat for about 10 minutes,
stirring occasionally. The semolina
should become scorched or 'toasted',
but not burnt.

Remove from the heat and stir in the
brown sugar, salt, creamed coconut (coconut milk) and water. Leave to stand for
at least 30 minutes, then cook over low
heat for about 15 minutes or until quite
thick, stirring occasionally.

Remove from the heat, add the butter
or margarine and stir until melted. Stir in
the oil, leave to cool slightly, then stir in
the eggs.

Return to the heat and cook gently for 5
minutes, stirring constantly. Stir in the
raisins and cook for 5 to 10 minutes until
the mixture is thick, but not solid.

Pour into a greased shallow ovenproof
square dish and sprinkle with the sesame
or poppy seeds. Bake in a preheated
moderately hot oven (200°C/400°F, Gas
Mark 6) for about 1½ hours until the
pudding has begun to shrink away from
the sides of the dish and the seeds are
brown.

Leave until cold, then cut into squares
or diamond shapes to serve.
SERVES 6 to 8

# Thailand

## Ornsiri Selby-Lowndes

'*Nai nam mee pla, Nai nar mee Kow*': 'In the water there is fish, in the field there is rice', so wrote King Ramkhamkaeng, son of the founder of Siam in AD 1292. This statement characterizes Thailand even today, for the word 'hunger' does not exist in the Thai language!

The modern name 'Thailand' or '*Moeng Tai*' means 'Land of Freedom', and it is the only country in South-East Asia which has never been a colony. Thailand has always been a monarchy, and although the king no longer has absolute power, he still forms a focal point for the people and, by his example, perpetuates the lifestyle set by his ancestors.

Because of their independence, the Thai people, their customs and cuisine, have hardly been affected by outside influences through the centuries. The majority of people are Buddhists and there are no religious restrictions in their basic diet. Different kinds of meat are eaten, as well as fresh fruit and vegetables. The favourable climate in Southern Thailand allows two or three rice harvests each year, and ensures a steady supply of many varieties of *pak* (green vegetables), *tua* (green beans) and *fuk* (squash).

Thai cooking favours the use of fresh rather than dried herbs and spices, and these are available throughout the year. Fruit is generally plentiful, but some varieties are restricted to special seasons. Raw vegetables also play an important part in the Thai diet.

### Cooking Utensils and Equipment

A simple charcoal stove is traditionally used for cooking. In urban areas, this has been replaced in recent years by rings fed by bottled gas, but these can only be used for boiling and frying. The most important utensil in Thai cooking is the wok, which is used for boiling, steaming and frying. For steaming, the food is placed in a covered bamboo sieve (strainer) which is suspended over boiling water in the wok. Food is often wrapped in banana leaves or stuffed into green bamboo before steaming to give it a special flavour.

Standard western kitchen equipment is suitable for preparing simple Thai dishes, but a few special items are needed for traditional cooking. One of these is a pestle and mortar. In Thailand these are made from granite with a rough interior, which makes it easier to grind fibrous materials such as prawns (shrimp) and meat. A large porcelain pestle and mortar is, however, generally satisfactory. Two other important items are the wok, now easily available, and a small

charcoal stove for grilled (broiled) dishes. A Chinese steamboat is excellent for cooking Thai soups and keeping them hot at the table.

### Serving

Rice is the staple diet in Thailand, as it is in most of Asia. Noodles may be eaten at noon or as a snack, but all main meals are based on rice. At least four dishes are served with the rice to form a meal. For example; a soup, a curry, a meat or fish dish and a raw vegetable salad with a spicy sauce.

Sweet dishes are not usually served as part of a meal, but are eaten as snacks; these are usually bought from street vendors rather than cooked at home. Fruit is plentiful in Thailand and is frequently served after meals. Pineapple and mangoes are particularly popular. Often the fruit is cut into small pieces, chilled and then served with a bowl of salt or spiced salt for dipping.

### Rice

Long-grain or Patna rice may be used, but if you can obtain real Thai rice, it is well worth buying. The best rice, often called 'fragrant rice', comes from Nakorn Pratom, famous for its huge pagoda. If the rice is fresh (the previous season's harvest), it will absorb about one and a half times its volume in water during cooking. As the rice becomes older and drier, the amount of water needed can increase to a volume twice that of the rice. Salt is never added.

### Soups

The two main types of soup eaten are *Kang Chud*, which is similar to consommé, and *Tom Yum*, which usually contains pieces of prawn (shrimp), pork, beef, chicken or fish. The flavour of *Tom Yum* is typically Thai – a blend of lemon grass,* lime juice and fish sauce. Both soups can be served along with other dishes during a meal.

### Salads

Thai salads are unusual in that they can be very hot to the taste. Small green chillis (bird's eye chillis) are concealed amongst the fresh vegetables and these can take one by surprise! Thais often include a sprig of flowers and tender young mango leaves in a salad. Leaves and young shoots from various other trees and shrubs are also added, according to the season. Lettuce and cauliflower make perfectly acceptable substitutes.

### Curries

In Thailand, curries are prepared with a spicy paste made from fresh ingredients, rather than a powdered dried spice base. This is because many of the ingredients, including lemon grass,* garlic, shallots, *kapi,* *kha,* *pak chee*,* lime peel and chillis have a superior flavour and have a much better flavour when used fresh. Unfortunately, the individual spices used in many of the Thai curries are not obtainable fresh outside Thailand and the dried equivalents, or the prepared curry pastes sold in Oriental food stores, must be used instead.

### Fish

Fish is plentiful in Thailand and normally at least one fish dish is included in every Thai meal. The commonest fish is *Pla Tu*, a small mackerel which is sold ready-steamed in the markets. Mackerel is suitable for most Thai dishes where the fish is unspecified. If a whole fish is required, use *Pla Jelamed* if possible. Known in this country as Pomfret, this fish has a flat, roundish body, and can often be found in the freezer section of Chinese supermarkets. Where fish is to be pounded to a fibrous pulp, cod fillets are fairly satisfactory, but will take a little longer to grind than the native fish.

Boiled *Pla Muek* (squid) is widely used in salads; it is also fried, stewed or grilled (broiled) and added to many other dishes. Choose young small squid for preference, as they respond well to a short cooking time, and do not take on the rubbery texture of the larger squid and octopus.

### Drinks to Accompany Thai Food

In Thailand, a meal is always accompanied by iced water or iced weak tea. Alcoholic drinks are less common as they are not really compatible with the hot spices used in cooking; any drink with a concentration of alcohol greater than 5 per cent is unsuitable. Thus beer should be chosen, rather than wine. Lager is particularly good; 'Singha' and 'Amarit' are the famous Bangkok brands. Alternatively, a glass of whisky heavily diluted with water is quite a pleasant accompaniment to Thai food.

# Prawns (Shrimp) and Squid Hot Soup

## Tom Yum Kung Lae Pla Muk

Ideally, the stock for this soup should be made with pork bones. If these are not available, however, use chicken stock (bouillon) cubes instead.

### METRIC/IMPERIAL

225 g/8 oz squid
1.2 litres/2 pints stock
3 lime leaves*
1 stalk lemon grass,* crushed
225 g/8 oz prawns, peeled and
   deveined
nam pla* to taste
2–4 fresh chillis, sliced into rounds
2 garlic cloves, peeled and crushed
juice of 1 lime or lemon, or to taste
chopped coriander leaves,* to garnish

### AMERICAN

½ lb squid
5 cups stock
3 lime leaves*
1 stalk lemon grass,* crushed
½ lb shrimp, shelled and deveined
nam pla* to taste
2–4 fresh chilis, sliced into rounds
2 garlic cloves, peeled and crushed
juice of 1 lime or lemon, or to taste
chopped coriander leaves,* to garnish

### METHOD

Clean the squid, cut off and chop the tentacles, then cut the body into rings.

Put the stock, lime leaves and lemon grass in a pan, bring to the boil, then lower the heat and simmer for 5 minutes. Add the prawns (shrimp), squid and nam pla. Cook until the prawns (shrimp) have turned pink, then add the chillis.

Pour the soup into 4 warmed individual bowls. Mix together the garlic and lime or lemon juice to taste, then stir into the soup. Sprinkle with coriander. Serve hot.
SERVES 4

# Transparent Vermicelli Soup
## Kang Ron

Dried squid is an acquired taste; if you do not like its rubbery texture omit it from this recipe. It is available from Chinese food stores.

### METRIC/IMPERIAL

100 g/4 oz wun sen,* soaked in water for 10 minutes
2 coriander roots,* finely chopped
2 garlic cloves, peeled and chopped
1 teaspoon freshly ground black pepper
100 g/4 oz pork, minced
1.2 litres/2 pints water
100 g/4 oz prawns, peeled and deveined
25 g/1 oz dried prawns* (optional)
25 g/1 oz dried squid, sliced (optional)
½ onion, peeled and sliced
2 tablespoons dried jelly mushrooms,* soaked in warm water for 20 minutes
pinch of monosodium glutamate*
1 egg
few spring onions, finely chopped, to garnish

### AMERICAN

¼ lb wun sen,* soaked in water for 10 minutes
2 coriander roots,* finely chopped
2 garlic cloves, peeled and chopped
1 teaspoon freshly ground black pepper
½ cup ground pork, firmly packed
5 cups water
3 large shrimp, shelled and deveined
⅓ cup dried shrimp* (optional)
1 oz dried squid, sliced (optional)
½ onion, peeled and sliced
2 tablespoons tree ears,* soaked in warm water for 20 minutes
pinch of msg*
1 egg
few scallions, finely chopped, to garnish

### METHOD

Drain the wun sen, then cut into 5 cm/2 inch lengths.

Put the coriander roots, garlic and pepper in a mortar and pound to a paste. Add the pork and continue pounding to a smooth paste. Shape the mixture into 10 to 12 balls, about 1 cm/½ inch in diameter.

Bring the water to the boil in a pan, then drop in the pork balls and cook for 5 minutes. Add the prawns (shrimp) and skim off any scum that comes to the surface with a slotted spoon. Simmer for a few minutes, stirring constantly.

Add the dried prawns (shrimp) and squid, if using, the onion, mushrooms, monosodium glutamate (msg) and the drained wun sen. Simmer for a few minutes, then stir the egg slowly into the soup and remove from the heat.

Pour into a warmed tureen and sprinkle with the spring onions (scallions). Serve hot.
SERVES 4

**Prawns (Shrimp) and Squid Hot Soup; Transparent Vermicelli Soup**

# Chicken Rice Porridge
## Kow Tom Kai

This dish is popular for breakfast or as a late supper; it is often served with chilli pickle. If possible, make the stock with pork bones. If these are not available, however, use chicken stock (bouillon) cubes instead.

### METRIC/IMPERIAL

1.2 litres/2 pints stock
2 large chicken breasts, skinned, boned and cut into 1 cm/½ inch cubes
100 g/4 oz boned pork loin, cut into 1 cm/½ inch cubes
350 g/12 oz rice, cooked
2 celery sticks, with leaves, chopped into 1 cm/½ inch lengths
2 spring onions, chopped
nam pla,* to taste
freshly ground black pepper
**To garnish:**
1 tablespoon vegetable oil
4 garlic cloves, peeled and finely chopped
100 g/4 oz bacon, derinded and cut into 1 cm/½ inch squares

### AMERICAN

5 cups stock
2 large boneless chicken breasts, skinned and cut into ½ inch cubes
¼ lb boneless pork loin, cut into ½ inch cubes
1½ cups rice, cooked
2 celery stalks, with leaves, chopped into ½ inch lengths
2 scallions, chopped
nam pla,* to taste
freshly ground black pepper
**To garnish:**
1 tablespoon vegetable oil
4 garlic cloves, peeled and finely chopped
¼ lb bacon, cut into ½ inch squares

### METHOD

Bring the stock to the boil in a pan, then add the chicken and pork. Cook until the meat turns white, then add the rice. Remove from the heat, add the celery and spring onions (scallions), then add nam pla and pepper to taste. Set aside.

Heat the oil in a frying pan (skillet), add the garlic and fry until golden brown. Remove from the pan with a slotted spoon and set aside. Add the bacon to the pan and fry until brown and crisp.

Pour the soup into 4 warmed individual bowls and sprinkle with the garlic and bacon. Serve hot.
SERVES 4

# Deep-fried Rice Vermicelli with Sauce

## Pad Mee Krob

METRIC/IMPERIAL

vegetable oil for deep-frying
175 g/6 oz rice vermicelli,* broken into
  pieces
**Sauce:**
1 tablespoon vegetable oil
1 onion, peeled and finely chopped
2 garlic cloves, peeled and finely
  chopped
225 g/8 oz prawns, peeled and
  deveined
75 g/3 oz crabmeat
2 teaspoons brown sugar
2 tablespoons tamarind water*
1 teaspoon salt
1 tablespoon soy sauce
**To garnish:**
2 teaspoons finely grated orange rind
2 red chillis, shredded
chopped coriander leaves*
100 g/4 oz fresh bean sprouts

AMERICAN

vegetable oil for deep-frying
6 oz rice noodles,* broken into pieces
**Sauce:**
1 tablespoon vegetable oil
1 onion, peeled and finely chopped
2 garlic cloves, peeled and finely
  chopped
½ lb shrimp, shelled and deveined
½ cup crabmeat
2 teaspoons brown sugar
2 tablespoons tamarind water*
1 teaspoon salt
1 tablespoon soy sauce
**To garnish:**
2 teaspoons finely grated orange rind
2 red chilis, shredded
chopped coriander leaves*
2 cups fresh bean sprouts

METHOD

Heat the oil in a deep-fat fryer and fry the rice vermicelli (noodles), in batches, for about 30 seconds until the strands swell and float. Drain and set aside.

To make the sauce: Heat the oil in a wok or deep frying pan (deep-fat fryer), add the onion and garlic and fry until lightly brown. Add the prawns (shrimp) and crab and cook until they turn pink.

Stir in the remaining ingredients, with the fried vermicelli (noodles). Taste and adjust the seasoning. Heat through, then transfer to a warmed serving dish.

Garnish with the orange rind, chillis and coriander, and arrange the bean sprouts around the edge of the dish. Serve hot.
SERVES 4

# Fried Mackerel with Tamarind Sauce

## Pla Prio Wan

METRIC/IMPERIAL

4 medium mackerel
2 tablespoons vegetable oil
3 garlic cloves, peeled and finely
  chopped
2 tablespoons shredded fresh root
  ginger*
3 tablespoons water
1 teaspoon sugar
3 tablespoons tamarind water*
**To serve:**
few spring onions, chopped
1 cucumber, skinned and cut into
  1 cm/½ inch slices

AMERICAN

4 medium mackerel
2 tablespoons vegetable oil
3 garlic cloves, peeled and finely
  chopped
2 tablespoons shredded fresh ginger
  root*
3 tablespoons water
1 teaspoon sugar
3 tablespoons tamarind water*
**To serve:**
few scallions, chopped
1 cucumber, skinned and cut into
  ½ inch slices

METHOD

Clean the fish, but do not remove the skin. Wrap the fish together in well-buttered foil, then bake in a preheated cool oven (150°C/300°F, Gas Mark 2) for 45 minutes or until tender. Unwrap the fish, then leave until cool and dry.

Heat the oil in a wok or deep frying pan (deep-fat fryer), add the fish and fry gently until golden brown. Remove from the pan carefully and drain. Transfer to a warmed serving dish and keep hot.

To make the sauce: Add the garlic to the pan in which the fish was fried and fry over high heat until light brown. Add the ginger and fry for a further 1 minute. Stir in the water, sugar and tamarind water. Heat through, then pour over the fish.

Sprinkle with the spring onions (scallions). Serve hot, with the cucumber as a side dish.
SERVES 4

# Fried Hot Fish Balls

## Tod Mun Pla

METRIC/IMPERIAL

4 garlic cloves, peeled and chopped
20 peppercorns
4 coriander roots,* finely chopped
pinch of sugar
3 dried chillis
750 g/1½ lb cod fillets, skinned
1 tablespoon plain flour
1 tablespoon soy sauce
5 tablespoons vegetable oil
**To serve:**
½ cucumber, peeled and thinly sliced
1 teaspoon distilled vinegar
2 tablespoons water
1 teaspoon sugar
2 shallots, peeled and finely chopped
1 small carrot, peeled and grated

AMERICAN

4 garlic cloves, peeled and chopped
20 peppercorns
4 coriander roots,* finely chopped
pinch of sugar
3 dried chilis
1½ lb cod fillets, skinned
1 tablespoon all-purpose flour
1 tablespoon soy sauce
⅓ cup vegetable oil
**To serve:**
½ cucumber, peeled and thinly sliced
1 teaspoon distilled vinegar
2 tablespoons water
1 teaspoon sugar
2 shallots, peeled and finely chopped
1 small carrot, peeled and grated

METHOD

Put the garlic, peppercorns, coriander, sugar and chillis in a mortar and pound to a paste. Add the fish a little at a time and continue pounding to a smooth paste. Add the flour and soy sauce. Pound the mixture for a further 1 minute, then shape into 20 to 25 balls, about 2.5 cm/1 inch in diameter.

Heat the oil in a wok or deep frying pan (deep-fat fryer) and fry the fish balls, a few at a time, until golden brown all over. Remove from the pan with a slotted spoon, drain and arrange on a serving dish. Keep hot while frying the remainder.

Arrange the cucumber slices in a separate serving dish. Mix together the vinegar, water, sugar, shallots and carrot. Sprinkle over the cucumber. Serve the fish balls hot, with the cucumber salad as a side dish.
SERVES 4

# Dry Chicken Curry

## Kai P'Anang

METRIC/IMPERIAL

150 g/5 oz creamed coconut,* roughly
   chopped
150 ml/¼ pint water
2–3 large chicken breasts, skinned,
   boned and cut into serving pieces

**Curry paste:**
½ teaspoon caraway seeds
2 large chillis, seeded and chopped
½ teaspoon coriander seeds
2 teaspoons shredded lemon grass*
3 shallots, peeled
1 teaspoon finely chopped coriander
   root*
5 garlic cloves, peeled
3 slices kha*
½ teaspoon makrut peel,* grated
½ teaspoon kapi*

AMERICAN

1⅓ cups thick coconut milk*
2–3 large boneless chicken breasts,
   skinned, cut into serving pieces

**Curry paste:**
½ teaspoon caraway seeds
2 large chilis, seeded and chopped
½ teaspoon coriander seeds
2 teaspoons shredded lemon grass*
3 shallots, peeled
1 teaspoon finely chopped coriander
   root*
5 garlic cloves, peeled
3 slices kha*
½ teaspoon makrut peel,* grated
½ teaspoon kapi*

Put the creamed coconut (coconut milk) in
a large pan. If using creamed coconut,
add the water and heat gently until the
coconut has melted, stirring frequently.

Add the chicken to the coconut and
cook for about 10 minutes until almost
tender. Remove the chicken from the pan.
Boil the liquid for a few minutes until it
becomes oily.

Meanwhile, make the curry paste:
Pound the caraway seeds in a mortar. Add
the remaining ingredients one at a time,
pounding between each addition, to
obtain a smooth paste. Add the paste to the
coconut liquid and heat gently, stirring
constantly. Return the chicken to the pan
and reheat, turning to coat with the sauce.
Transfer to a warmed serving dish. Serve
hot.
SERVES 4

Fried Mackerel with Tamarind Sauce;
Deep-Fried Rice Vermicelli with Sauce

# Fried Pork Balls
## Moo Tod

### METRIC/IMPERIAL

*2 coriander roots,\* finely chopped*
*2 teaspoons freshly ground black*
*  pepper*
*4 garlic cloves, peeled*
*pinch of sugar*
*450 g/1 lb minced pork*
*2 tablespoons nam pla\**
*flour for coating*
*4–5 tablespoons vegetable oil*
*coriander leaves\* to garnish*

### AMERICAN

*2 coriander roots,\* finely chopped*
*2 teaspoons freshly ground black*
*  pepper*
*4 garlic cloves, peeled*
*pinch of sugar*
*2 cups ground pork*
*2 tablespoons nam pla\**
*flour for coating*
*4–5 tablespoons vegetable oil*
*coriander leaves\* to garnish*

### METHOD

Put the coriander roots, pepper, garlic and sugar in a mortar and pound to a smooth paste.

Add the pork and pound to a pulp, then transfer to a bowl and add the nam pla. Stir well, then form into about 20 balls, approximately 2.5 ml/1 inch in diameter, and coat lightly with flour.

Heat the oil in a wok or deep frying pan (deep-fat fryer). Add about 5 pork balls and fry over moderate heat for 2 to 3 minutes, or until no liquid is released from the balls when pierced with a sharp knife. Remove from the pan with a slotted spoon and keep hot while frying the remainder.

Pile the pork balls in a warmed serving dish and garnish with the coriander. Serve hot.
SERVES 4

**Chicken Ginger with Honey; Fried Pork Balls**

# Fried Chicken with Garlic

## Kai Tod Karb Kratiem

### METRIC/IMPERIAL

4 chicken breasts, skinned and boned
3 garlic cloves, peeled and crushed
1 tablespoon freshly ground black
    pepper
2 tablespoons soy sauce
1 teaspoon sugar
1 teaspoon salt
1 teaspoon sesame seed oil*
vegetable oil for shallow-frying

### AMERICAN

4 boneless chicken breasts, skinned
3 garlic cloves, peeled and crushed
1 tablespoon freshly ground black
    pepper
2 tablespoons soy sauce
1 teaspoon sugar
1 teaspoon salt
1 teaspoon sesame seed oil*
vegetable oil for shallow-frying

### METHOD

Slit the surface of the chicken breasts on both sides, using a very sharp knife. Put the remaining ingredients in a bowl, mix well, then rub into the chicken breasts. Leave to marinate for 2 hours.

Heat about 5 tablespoons vegetable oil in a wok or frying pan (skillet). Add 2 chicken breasts and fry over moderate heat for about 4 minutes on each side until golden brown. Remove from the pan and drain. Fry the remaining chicken breasts in the same way, adding more oil to the pan if necessary.

Cut each chicken breast in half, return to the pan and fry until the cut edges of the meat are no longer pink. Serve hot.
SERVES 4

# Chicken Ginger with Honey

## Pad King Kai

The flavour of this dish is greatly improved if it is cooked the day before it is required, then reheated just before serving.

### METRIC/IMPERIAL

5 spring onions, cut into 1 cm/½ inch
    pieces
100 g/4 oz fresh root ginger,*
    shredded
2 tablespoons vegetable oil
3 chicken breasts, skinned, boned and
    cut into small pieces
3 chicken livers, chopped
1 onion, peeled and sliced
3 garlic cloves, peeled and chopped
2 tablespoons dried jelly mushrooms,*
    soaked in warm water for 20 minutes
2 tablespoons soy sauce
1 tablespoon honey

### AMERICAN

5 scallions, cut into ½ inch pieces
1¼ cups shredded fresh ginger root*
2 tablespoons vegetable oil
3 boneless chicken breasts, skinned
    and cut into small pieces
3 chicken livers, chopped
1 onion, peeled and sliced
3 garlic cloves, peeled and chopped
2 tablespoons tree ears,* soaked in
    warm water for 20 minutes
2 tablespoons soy sauce
1 tablespoon honey

### METHOD

Put the spring onions (scallions) in a bowl, cover with cold water and leave to soak.

Mix the ginger with a little cold water, then drain and squeeze to reduce the hot taste. Rinse under cold running water, then drain well.

Heat the oil in a wok or frying pan (skillet), add the chicken and liver pieces and fry for 5 minutes. Remove from the pan with a slotted spoon and set aside.

Add the onion to the pan and fry gently until soft, then add the garlic and mushrooms (tree ears) and stir-fry for 1 minute. Return the chicken pieces to the pan.

Mix the soy sauce and honey together, pour over the chicken and stir well. Add the ginger and stir-fry for 2 to 3 minutes, then add the drained spring onions (scallions).

Transfer the mixture to a bowl, cover and leave overnight. Reheat when required. Serve hot.
SERVES 4

# Stuffed Pancakes (Crêpes)

## Kai Yad Sai

### METRIC/IMPERIAL

*225 g/8 oz minced pork*
*2 tablespoons tung chai\**
*1 teaspoon sugar*
*2 tablespoons soy sauce*
*2 onions, peeled and finely chopped*
*2 tablespoons vegetable oil*
*6 eggs, beaten*
*coriander leaves\* to garnish*

### AMERICAN

*1 cup ground pork*
*2 tablespoons tung chai\**
*1 teaspoon sugar*
*2 tablespoons soy sauce*
*2 onions, peeled and finely chopped*
*2 tablespoons vegetable oil*
*6 eggs, beaten*
*coriander leaves\* to garnish*

### METHOD

Put the pork, tung chai, sugar, soy sauce and onions in a bowl and mix well. Heat 1 tablespoon oil in a wok or frying pan (skillet), add the pork mixture and fry gently for 3 minutes. Remove from the pan and set aside.

Add the remaining oil to the cleaned pan and tilt to coat the entire surface with oil. Pour off any excess oil, then heat the pan until smoking. Pour in half the beaten eggs to make a thin omelet. Spoon half the pork mixture into the centre, then fold over the edges. Turn the omelet over and cook quickly on the underside until lightly browned. Remove from the pan and keep hot while cooking the remaining eggs and pork in the same way. Cut the pancakes (crêpes) into slices and arrange in a serving dish. Garnish with coriander. Serve immediately.

SERVES 4

# Beef with Hot Salad
## Nua Nam Toak

Braising steak can be used instead of
fillet steak for a more economical meal;
after slicing the meat treat it with meat
tenderizer, then leave for about 10 minutes before cooking. In Thailand,
papaya (pawpaw) peel is used to make
the meat tender.

The flavour of this dish is greatly improved if the onion, chillis and beef are
grilled (broiled) over glowing charcoals
rather than using a conventional grill
(broiler).

### METRIC/IMPERIAL

*450 g/1 lb fillet steak*
*1 large onion, peeled and sliced into*
  *rings*
*2 fresh chillis*
*2 garlic cloves, peeled and crushed*
*½ teaspoon sugar*
*1 teaspoon salt*
*½ teaspoon soy sauce*
*juice of 1 lime or lemon*
*1 teaspoon chopped mint*
**To serve:**
*fresh green seasonal vegetables*
  *(cucumber, tomatoes, Chinese*
  *cabbage, bean sprouts, etc.),*
  *chopped*

### AMERICAN

*1 lb fillet steak*
*1 large onion, peeled and sliced into*
  *rings*
*2 fresh chilis*
*2 garlic cloves, peeled and crushed*
*½ teaspoon sugar*
*1 teaspoon salt*
*½ teaspoon soy sauce*
*juice of 1 lime or lemon*
*1 teaspoon chopped mint*
**To serve:**
*fresh green seasonal vegetables*
  *(cucumber, tomatoes, bok choy,*
  *bean sprouts, etc.), chopped*

### METHOD

Cut the beef along the grain into strips
about 6 cm/2½ inches long, 2.5 cm/1 inch
wide and 1 cm/½ inch thick. Put the onion
rings and chillis on a skewer and grill
(broil) until soft. Remove from the
skewer, then mash together.

Grill (broil) the beef until just cooked
to taste, then mix with the mashed onion
and chillis. Add the remaining ingredients and mix well.

Arrange the chopped vegetables
around the edge of a warmed serving
dish, then pile the beef mixture in the
centre. Alternatively, toss the vegetables
quickly with the beef and pile into a
warmed serving dish. Serve hot.
SERVES 4

# Fried Beef and Horapa
## Pad Ho-ra-pa kub Nua

### METRIC/IMPERIAL

*2 tablespoons plus 1 teaspoon*
  *vegetable oil*
*750 g/1½ lb braising steak, thinly sliced*
*2 onions, peeled and sliced*
*3 garlic cloves, peeled and finely*
  *chopped*
*3 tablespoons freshly chopped horapa*
  *leaves\**
*3 fresh chillis, sliced*
*nam pla\* to taste*
*monosodium glutamate\* to taste*
*few chopped spring onions to garnish*

### AMERICAN

*2 tablespoons plus 1 teaspoon*
  *vegetable oil*
*1½ lb chuck steak, thinly sliced*
*2 onions, peeled and sliced*
*3 garlic cloves, peeled and finely*
  *chopped*
*3 tablespoons freshly chopped horapa*
  *leaves\**
*3 fresh chilis, sliced*
*nam pla\* to taste*
*msg\* to taste*
*few chopped scallions to garnish*

### METHOD

Heat 1 teaspoon of the oil in a wok or frying
pan (skillet), add the beef and fry until the
juices are extracted from the meat. Stir
twice and cook for about 3 minutes, then
remove from the pan and set aside.

Heat the remaining oil in the pan, add
the onions and garlic and fry over brisk
heat until brown. Stir in the horapa, then
return the beef to the pan. Add the chillis,
fry for a further 1 minute, then add nam
pla and monosodium glutamate (msg) to
taste.

Transfer to a serving dish and garnish
with the chopped spring onions (scallions). Serve hot.
SERVES 4

# Son-in-Law Eggs
## Kai Look Koei

### METRIC/IMPERIAL

*2 tablespoons vegetable oil*
*5 shallots, peeled and finely chopped*
*4 hard-boiled eggs, shelled and*
  *quartered*
*2 tablespoons tamarind water\**
*1 tablespoon water*
*2 teaspoons brown sugar*
*nam pla\* to taste*

### AMERICAN

*2 tablespoons vegetable oil*
*5 shallots, peeled and finely chopped*
*4 hard-cooked eggs, shelled and*
  *quartered*
*2 tablespoons tamarind water\**
*1 tablespoon water*
*2 teaspoons brown sugar*
*nam pla\* to taste*

### METHOD

Heat the oil in a wok or deep frying pan
(deep-fat fryer). Add the shallots and fry
until brown. Remove from the pan with a
slotted spoon and set aside.

Add the eggs to the pan and fry until
crisp and blistered on the outside, then
remove from the pan with a slotted spoon
and set aside.

Add the remaining ingredients to the
pan and cook for 5 minutes, stirring
constantly. Return the eggs to the pan
and heat gently for 2 minutes, stirring
carefully. Transfer to a warmed serving
dish and garnish with the fried shallots.
Serve hot.
SERVES 4

**Left: Beef with Hot Salad; Fried Beef
and Horapa
Below: Stuffed Pancakes (Crêpes)**

# Thai Salad

## Som Tum

In Thailand, papaya (pawpaw) is normally used in this salad, together with vegetables such as tomatoes and lettuce. It is a good side dish to serve with *Fried Pork Balls* (see page 58) and *Fried Chicken with Garlic* (see page 59).

### METRIC/IMPERIAL

*75 g/3 oz cabbage, shredded*
*1 large carrot, peeled and shredded*
*25 g/1 oz peanuts, roasted and crushed (see page 81)*
*25 g/1 oz dried prawns,\* ground*
**Dressing:**
*1 tablespoon nam pla\**
*2 teaspoons sugar*
*freshly ground black pepper*
*2 garlic cloves, peeled and crushed*
*2 tablespoons lime or lemon juice*

### AMERICAN

*1 cup shredded cabbage*
*½ cup shredded carrots*
*3 tablespoons peanuts, roasted and crushed (see page 81)*
*⅓ cup dried shrimp,\* ground*
**Dressing:**
*1 tablespoon nam pla\**
*2 teaspoons sugar*
*freshly ground black pepper*
*2 garlic cloves, peeled and crushed*
*2 tablespoons lime or lemon juice*

### METHOD

Put all the salad ingredients in a bowl and stir well. Mix together the dressing ingredients, pour over the salad and toss well to coat. Serve cold.

# Masaman Curry

## Kang Masaman

This is an unusual Thai curry in that it contains peanuts and tamarind water\* and there are many variations. It is equally good prepared with chicken, rather than beef.

King Rama VI said in one of his poems, 'A lady who makes a good *masaman* will never be short of suitors'.

### METRIC/IMPERIAL

*1 kg/2–2¼ lb braising steak, cut into 2.5 cm/1 inch squares*
*1.2 litres/2 pints water*
*200 g/7 oz creamed coconut,\* roughly chopped*
*100 g/4 oz peanuts, roasted (see page 81)*
*nam pla\* to taste*
*3 tablespoons tamarind water\**
*coconut sugar,\* to taste*
**Curry paste:**
*7 dried chillis, deseeded and finely chopped*
*½ teaspoon freshly ground black pepper*
*2 tablespoons coriander seeds*
*2 tablespoons cumin seeds*
*1 tablespoon shredded lemon grass\**
*1 cinnamon stick*
*5 cardamom seeds*
*¼ whole nutmeg, grated*
*1 teaspoon salt*
*7 shallots, peeled and grilled*
*5 garlic cloves, peeled*
*½ teaspoon kapi\**

### AMERICAN

*2¼ lb chuck steak, cut into 1 inch squares*
*5 cups water*
*1 cup coconut milk\**
*1 cup peanuts, roasted (see page 81)*
*nam pla\* to taste*
*3 tablespoons tamarind water\**
*coconut sugar,\* to taste*
**Curry paste:**
*7 dried chilis, deseeded and finely chopped*
*½ teaspoon freshly ground black pepper*
*2 tablespoons coriander seeds*
*2 tablespoons cumin seeds*
*1 tablespoon shredded lemon grass\**
*1 cinnamon stick*
*5 cardamom seeds*
*¼ whole nutmeg, grated*
*1 teaspoon salt*
*7 shallots, peeled and broiled*
*5 garlic cloves, peeled*
*½ teaspoon kapi\**

## METHOD

Put the steak and water in a pan and bring to the boil. Lower the heat, cover and simmer for about 1 hour or until the meat is tender.

To make the curry paste: Put the chillis in a pan with the pepper, coriander, cumin, lemon grass, cinnamon, cardamom and nutmeg. Cook over low heat until the mixture browns, stirring constantly. Transfer to a mortar and pound to a smooth paste. Add the remaining ingredients and pound the mixture until smooth.

Remove the meat from the pan with a slotted spoon and set aside. Add the coconut cream (coconut milk) to the liquid in the pan and heat gently, stirring frequently. Add the peanuts and a little nam pla. Boil the liquid until reduced in volume by one third. Add the prepared curry paste and simmer for about 5 minutes, stirring constantly.

Return the meat to the pan and cover with a tight-fitting lid. Bring back to the boil and continue cooking until the meat is very tender. Add the tamarind water with coconut sugar and nam pla to taste. Serve hot.
SERVES 6

# Soya Bean and Coconut Dip

## Tao Chiew Lon

Serve this dip with a salad of chopped fresh vegetables according to availability. Cucumber, red and green peppers, chicory (Belgian endive) or celery, and crisp lettuce make a good combination.

### METRIC/IMPERIAL

*100 g/4 oz creamed coconut,\* roughly chopped*
*300 ml/½ pint water*
*3 tablespoons tao chiew\**
*1 tablespoon finely chopped shallots or onion*
*50 g/2 oz cooked peeled prawns*
*50 g/2 oz mashed potato*
*2 chillis, finely chopped*
*1 teaspoon brown sugar*
*3 tablespoons tamarind water\**
*chillis to garnish*

### AMERICAN

*1¾ cups thick coconut milk\**
*3 tablespoons tao chiew\**
*1 tablespoon finely chopped shallots or onion*
*2 cooked shelled shrimp*
*¼ cup mashed potato*
*2 chilis, finely chopped*
*1 teaspoon brown sugar*
*3 tablespoons tamarind water\**
*chilis to garnish*

### METHOD

If using creamed coconut, place in a pan with the water and heat gently until the coconut has melted, stirring frequently.

Work the tao chiew and shallots to a paste, using an electric blender or a pestle and mortar then add to the coconut liquid with the prawns (shrimp) and potato.

Cook until the fat from the coconut floats to the surface of the sauce, stirring constantly to prevent sticking. Stir in the remaining ingredients and bring to the boil.

Transfer to a serving dish and garnish with chillis. Serve hot, as a dip with a crisp salad.
SERVES 4

Thai Salad; Masaman Curry; Soya Bean and Coconut Dip

Sweet Mung Beans with Coconut; Sticky
Rice with Black Beans; Sticky Rice and
Custard

# Sweet Mung Beans with Coconut
## Maled Khanun

### METRIC/IMPERIAL

*150 g/5 oz mung beans\**
*150 g/5 oz creamed coconut,\* roughly
    chopped*
*450 ml/¾ pint water*
*225 g/8 oz sugar*
*4 egg yolks, beaten*

### AMERICAN

*1 cup mung beans\**
*1¼ cups thick coconut milk\**
*1⅓ cups water*
*1 cup sugar*
*4 egg yolks, beaten*

### METHOD

Crush the beans, using a pestle and
mortar, then leave to soak in cold water
overnight.

Drain the beans and wash to remove
the green skins. Put the beans in a pan,
add enough water to cover, then simmer,
covered, for about 20 minutes or until
soft. Drain, then return to the cleaned pan
and heat gently until the beans are dry
and completely cooked, stirring occasionally. Mash to a smooth paste.

Put the creamed coconut (coconut
milk) in a pan. If using creamed coconut,
add 150 ml/¼ pint/⅓ cup of the water and
heat gently until melted, stirring
frequently.

Add 150 g/5 oz/¾ cup of the sugar to the
coconut liquid, then stir in the mashed
beans. Bring to the boil, then boil, uncovered, for about 30 minutes until the
mixture is thick, stirring frequently with
a wooden spoon. Remove from the heat
and leave until completely cold.

Form the paste into about 50 small
balls, approximately 1 cm/½ inch in diameter. Put the remaining sugar and
water in a pan. Heat gently until the sugar
has dissolved, then boil until a thin syrup
is formed.

Dip each ball into beaten egg yolk to
coat, then immerse in the hot syrup and
cook for about 30 seconds. Remove with
a slotted spoon and arrange in a single
layer on a serving dish, taking care that
the balls are not touching or they will
stick together. Chill in the refrigerator
for at least 3 hours before serving. Serve
very cold.
SERVES 4

# Sticky Rice with Black Beans
## Kow Neo Tua Dom

In Thailand, this dish is cooked and sold
in hollow sticks of green bamboo which
have been cooked over charcoal. This
recipe has been adapted for a domestic
oven. Dried black beans are available at
Chinese, Indian and Italian supermarkets.

### METRIC/IMPERIAL

*150 g/5 oz creamed coconut,\* roughly
    chopped*
*600 ml/1 pint water*
*50 g/2 oz dried black beans, soaked in
    cold water for 12 hours*
*40 g/1½ oz glutinous (sweet) rice\**
*25 g/1 oz coconut sugar\**

### AMERICAN

*1¼ cups thick coconut milk\**
*1¾ cups water*
*½ cup dried black beans, soaked in
    cold water for 12 hours*
*¼ cup glutinous (sweet) rice\**
*2 tablespoons coconut sugar\**

### METHOD

Put the creamed coconut (coconut milk)
and water in a pan and heat gently,
stirring frequently.

Drain the beans, then mix with the rice,
sugar and coconut milk. Pour into a
baking dish, cover and bake in a preheated very cool (120°C/250°F, Gas Mark
½) for about 3 hours, stirring after 2 hours.
Serve hot.
SERVES 4

# Sticky Rice and Custard
## Kow Neo Sang Kaya

### METRIC/IMPERIAL

**Custard:**
*159 g/5 oz creamed coconut,\* roughly
    chopped*
*300 ml/½ pint water*
*2 tablespoons rose water*
*2 tablespoons brown sugar*
*4 eggs, beaten*
**Sticky rice:**
*175 g/6 oz glutinous (sweet) rice\**
*100 g/4 oz creamed coconut,\* roughly
    chopped*
*300 ml/½ pint water*
*1 teaspoon salt*
*1 tablespoon sugar*
**To decorate:**
*lime slices*

### AMERICAN

**Custard:**
*2 tablespoons rose water*
*2 tablespoons brown sugar*
*1¾ cups thick coconut milk\**
*4 eggs, beaten*
**Sticky rice:**
*1 cup glutinous (sweet) rice\**
*1¾ cups coconut milk\**
*1 teaspoon salt*
*1 tablespoon sugar*
**To decorate:**
*lime slices*

## METHOD

To make the custard: If using creamed coconut, place in a pan, add the water and heat gently until the coconut has melted, stirring frequently.

Add the rose water and sugar to the coconut milk. Stir well, then beat in the eggs. Strain into a heatproof bowl and steam for about 1½ hours or until the custard has set. Alternatively, place the bowl in a baking dish of water and bake in a preheated cool oven (140°C/275°F, Gas Mark 1).

Meanwhile, make the sticky rice: Put the rice in a bowl in the top of a steamer or double boiler. If using creamed coconut, place in a pan, add the water and heat gently until the coconut has melted, stirring frequently. Mix the coconut milk with the salt and sugar, then pour over the rice. Steam for 30 minutes or until the rice is cooked.

To serve: Place the cooked custard on top of the rice and decorate with lime slices. Serve hot or cold.

SERVES 4

# Kampuchea, Laos and Vietnam

## Gloria Zimmerman
## Bach Ngo

Few cultures of the world have been as misunderstood in the West as those of South-East Asia. Among them, the lands of Vietnam, Kampuchea and Laos are probably the least understood. Variously dismissed as a conglomeration of Chinese, Indian and French influence, these countries essentially have cultures of their own. Recent research indicates that such basic words as plough and seed, kiln and pottery, axe and boat, iron and gold, went from South-East Asian language into Chinese. Archaeological finds point to the probability that rice was first domesticated here 1,000 years earlier than in India or China; the same appears to be true in the making of polished stone tools, pottery and bronze implements. Scholars now ask themselves if the Chinese and Indians learned from the South-East Asians, rather than the other way round.

Vietnamese culture, after centuries of struggle against Chinese domination, has maintained its own distinct, sophisticated and highly complex identity. Despite 1,000 years of Chinese occupation and repeated attempts at conquest, this ancient culture – dating back over 4,000 years – has retained its own language, folklore, customs and arts. The University of Hanoi is older than any university in Europe.

Although there are overtones which reflect Chinese, Indian and a later French influence, authentic Vietnamese cuisine is unique. Craig Claiborne, leading food critic of the 'New York Times', acclaims the Vietnamese kitchen as 'one of the most outstanding on earth'. In France, home of *haute cuisine*, Vietnamese restaurants far outnumber Chinese. Vietnamese chefs have earned so enviable a reputation that soon after John F Kennedy became president, a Vietnamese chef was invited to take charge of the White House kitchen.

The diversity of Vietnamese cuisine is at least partially explained by the country's geography The extensive coastline, stretching over 1,400 miles along the eastern seaboard of South-East Asia, provides all kinds of fish and shellfish. Most of the population is concentrated in the north and south, which are connected by a narrow stretch of mountainous country in the centre. The Red River Delta of the north and the Mekong River Delta in the south provide very fertile, low lying country.

In the hot, humid south a much broader range of vegetables, fruits and other foods are grown than in the cooler north. The highlands of the centre, with their temperate climate, provide a variety of vegetables, including asparagus, cauliflower, potatoes and artichokes. As might be expected, the regional cuisines are divided in the same way: Hanoi in the north, Hue in the centre and Saigon in the south.

Laos is a small, landlocked country which is relatively undeveloped and sparsely populated by a collection of tribes without a national history. Neighbouring China and Thailand have had the greatest influence on the Laotian culture.

Kampuchea, previously known as Cambodia, was a centre of power in South-East Asia about

1,000 years ago. With its capital at Angkor, the Khmer kingdom of Cambodia developed a great civilization. The remains of this can be seen today, with such enormous structures as the Temple at Angkor Wat, the world's largest religious building. From the twelfth century, the Khmer culture and power gradually declined.

Rice, staple food of the vast majority of Asian kitchens, is no less important in the cooking of Vietnam, Kampuchea and Laos. Prepared in infinite variety, it appears at every meal and is, indeed, the 'bread' of life. The most unusual feature of Laotian food is the emphasis on glutinous (sweet) rice* at every meal. In this respect, the Laotian cuisine is unique. In Vietnam, Kampuchea and other Asian countries, glutinous (sweet) rice* is normally only used for sweets or snacks. For all-round use, the Vietnamese prefer rice that is very dry and flaky.

All three cuisines make good use of home-grown fruits and vegetables. The markets are a feast to Western eyes with their colourful display of unfamiliar fruits, vegetables and fresh herbs. A variety of mints, lemon grass* and coriander* are used in dishes.

Fish, both fresh and dried, are a major source of protein. In landlocked Laos, freshwater fish from the many streams and rivers predominate. Likewise Kampuchea, with its Tonle Sap (Great Lake), the Mekong river and the sea, has a plentiful supply of fish and shellfish. The long coastline of Vietnam, the Red river in the north and the Mekong in the south, similarly supply an abundance of seafood and freshwater fish.

Meat is less widely used than fish and seafood, primarily because it is relatively expensive. Lamb and mutton are not seen at all. Pork is cheaper than other types of meat and is therefore more frequently eaten. Vietnamese pigs, fed on chopped banana tree trunks, produce a superior pork that is much prized. Chicken and duck, much leaner than their Western counterparts, are seen on special occasions. Beef is very expensive and is served only at very special feasts. In Laos, deer and other game are hunted in the mountains and forests; these are eaten on festive occasions, rather than beef.

Nuoc Cham (see page 77), also known as Nuoc Mam, is a universal condiment, used in many different ways. This clear, salty liquid is prepared by layering fresh anchovies, sardines and other small fish, with salt, in large barrels; these are then set out in the sun. As salt is to the Western cuisine and soy sauce is to the Chinese cuisine, so Nuoc Cham is to these cuisines. It is added to all kinds of dishes during preparation; it also serves as the base for sauces to be sprinkled on prepared dishes or served as a dip. In Vietnam, Nuoc Cham is combined with garlic, lime or lemon juice, sugar and fresh chillis, and used to enhance flavours of other foods. In Kampuchea and Laos, roasted peanuts are added and, in Laos, Nuoc Cham is also mixed with anchovy paste.

The hallmarks of Vietnamese cuisine are lightness and subtlety, with a delicacy and clarity of flavour. Although Chinese influences are apparent, they have been so assimilated that even a stir-fried dish which looks somewhat Chinese will have a taste and aroma unmistakably Vietnamese, while their curry is quite unlike any Indian curry. The Vietnamese aversion to fats is apparent in their stir-frying technique in which even less oil is used than in Chinese cooking. Their dislike of fat is probably one reason why the Vietnamese simmer so many of their dishes. The light and delicate nature of this cuisine can be attributed to this limited use of fats and the emphasis on fresh, raw vegetables.

The food of the north is not as spicy as that of the south, although black pepper is widely used as a condiment. Northerners like their vegetables cooked and tend to prefer more complex and delicate flavours. Fish is not as important in the north, but shellfish, such as crab, is exceedingly popular. Stir-fried dishes are seen more often in the north than in the centre and south – undoubtedly because of the proximity of the Chinese border.

The centre mountainous neck of land connecting the north and south, is where Hue, the ancient capital of the kings of Vietnam is located. Here the influence of the royal palate is evident in the emphasis on food presentation. Small portions of a variety of dishes are served at each meal and spicy foods predominate, with the frequent use of hot chilli peppers and Nuoc Cham.*

The hot climate and fertile fields of the south provide a great variety of vegetables, fruit, meat and game. Large quantities of fresh fruits and raw vegetables are consumed. A tropical people, the South Vietnamese traditionally prefer spicy food; they also make good use of locally grown coconut and sugar cane. The influence of the French is more evident here – in the use of Western vegetables, such as potatoes and asparagus, though prepared in Vietnamese style.

Kampuchea and Laos are relatively underdeveloped countries with very low per capita incomes. In addition, they do not have the extensive range of foods that are available to the Vietnamese and this is reflected in their relatively limited cuisines. The Kampuchean diet is largely based on rice, freshwater and dried fish. It is heavily spiced and tends to be somewhat strong in flavour for Western tastes. Barbecuing over charcoal is a favourite way of preparing meat or fish, which is generally served with a raw Vegetable Platter (see page 77). Laotian dishes are more influenced by the Thai kitchen, although their prolific use of glutinous rice* clearly distinguishes them from others. Here, too, barbecuing is very popular, though frequently it is only the first step in the preparation of a dish. The liberal use of red chilli peppers makes for many fiery dishes.

## Serving

In neither Laos or Kampuchea are there restaurants serving the national cuisine. The foreigner must be invited to a family meal to sample the food. Meals are served in very simple fashion and the family are seated on straw mats on the floor, as compared to Vietnam where even simple family meals are served at the table. Chopsticks are not used in Laos and Kampuchea, but food is generally eaten with the fingers. Soup is eaten with a soup spoon out of a large communal bowl placed in the centre of the serving area. In Vietnam, the Chinese influence is evident in the universal use of chopsticks, but the Vietnamese use metal spoons rather than the ceramic soup spoons favoured by the Chinese.

## Cooking Utensils and Equipment

All three cuisines tend to use the same kitchen equipment, although with a different emphasis. The mortar and pestle, the wok, a sharp chopper and chopping board are common items. In Laos, the glutinous rice* is cooked in a steamer made of woven bamboo, whereas in Vietnam and Kampuchea the steamers are metal. In all three countries, cooking in the cities is generally done over kerosene or bottled gas, whereas in rural areas charcoal is most commonly used.

# Rice Noodle
# Fish Soup

## Num Banh Choc
### Kampuchea

This soup is usually served at breakfast in
Kampuchea. *Khcheay* (white turmeric) is
available in dried powdered form at
oriental groceries.

#### METRIC/IMPERIAL

1.5 litres/2½ pints water
1 fish (carp, mackerel, sea bass, etc);
   weighing 1.5 kg/3–3½ lb
3 tablespoons khcheay
2 garlic cloves, peeled
5 lemon grass leaves,* thinly sliced
1 teaspoon turmeric powder
2 tablespoons fish paste*
2 tablespoons fish sauce*
1 teaspoon salt
pinch of monosodium glutamate*
1 teaspoon sugar
250 ml/8 fl oz coconut milk*
**To serve:**
225 g/8 oz medium rice vermicelli*
40 g/1½ oz fresh bean sprouts
50 g/2 oz cucumber, shredded
50 g/2 oz green papaya, shredded
2 tablespoons chopped dill
50 g/2 oz cabbage, shredded
50 g/2 oz fresh or canned banana
   blossoms, shredded (optional)

# Chicken Soup

## Môn Sngôr
### Kampuchea

#### METRIC/IMPERIAL

1 chicken, weighing 1–1.25 kg/2–2½ lb
2 litres/3½ pints water
3 tablespoons fish sauce*
1 teaspoon sugar
pinch of monosodium glutamate*
juice of 1 lime
2 spring onions, chopped
4 tablespoons shredded culantro*
1 red chilli, sliced

#### AMERICAN

1 chicken, weighing 2–2½ lb
4½ pints water
3 tablespoons fish sauce*
1 teaspoon sugar
pinch of msg*
juice of 1 lime
2 scallions, chopped
¼ cup shredded culantro*
1 red chili, sliced

#### METHOD

Put the chicken and water in a large pan
and bring to the boil. Boil for 20 minutes
or until the chicken is cooked. Remove
the chicken from the pan and tear the
meat from the bones in bite-sized pieces.
Return the meat and bones to the pan and
bring back to the boil. Boil for 5 minutes,
then remove from the heat.

Put the fish sauce, sugar, monosodium
glutamate (msg) and lime juice in a
warmed soup tureen. Pour the hot soup
into the tureen and stir well, then
sprinkle over the spring onions (scallions), culantro and chilli. Serve hot with
rice as part of a family dinner.
SERVES 4

#### AMERICAN

6¼ cups water
1 fish (bluefish, catfish, etc.), weighing
   3–3½ lb
3 tablespoons khcheay
2 garlic cloves, peeled
5 lemon grass leaves,* thinly sliced
1 teaspoon turmeric powder
2 tablespoons fish paste*
2 tablespoons fish sauce*
1 teaspoon salt
pinch of msg*
1 teaspoon sugar
1 cup coconut milk*
**To serve:**
½ lb medium rice vermicelli*
¾ cup fresh bean sprouts
½ cup shredded cucumber
½ cup shredded green papaya
2 tablespoons chopped dill
¾ cup shredded cabbage
½ cup fresh or canned banana
   blossoms, shredded (optional)

#### METHOD

Bring the water to the boil in a large pan.
Add the fish and bring back to the boil,
then simmer for about 15 minutes or until
the fish flakes easily. Remove the fish
from the pan and reserve the cooking
liquid.

Remove all the flesh from the fish and
discard the carcass. Put the khcheay,
garlic, lemon grass and turmeric in a
mortar and pound to a paste. Add the fish
and pound again to a smooth paste.

Bring the reserved cooking liquid to
the boil. Add the fish paste, fish sauce,
salt, monosodium glutamate (msg), sugar
and coconut milk. Bring back to the boil,
add the pounded fish mixture, then boil
for 10 to 15 minutes.

Boil the rice vermicelli in about 2
litres/3½ pints/4½ pints water for 5 minutes, then drain and rinse under cold
running water. Drain again.

Pour the hot soup into a warmed soup
tureen. Divide the rice vermicelli between 4 individual warmed soup bowls,
add the remaining ingredients and ladle
the soup over the top. Serve hot.
SERVES 4

# Stir-Fried Chicken with Ginger

## Sach Môn Chha Khnhei
Kampuchea

### METRIC/IMPERIAL

2.5 cm/1 inch piece of fresh root
    ginger,* peeled and shredded
salt
2 tablespoons pork fat or vegetable oil
2 garlic cloves, peeled and chopped
4 chicken thighs, chopped into
    2.5 cm/1 inch squares
1 tablespoon fish sauce*
1 teaspoon sugar
1 tablespoon water
2 spring onions, cut into 5 cm/2 inch
    pieces
coriander leaves* or parsley sprigs to
    garnish

### AMERICAN

1 inch piece of fresh ginger root,*
    peeled and shredded
salt
2 tablespoons pork fat or vegetable oil
2 garlic cloves, peeled and chopped
4 chicken thighs, chopped into 1 inch
    squares
1 tablespoon fish sauce*
1 teaspoon sugar
1 tablespoon water
2 scallions, cut into 2 inch pieces
coriander leaves* or parsley sprigs to
    garnish

### METHOD

Sprinkle the ginger with a little salt, leave to stand for a few minutes, then squeeze and discard the liquid. Rinse the ginger with water and squeeze out the liquid again.

Heat the pork fat or oil in a frying pan (skillet). Add the garlic and stir-fry until lightly browned. Add the ginger and stir-fry for 1 minute, then add the chicken. Stir in the remaining ingredients, except the spring onions (scallions), then cover and cook over moderate heat for 10 minutes or until the chicken is completely cooked. Stir in the spring onions (scallions).

Transfer to a serving dish and garnish with coriander or parsley. Serve hot with rice as part of a family dinner.
SERVES 4

Stir-Fried Chicken with Ginger; Fried
Pork Spareribs; Sour Beef Stew

# Sour Beef Stew

## Somlâr Mochu Sachko
Kampuchea

### METRIC/IMPERIAL

2 stalks lemon grass,* thinly sliced
3 garlic cloves, peeled
5 fresh or dried lime leaves,* shredded
4 tablespoons tamarind paste*
1 tablespoon turmeric powder
2 tablespoons dried galingale,* soaked
   in hot water for 1 hour
1 red chilli
2 tablespoons fish paste*
2 tablespoons pork fat or vegetable oil
2 tablespoons fish sauce*
1 kg/2–2¼ lb stewing beef, cut into
   2.5 cm/1 inch cubes
120 ml/4 fl oz water
**To garnish:**
2 tablespoons chopped spring onion,
   green part only

### AMERICAN

2 stalks lemon grass,* thinly sliced
3 garlic cloves, peeled
5 fresh or dried lime leaves,* shredded
¼ cup tamarind paste*
1 tablespoon turmeric powder
2 tablespoons dried galingale,* soaked
   in hot water for 1 hour
1 red chili
2 tablespoons fish paste*
2 tablespoons pork fat or vegetable oil
2 tablespoons fish sauce*
2–2¼ lb stewing beef, cut into 1 inch
   cubes
½ cup water
**To garnish:**
2 tablespoons chopped scallion, green
   part only

### METHOD

Put all the ingredients except the beef,
fish sauce, paste and pork fat in a mortar
and pound to a paste.

Work the fish paste through a sieve
(strainer) and discard the pulp remaining in the sieve.

Heat the pork fat or oil in a pan. Add the
fish paste, stir-fry for a few seconds, then
add the pounded ingredients. Stir again,
then add the fish sauce. Stir in the meat
and water. Bring to the boil and simmer,
uncovered, for 15 minutes.

Add more water as necessary to
ensure the meat is just covered with
liquid. Cover and simmer for 1 hour or
until the meat is tender, adding more
water if necessary during cooking.

Transfer to a serving dish and garnish
with spring onion (scallion). Serve hot
with rice as a main dish for a family
dinner.
SERVES 6

# Fried Pork Spareribs

## Choeeng Chomni Chrouc Chean

Kampuchea
These spareribs can alternatively be
cooked over charcoal.

### METRIC/IMPERIAL

1 kg/2–2¼ lb pork spareribs, cut into
   separate pieces
2 tablespoons fish sauce*
1 tablespoon sugar
3 garlic cloves, peeled and chopped
pinch of freshly ground black pepper
3 tablespoons pork fat or vegetable oil
**To garnish:** (optional)
thinly pared strip of chilti
parsley sprig

### AMERICAN

2–2¼ lb pork spareribs, cut into
   separate pieces
2 tablespoons fish sauce*
1 tablespoon sugar
3 garlic cloves, peeled and chopped
pinch of freshly ground black pepper
3 tablespoons pork fat or vegetable oil
**To garnish:** (optional)
thinly pared strip of chili
parsley sprig

### METHOD

Put the spareribs in a bowl, cover with
the remaining ingredients except the fat
or oil; leave to marinate for 30 minutes.

Heat the pork fat or oil in a frying pan
(skillet). Add the spareribs and fry
gently for about 10 minutes on each side
until golden brown and cooked through.

Drain the spareribs and arrange on a
serving dish. Garnish with red chilli and
parsley, if liked, arranged to resemble a
flower head. Serve hot with rice.
SERVES 4

# Chicken Lap

## Lap Kay

### Laos

A dish of Lap Kay, a bowl of chicken soup, a bamboo steamer containing glutinous (sweet) rice* and a *Vegetable Platter* (see page 77) – all of these are placed in the centre of the table. (In Laos, this would be a straw mat on the floor.)

Each diner is given a plate and a spoon. He then picks up about 1 table-spoon rice, squeezes it into a ball, presses it against the mound of Chicken Lap, then eats the rice and the food that adheres to it. A spoonful of soup is eaten after each mouthful, followed by a few pieces of vegetable from the platter.

METRIC/IMPERIAL

225 g/8 oz boned chicken meat,
    skinned and finely diced
100 g/4 oz chicken livers, finely diced
100 g/4 oz chicken gizzards, finely
    diced (optional)
2 teaspoons anchovy paste
2 teaspoons fish sauce*
1 tablespoon whole dried red chillis
2 tablespoons dried galingale,* soaked
    in hot water for 1 hour and finely
    chopped
4 teaspoons lime juice
¼ teaspoon salt
¼ teaspoon freshly ground black
    pepper
**To garnish:**
2 tablespoons chopped spring onion,
    green part only
coriander leaves*

AMERICAN

½ lb skinned boneless chicken meat,
    finely diced
¼ lb chicken livers, finely diced
¼ lb chicken gizzards, finely diced
    (optional)
2 teaspoons anchovy paste
2 teaspoons fish sauce*
1 tablespoon whole dried red chilis
2 tablespoons dried galingale,* soaked
    in hot water for 1 hour and finely
    chopped
4 teaspoons lime juice
¼ teaspoon salt
¼ teaspoon freshly ground black
    pepper
**To garnish:**
2 tablespoons chopped scallion, green
    part only
coriander leaves*

METHOD

Mix together the chicken, livers and gizzards, if using. Place in a 20 cm/8 inch square baking tin (pan) and press the mixture down firmly until about 1 cm/½ inch thick. Bake in a preheated moderate oven (180°C/350°F, Gas Mark 4) for 20 minutes.

Allow to cool slightly, then add the remaining ingredients and work into the mixture, with the hands, squeezing out all the excess liquid.

Arrange on a warmed serving dish and garnish with the spring onion (scallion) and coriander. Serve hot or allow to cool before serving.
SERVES 4

# Chicken Soup

## Ken Kay

### Laos

This is always served as an accompaniment to *Lap Kay*.

METRIC/IMPERIAL

1 tablespoon dried tamarind pulp*
750 g/1½ lb chicken, chopped into
    5 cm/2 inch pieces, with the bones
1.6 litres/2¾ pints water
2 tomatoes, cut into wedges
6 lime leaves*
2 tablespoons fish sauce*
½ teaspoon salt
pinch of freshly ground black pepper
**To garnish:**
2 tablespoons chopped spring onion,
    green part only
2 tablespoons chopped coriander
    leaves*

AMERICAN

1 tablespoon dried tamarind pulp*
1½ lb chicken, chopped into 2 inch
    pieces, with the bones
7 cups water
2 tomatoes, cut into wedges
6 lime leaves*
2 tablespoons fish sauce*
½ teaspoon salt
pinch of freshly ground black pepper
**To garnish:**
2 tablespoons chopped scallion, green
    part only
2 tablespoons chopped coriander
    leaves*

## METHOD

Soak the tamarind pulp in 120 ml/4 fl oz/ ½ cup hot water for 10 minutes, then knead to extract the flavour. Strain the liquid, discarding the pulp.

Put the chicken, water, tomatoes, tamarind water and lime leaves in a pan and bring to the boil. Skim, then lower the heat and simmer, uncovered, for 20 minutes or until the chicken is tender. Add the fish sauce, salt and pepper.

Pour the hot soup into a warmed tureen and garnish with the spring onion (scallion) and coriander. Serve hot.

SERVES 4

# Sour Carrot

## Tam Sôm

### Laos

Tam Sôm appears as an appetizer at all social occasions. It has an amalgam of flavours – sour, salty, sweet and very hot. If pork stomach cannot be obtained, it may be omitted.

## METRIC/IMPERIAL

*225 g/8 oz pork stomach*
*5 garlic cloves, peeled*
*5 dried red chillis*
*2 tomatoes*
*1 teaspoon monosodium glutamate\**
*2 tablespoons fish sauce\**
*3 medium carrots, peeled and shredded*

## AMERICAN

*½ lb pork stomach*
*5 garlic cloves, peeled*
*5 dried red chilis*
*2 tomatoes*
*1 teaspoon msg\**
*2 tablespoons fish sauce\**
*3 medium carrots, peeled and shredded*

## METHOD

Put the pork stomach in a pan, cover with water and boil for about 30 minutes.

Meanwhile, pound the garlic, chillis, tomatoes and monosodium glutamate (msg) in a mortar. Stir in the fish sauce.

Place the shredded carrot on a serving dish and pour over the sauce. Drain the pork stomach, slice thinly and arrange on top of the salad. Mix well with chopsticks just before serving. Serve cold.

SERVES 4

**Chicken Lap, served with Chicken Soup, Glutinous Rice (see page 74) and Vegetable Platter (see page 77)**

# Glutinous (Sweet) Rice*

In Laos, rice is always served in the bamboo basket in which it has been steamed. In the West, however. it can be steamed by putting a layer of cheese-cloth (muslin) on one of the layers of an oriental aluminium steamer, and placing the soaked glutinous (sweet) rice* on the cheesecloth (muslin). For this method of cooking rice, no measurements are necessary: every cup of glutinous (sweet) rice* doubles in volume when cooked.

## METHOD

Soak the rice in water to cover for at least 6 hours, then drain. Bring water to the boil in the lower level of a steamer, making sure that the water does not touch the steaming level. Place the rack containing the rice on top of the boiling water, then cover and steam for about 15 minutes until the rice looks clear and is soft to the touch. The longer the soaking period, the shorter the cooking time.

# Barbecued Pork with Mushrooms and Beans

## Ocklam

Laos

This is the national dish of Laos. Beef or chicken may be substituted for the pork used here. Fresh pork skin is easily obtainable at butchers' shops while dried pork skin can be obtained at Vietnamese grocery stores – it should be soaked in warm water for 30 minutes before use.

### METRIC/IMPERIAL

225 g/8 oz pork, sliced into strips 2.5 cm/1 inch wide and 5 mm/¼ inch thick
250 g/9 oz glutinous (sweet) rice*
2 tablespoons fish sauce*
½ teaspoon salt
1 aubergine, weighing about 450 g/1 lb
1 tablespoon whole dried red chillis
100 g/4 oz French beans or Chinese long beans, cut into 2.5 cm/1 inch pieces
8 large Chinese dried mushrooms,* soaked in warm water for 30 minutes and shredded
3 bay leaves
10 cm/4 inch square piece of fresh or dried pork skin, shredded into thin strips

**To garnish:**
few lemon slices
thinly pared strip of chilli
2.5 cm/1 inch piece of spring onion

**Barbecued Pork with Mushrooms and Beans, served with Vegetable Platter (see page 77)**

### AMERICAN

½ lb pork, sliced into strips 1 inch wide and ¼ inch thick
1½ cups glutinous (sweet) rice*
2 tablespoons fish sauce*
½ teaspoon salt
1 eggplant, weighing about 1 lb
1 tablespoon whole dried red chilis
¼ lb string beans or Chinese long beans, cut into 1 inch pieces
8 large Chinese dried mushrooms,* soaked in warm water for 30 minutes and shredded
3 bay leaves
4 inch square piece of fresh or dried pork skin, shredded into thin strips

**To garnish:**
few lemon slices
thinly pared strip of chili
1 inch piece of scallion

### METHOD

Roast the pork in a preheated moderate oven (180°C/350°F, Gas Mark 4) for 15 minutes. Meanwhile, put the glutinous rice in a mortar, add just enough water to cover, then crush with a pestle.

Pour 1.75 litres/3 pints/7½ cups water into a pan and bring to the boil. Add the fish sauce and salt, then the pork, aubergine (eggplant) and chillis. Boil for 10 minutes or until the aubergine (eggplant) is soft, then remove from the pan together with the chillis.

Pound the aubergine (eggplant) and chillis, using a pestle and mortar, then return to the pan. Add the beans, mushrooms and bay leaves. Bring to the boil, then add the glutinous rice with its soaking liquid and the pork skin. Boil for 20 minutes or until the glutinous rice is cooked.

Transfer to a serving dish and garnish with lemon slices, chilli and spring onion (scallion), coiling the chilli around the onion (scallion) to resemble a flower head. Serve hot with boiled rice and a *Vegetable Platter* (see page 77).
SERVES 4

# Spicy Beef

## Shin Ngoa Lap

Laos

### METRIC/IMPERIAL

3 tablespoons glutinous rice*
450 g/1 lb beef topside, cut into 3 pieces
1 tablespoon fish sauce*
2 teaspoons anchovy paste
1 teaspoon monosodium glutamate* (optional)
1 tablespoon dried galingale,* soaked in hot water for 1 hour and finely chopped
1 tablespoon chopped coriander leaves*
1 tablespoon chopped spring onion, green part only

**To finish:**
1 red chilli, sliced into rings
juice of ½ lime

### AMERICAN

3 tablespoons glutinous rice*
1 lb beef top round, cut into 3 pieces
1 tablespoon fish sauce*
2 teaspoons anchovy paste
1 teaspoon msg* (optional)
1 tablespoon dried galingale,* soaked in hot water for 1 hour and finely chopped
1 tablespoon chopped coriander leaves*
1 tablespoon chopped scallion, green part only

**To finish:**
1 red chili, sliced into rings
juice of ½ lime

### METHOD

Fry the glutinous rice in a hot, dry frying pan (skillet) until brown, then pound to a powder in a mortar or electric blender.

Roast the beef in a preheated moderately hot oven (200°C/400°F, Gas Mark 6) for 15 minutes. Leave until cool enough to handle, then shred into thin strips and mix with the powdered rice.

Combine the fish sauce and anchovy paste in a pan, then cook over moderate heat until smooth. Add to the beef with the monosodium glutamate (msg), if using, the galingale, coriander and spring onion (scallion); stir well.

Arrange the meat mixture on a warmed serving dish and garnish with the chilli. Sprinkle with the lime juice just before serving. Serve hot, or at room temperature.
SERVES 4

# Chicken Spring Rolls

## Cha Gio Ga

### Vietnam

Cha Gio Ga is the most popular dish in Vietnamese cuisine, for both rich and poor. It is usually filled with pork and crab, but a combination of any meat or seafood may be used. Serve as an appetizer with a bowl of *Nuoc Cham* or as a main course accompanied by a *Vegetable Platter* with *Nuoc Cham* served separately as a dip.

Cooked spring rolls can be frozen, then reheated in a moderate oven (180°C/350°F, Gas Mark 4). Alternatively they can be partially cooked, refrigerated for 1 day, then completed the following day.

METRIC/IMPERIAL

**Filling:**

*50 g/2 oz transparent noodles,\* soaked in water for 10 minutes, then cut into 2.5 cm/1 inch pieces*

*450 g/1 lb chicken breast meat, skinned and cut into thin strips*

*2 tablespoons dried wood ears,\* soaked in warm water for 20 minutes, then finely chopped*

*3 garlic cloves, peeled and finely chopped*

*3 shallots, finely chopped*

*225 g/8 oz crabmeat*

*½ teaspoon freshly ground black pepper*

**Wrappers:**

*4 eggs, beaten*

*20 dried rice papers\**

*450 ml/¾ pint vegetable oil*

**To garnish:**

*shredded spring onion*

AMERICAN

**Filling:**

*2 oz cellophane noodles,\* soaked in water for 10 minutes, then cut into 1 inch pieces*

*1 lb skinned and boned chicken breast meat, cut into thin strips*

*2 tablespoons tree ears,\* soaked in warm water for 20 minutes, then finely chopped*

*3 garlic cloves, peeled and finely chopped*

*3 shallots, finely chopped*

*½ lb crabmeat*

*½ teaspoon freshly ground black pepper*

**Wrappers:**

*4 eggs, beaten*

*20 dried rice papers\**

*2 cups vegetable oil*

**To garnish:**

*shredded scallion*

METHOD

To make the filling: Put all the ingredients in a bowl and mix well, using the hands.

Brush beaten egg over the entire surface of each piece of rice paper. Leave for a few seconds until soft and flexible. Place 1 teaspoon filling in a rectangular shape along the curved edge of the paper, roll once, then fold over the sides to enclose the filling and continue rolling. (The beaten egg not only makes the wrapper flexible, it also holds it together.)

Pour the cold oil into a 30 cm/12 inch frying pan (skillet), then add about one third of the spring rolls. Fry over moderate heat for about 30 minutes until golden brown, then remove with a slotted spoon and drain on absorbent kitchen paper towels. Fry the remaining spring rolls in the same way. Serve hot or at room temperature, garnished with shredded spring onion (scallion).
MAKES ABOUT 20

**Chicken Spring Rolls, served with Nuoc Cham**

## Nuoc Cham

### Vietnam

No Vietnamese meal is served without Nuoc Cham – a hot, tangy sauce which is sprinkled on food as desired. If you do not have a pestle and mortar, mash the ingredients with the back of a spoon. Do not use an electric blender – it will not give the right consistency. Nuoc Cham can be made in larger quantities and stored in the refrigerator for up to 1 week.

METRIC/IMPERIAL

*2 garlic cloves, peeled*
*4 dried red chillis, or 1 fresh red chilli*
*5 teaspoons sugar*
*juice and pulp of ¼ lime*
*4 tablespoons fish sauce\**
*5 tablespoons water*

AMERICAN

*2 garlic cloves, peeled*
*4 dried red chilis, or 1 fresh red chili*
*5 teaspoons sugar*
*juice and pulp of ¼ lime*
*¼ cup fish sauce\**
*⅓ cup water*

METHOD

Pound the garlic, chillis and sugar using a pestle and mortar. Add the lime juice and pulp, then the fish sauce and water. Mix well to combine the ingredients. Use as required.
SERVES 4

## Vegetable Platter

### Dia Rau Song

A platter of raw vegetables is an important part of almost every Laotian, Cambodian or Vietnamese meal. In South-East Asia, a variety of vegetables and different herbs are used. A satisfactory vegetable platter can however be made with fewer ingredients.

METRIC/IMPERIAL/AMERICAN

*soft lettuce leaves*
*mint leaves*
*coriander leaves\**
*cucumber, partially peeled and thinly sliced into half-moon shapes*

METHOD

Pile the lettuce in a mound in the centre of a serving dish, then place the mint and coriander around the lettuce in separate mounds. Arrange the cucumber slices overlapping around the rim of the dish. Serve cold.
SERVES 4

# Crabmeat and Tapioca Pearl Soup

## Cua Nâú Bôt Báng

Vietnam

Fresh, frozen or canned crabmeat can be used for this soup. If using live fresh crabs, boil 1 or 2 crabs in just enough water to cover for 10 minutes, then drain and remove the meat. Reserve the cooking liquid and use in place of the chicken stock listed in the ingredients.

### METRIC/IMPERIAL

*1 tablespoon vegetable oil*
*4 shallots, peeled*
*225 g/8 oz crabmeat*
*1.2 litres/2 pints chicken stock*
*2 tablespoons fish sauce\**
*125 g/4½ oz tapioca pearls, soaked in water for 10 minutes*

### To garnish:

*freshly ground black pepper*
*2 tablespoons chopped coriander leaves\**
*2 tablespoons chopped spring onion, green part only*

### AMERICAN

*1 tablespoon vegetable oil*
*4 shallots, peeled*
*½ lb crabmeat*
*5 cups chicken stock*
*2 tablespoons fish sauce\**
*⅔ cup tapioca pearls, soaked in water for 10 minutes*

### To garnish:

*freshly ground black pepper*
*2 tablespoons chopped coriander leaves\**
*2 tablespoons chopped scallion, green part only*

### METHOD

Heat the oil in a pan, add the shallots and fry gently until lightly browned. Add the crabmeat and stir-fry until beginning to brown, then add the stock and fish sauce.

Drain the tapioca, add to the pan and boil for 5 minutes or until the tapioca pearls are clear. Pour into warmed individual soup bowls and sprinkle with pepper, coriander and spring onions (scallions). Serve hot.

SERVES 4

# Chrysanthemum Soup with Minced (Ground) Pork

## Canh Tân Ô Thit Heo

Vietnam

Chrysanthemum choy is a cultivated edible chrysanthemum, eaten before it blooms. The tough stems are discarded and only the top, tender stems and leaves are eaten. It is available at Oriental groceries.

### METRIC/IMPERIAL

*100 g/4 oz minced pork*
*freshly ground black pepper*
*2 tablespoons plus 1 teaspoon fish sauce\**
*1 shallot, peeled and finely chopped*
*1.5 litres/2½ pints chicken stock*
*450 g/1 lb chrysanthemum choy*
*2 spring onions, cut into 5 cm/2 inch lengths*

## AMERICAN

½ cup ground pork
freshly ground black pepper
2 tablespoons plus 1 teaspoon fish
  sauce*
1 shallot, peeled and finely chopped
6¼ cups chicken stock
1 lb chrysanthemum choy
2 scallions, cut into 2 inch lengths

## METHOD

Put the pork in a bowl with a pinch of black pepper, 1 teaspoon fish sauce and the shallot. Mix well, then leave to stand for about 15 minutes. Shape the mixture into about 24 small balls, using about 1 teaspoonful for each.

Put the stock in a pan and bring to the boil. Add the pork balls and boil for 12 minutes, then add the remaining fish sauce and black pepper to taste.

Put the chrysanthemum choy and spring onions (scallions) in a warmed large soup tureen. Pour over the boiling stock and meatballs. Serve hot with rice and fish sauce.

SERVES 4

# Duck Soup with Dried Bamboo Shoot
## Vit Xáo Măng
### Vietnam

At some stage during the New Year celebrations, every Vietnamese home will serve a dish containing dried bamboo shoots.* This soup is substantial enough to be served as a complete meal.

## METRIC/IMPERIAL

1 duck, weighing 1.5–2 kg/3–4¾ lb
1 tablespoon salt
¼ teaspoon freshly ground black pepper
5 shallots, peeled and crushed
25 g/1 oz dried bamboo shoot,* soaked
  in hot water for 2 hours
1 lump rock sugar*
4 tablespoons fish sauce*
225 g/8 oz medium rice vermicelli*
**To serve:**
1 tablespoon chopped spring onion,
  green part only
1 tablespoon chopped coriander
  leaves*
Nuoc Cham (see page 77)

## AMERICAN

1 duck, weighing 3–4¾ lb
1 tablespoon salt
¼ teaspoon freshly ground black
  pepper
5 shallots, peeled and crushed
1 cup dried bamboo shoot,* soaked in
  hot water for 2 hours
1 lump rock sugar*
¼ cup fish sauce*
½ lb medium rice vermicelli*
**To serve:**
1 tablespoon chopped scallion, green
  part only
1 tablespoon chopped coriander
  leaves*
Nuoc Cham (see page 77)

## METHOD

Sprinkle the duck with the salt and pepper, then rub all over with the crushed shallots. Leave to marinate for 1 hour.

Pour 1.2 litres/2 pints/5 cups water into a large pan and bring to the boil. Add the duck and bamboo shoot, bring back to the boil and simmer for 15 minutes, skimming frequently until no further scum is formed.

Add the rock sugar, cover and simmer for 1 hour. Add the fish sauce, cover and simmer for 30 minutes or until the bamboo shoot is tender; it should have a chewy texture.

Meanwhile, cook the rice vermicelli in about 2 litres/3½ pints/4½ pints boiling water for 5 minutes, then drain and rinse under cold running water.

Cut the duck into 8 pieces. Divide the vermicelli between 8 individual warmed soup bowls. Place a piece of duck and a few pieces of bamboo shoot on top, then cover with the hot soup. Sprinkle with the spring onion (scallion) and coriander. Serve hot with the Nuoc Cham as an accompaniment.

SERVES 8

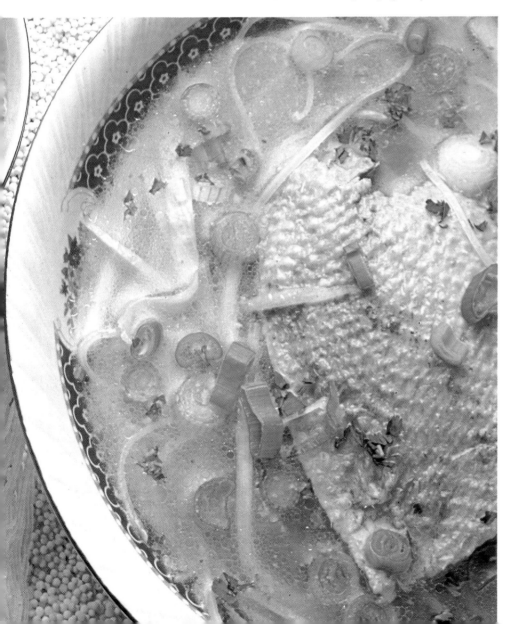

Crabmeat and Tapioca Pearl Soup; Chrysanthemum Soup with Minced (Ground) Pork; Duck Soup with Dried Bamboo Shoot

# Simmered Pineapple with Fish

## Cá Kho Thòm
Vietnam

### METRIC/IMPERIAL

2 tablespoons vegetable oil
450 g/1 lb fish steaks (halibut, sea
  bass, etc.)
1 shallot, peeled and sliced
150 g/5 oz fresh pineapple, cut into
  2.5 cm/1 inch squares about 5 mm/
  $\frac{1}{4}$ inch thick
6 tablespoons fish sauce*
4 tablespoons sugar
1 tablespoon Caramelized Sugar (see
  opposite)
freshly ground black pepper

### AMERICAN

2 tablespoons vegetable oil
1 lb fish steaks (bluefish, king
  mackerel, blackfish, etc.)
1 shallot, peeled and sliced
1 cup fresh pineapple, cut into 1 inch
  squares about $\frac{1}{4}$ inch thick
6 tablespoons fish sauce*
$\frac{1}{4}$ cup sugar
1 tablespoon Caramelized Sugar (see
  opposite)
freshly ground black pepper

### METHOD

Heat 1 tablespoon of the oil in a frying pan (skillet). Add the fish and fry gently until lightly browned on both sides, turning once.

Heat the remaining oil in a separate pan, add the shallot and fry gently until lightly browned. Add the pineapple and fry for about 3 minutes, then remove from the pan, using a slotted spoon. Discard the liquid.

Put half the fried pineapple and shallot in a small flameproof casserole. Place the fish steaks on top, then cover with the remaining pineapple and shallot. Add the remaining ingredients, cover with a tight-fitting lid and simmer for about 20 to 30 minutes until there is about 120 ml/ 4 fl oz/$\frac{1}{2}$ cup liquid remaining in the pan. Serve hot with rice.
SERVES 4

### Caramelized Sugar

Put 1 tablespoon sugar in a small frying pan (skillet) with 4 tablespoons ($\frac{1}{4}$ cup) water. Stir well, then cook over high heat until the mixture turns brown, stirring constantly; remove from the heat when it turns a very dark brown colour and steam forms. Stir well and add 2 tablespoons water. Return to a high heat and cook for about 5 minutes, stirring all the time, then add a squeeze of lemon juice. Stir rapidly, remove from heat and leave to cool. Store in a screwtop jar until required.

# Barbecued Prawns (Shrimp)

## Tôm Nùồng Bánh Hòi
Vietnam

### METRIC/IMPERIAL

450 g/1 lb uncooked prawns, unpeeled
175 g/6 oz very thin rice vermicelli*
2 teaspoons vegetable oil
3 spring onions, chopped
20 roasted peanuts (see below)
**To serve:**
few lemon slices, quartered
coriander leaves*
Nuoc Cham (see page 77)

### AMERICAN

1 lb large raw shrimp, unpeeled
6 oz very thin rice vermicelli*
2 teaspoons vegetable oil
3 scallions, chopped
20 roasted peanuts (see below)
**To serve:**
few lemon slices, quartered
coriander leaves*
Nuoc Cham (see page 77)

### METHOD

Cook the prawns (shrimp) over charcoal, for about 7 minutes, turning once. Alternatively, bake them in a preheated moderately hot oven (200°C/400°F, Gas Mark 6) for 10 minutes. Peel the prawns (shrimp), then cut each one in half and set aside.

Add the rice vermicelli to about 2 litres/3$\frac{1}{2}$ pints/9 cups boiling water and boil for 2 minutes, then drain and rinse under cold running water. Drain again.

Heat the oil in a frying pan (skillet), add the spring onions (scallions) and fry gently until softened.

Arrange the rice vermicelli on a warmed serving plate, top with prawns (shrimp), then sprinkle with spring onions (scallions) and peanuts. Garnish with lemon slices and coriander. Serve hot with Nuoc Cham.
SERVES 4

### Chopped Roasted Peanuts

Heat a small frying pan (skillet) until very hot, then add shelled red-skinned peanuts. Fry over dry heat until the skins turn black, stirring constantly, then transfer to a colander. Leave to cool for about 3 minutes, then rub between the hands to loosen the skins. Discard the skins. Chop the peanuts coarsely using a pestle and mortar or electric blender, if required.

# Fried Chicken with Coconut Milk and Lemon Grass

## Gà Xào Sã Nùòć Dùà

Vietnam

### METRIC/IMPERIAL

4 chicken thighs, or 2 legs and 2 thighs, chopped into small pieces
2 garlic cloves, peeled and chopped
1 shallot, peeled and chopped
½ teaspoon sugar
¼ teaspoon salt
pinch of freshly ground black pepper
½ teaspoon curry powder
pinch of crushed dried red chillis, or more to taste
1 tablespoon fish sauce*
1 tablespoon vegetable oil
1 stalk lemon grass,* very finely chopped
250 ml/8 fl oz coconut milk*

**To garnish:**
2 tablespoons chopped roasted peanuts
1 spring onion, cut into 5 cm/2 inch pieces
4 lime slices, halved (optional)

### AMERICAN

4 chicken thighs, or 2 legs and 2 thighs, chopped into small pieces
2 garlic cloves, peeled and chopped
1 shallot, peeled and chopped
½ teaspoon sugar
¼ teaspoon salt
pinch of freshly ground black pepper
½ teaspoon curry powder
pinch of crushed dried red chilis, or more to taste
1 tablespoon fish sauce*
1 tablespoon vegetable oil
1 stalk lemon grass,* very finely chopped
1 cup coconut milk*

**To garnish:**
2 tablespoons chopped roasted peanuts
1 scallion, cut into 2 inch pieces
4 lime slices, halved (optional)

### METHOD

Put the chicken in a bowl with half the garlic, the shallot, sugar, salt, black pepper, curry powder, crushed chillis and fish sauce. Stir well, then leave to marinate for 30 minutes.

Heat the oil in a wok or deep frying pan (deep-fat fryer). Add the remaining garlic and the lemon grass, stir-fry for a few seconds, then add the chicken. Stir-fry for about 10 minutes until the chicken is lightly browned, then add the coconut milk. Simmer, uncovered, for 10 minutes or until the chicken is tender and the liquid is reduced to a thick sauce.

Place the chicken on a warmed serving plate. Top with the peanuts and spring onion (scallion). Arrange lime slices around the edge of the plate, if liked. Serve hot with rice.
SERVES 4

**Fried Chicken with Coconut Milk and Lemon Grass; Barbecued Prawns (Shrimp)**

# Barbecued Spareribs

## Sùòn Nùòng

Vietnam

In Vietnam, this dish is barbecued over charcoal, but in the West it can successfully be roasted in the oven. It is always served on a bed of plain boiled rice, as a one-dish meal.

### METRIC/IMPERIAL

*5 shallots, peeled*
*2 garlic cloves, peeled*
*2 tablespoons sugar*
*4 tablespoons fish sauce\**
*¼ teaspoon freshly ground black pepper*
*750 g/1½ lb pork spareribs*
**To serve:**
*plain boiled rice*
*Nuoc Cham (see page 77)*
*few cucumber slices*

### AMERICAN

*5 shallots, peeled*
*2 garlic cloves, peeled*
*2 tablespoons sugar*
*¼ cup fish sauce\**
*¼ teaspoon freshly ground black pepper*
*1½ lb pork spareribs*
**To serve:**
*plain boiled rice*
*Nuoc Cham (see page 77)*
*few cucumber slices*

### METHOD

Pound the shallots, garlic and sugar to a paste, using a pestle and mortar. Add the fish sauce and black pepper and stir well. Place the spareribs in a roasting pan and pour the pounded mixture over them. Turn to coat thoroughly. Leave to marinate for at least 1 hour.

Roast in a preheated moderate oven (180°C/350°F, Gas Mark 4) for 45 minutes until the spareribs are well browned. Cut the ribs into separate pieces.

Put the rice in a serving dish, arrange the spareribs on top and sprinkle with a little Nuoc Cham. Arrange cucumber slices around the edge of the dish. Serve hot, with a bowl of Nuoc Cham handed separately.
SERVES 4

# Barbecued Beef with Lime Juice

## Thit Bò Nùòng Vi 'Sǎt

Vietnam

The literal translation of the name of this dish is 'Beef Barbecued on a 'Steel Griddle'. The dish is usually served in restaurants, where each diner is given a very small charcoal burner, a small steel griddle and a portion of food to cook for himself at the table. At home, use an electric or ordinary frying pan (skillet), or griddle over an electric hotplate or gas burner.

### METRIC/IMPERIAL

*450 g/1 lb slice beef topside, about 2.5 cm/1 inch thick*
*2 tablespoons vegetable oil*
*1 tablespoon fish sauce\**
*freshly ground black pepper*
*1 onion, peeled and thinly sliced into rings*
**To serve:**
*12 dried rice papers\**
*Vegetable Platter (see page 77)*
*few lime wedges*
*Nuoc Cham (see page 77)*

### AMERICAN

*1 × 1 lb slice beef top round, about 1 inch thick*
*2 tablespoons vegetable oil*
*1 tablespoon fish sauce\**
*freshly ground black pepper*
*1 onion, peeled and thinly sliced into rings*
**To serve:**
*12 dried rice papers\**
*Vegetable Platter (see page 77)*
*few lime wedges*
*Nuoc Cham (see page 77)*

### METHOD

Slice the beef thinly against the grain, then arrange in overlapping circles on a serving dish. Sprinkle with 1 tablespoon of the oil, the fish sauce and pepper to taste, then arrange the onion slices on top.

To serve, each diner should place a rice paper on an individual serving plate and brush the surface with water. Leave for about 1 minute until the rice paper is soft and flexible, then place a lettuce leaf, a few pieces of cucumber and a sprig each of coriander and mint on the paper.

Meanwhile, heat the frying pan (skillet) at the table and, when very hot, add the remaining oil. Let each person put in a few slices of beef and a slice of onion. Cook for a few seconds, then turn over and squeeze a little lime juice onto the meat.

Transfer the meat and onion to the top of the salad vegetables, then fold over the sides of the rice paper to enclose the food and roll up. Serve Nuoc Cham in individual bowls as a dip. Continue with the remaining ingredients until all are used up, eating the food as soon as it is cooked.
SERVES 4

Barbecued Spareribs, served with Nuoc Cham (see page 77); Barbecued Beef with Lime Juice, served with Vegetable Platter (see page 77), Nuoc Cham and rice papers

# Orange-shaped Cakes

## Bánh Cam
Vietnam

### METRIC/IMPERIAL

**Filling:** ·
*100 g/4 oz yellow mung beans\**
*175 ml/6 fl oz water*
*100 g/4 oz sugar*
**Wrapping:**
*225 g/8 oz glutinous (sweet) rice flour\**
*1 teaspoon baking powder*
*½ teaspoon salt*
*100 g/4 oz sugar*
*2 medium potatoes, boiled, peeled and mashed*
*120 ml/4 fl oz boiling water*
**To finish:**
*50 g/2 oz toasted sesame seeds\* (see opposite)*
*450 ml/¾ pint vegetable oil for deep-frying*

### AMERICAN

**Filling:**
*¾ cup yellow mung beans\**
*¾ cup water*
*½ cup sugar*
**Wrapping:**
*2 cups glutinous (sweet) rice flour\**
*1 teaspoon baking powder*
*½ teaspoon salt*
*½ cup sugar*
*2 medium potatoes, boiled, peeled and mashed*
*½ cup boiling water*
**To finish:**
*½ cup toasted sesame seeds\* (see below)*
*2 cups vegetable oil for deep-frying*

### METHOD

To make the filling: Rinse the mung beans thoroughly under cold running water. Put the beans and water in a small pan and bring to the boil. Lower the heat, cover and simmer for about 30 minutes until the water has evaporated completely and the beans are tender and dry. Remove from the heat and mash the beans, then add the sugar and mix well.

To make the wrapping: Put all the ingredients in a bowl, except the boiling water. Mix well, then gradually stir in the boiling water. Knead the mixture until it forms a smooth ball.

Roll 2 tablespoons of the wrapping mixture into a small ball, then flatten into a 7.5 cm/3 inch circle. Place 1 teaspoon of the filling mixture in the centre of the circle and gather the wrapping together to enclose the filling, shaping it into a ball. Repeat with the remaining wrapping and filling mixture until all the ingredients are used up, making about 12 balls.

Put the toasted sesame seeds on a plate or piece of greaseproof (waxed) paper and roll the balls in the seeds until completely coated.

Heat the oil in a small pan to 190°C/375°F. Drop one ball at a time into the hot oil and, with the bottom of a soup ladle, press against the ball and move the ladle against it, using a circular motion. Deep-fry the balls, a few at a time, for about 10 minutes until golden brown, then remove from the pan with a slotted spoon and drain on kitchen paper towels, while frying the remainder. Serve hot.
MAKES ABOUT 12

**Toasted Sesame Seeds**
Heat a frying pan (skillet) until very hot. Add the sesame seeds and stir-fry in the dry pan until well browned. It is essential to use a very hot pan or the seeds will become oily and not stick to the dough.

# China

## Deh-ta Hsiung

Most people who enjoy eating Chinese food will not attempt to cook it themselves because they think there is a great mystery surrounding this oriental art, while those whose experience of Chinese food is limited to 'chop suey' and 'sweet and sour pork' may well wonder what is so special about this cuisine. You may be surprised to learn that 'chop suey' has never even been heard of in China, and the soggy 'sweet and sour pork' often served in restaurants would never be cooked in China.

There is really no mystery about the art of Chinese cooking: once you have learnt a few basic facts, you will discover that authentic Chinese food can be cooked even without using unusual and exotic ingredients. Essentially, there are three fundamental principles in Chinese cooking: flavour, texture and colour.

### Flavour

The essential elements for seasoning and bringing out subtle flavours are: soy sauce, rice wine* (medium or dry sherry is an excellent substitute), sugar, vinegar, fresh root ginger and spring onions (scallions). Garlic, peppers and chillis are also used occasionally, but discreetly, for their purpose is to enhance the flavour of the food rather than overpower it. Cornflour (cornstarch) is used in moderation for thickening sauces and for coating meat, particularly when this is finely sliced and shredded, as it helps to preserve flavour and tenderness. Cornflour (cornstarch) should never be used to excess, however, otherwise the food will look unappetizing and taste starchy.

The practice of blending different flavours in one dish is quite common in China. The idea is to give the dish contrasting tastes as well as promote an exchange of flavours between ingredients. Each item in the dish acts as a seasoning agent, imparting a little flavour to the other ingredients.

It is therefore important to choose the ingredients to be blended with care, with the emphasis on harmonized contrast.

Above all else, the Chinese believe in the freshness of their food: vegetables should be dawn-picked, or ideally picked just before they are cooked; meats are never hung; poultry and fish are always bought still alive! The Chinese claim that loss of freshness is loss of flavour.

### Texture and Colour

Every dish in a Chinese meal should include two or more of the following textures: tenderness, crispness, crunchiness, smoothness and softness. Ingredients should also be chosen to complement each other in colour.

Ingredients are therefore chosen to obtain a harmony of flavours, colours and textures. For example, the main ingredient in *Jieca chao jiding* (see page 105) is chicken, which is white and tender. Mushrooms (soft and black) and celery (crisp and pale green) are used as the subsidiary ingredients to give the dish a harmonized texture. A colourful red pepper is also added for contrast and bamboo shoot (smooth in texture) for extra flavour. This combination, with the addition of salt, egg white, cornflour (cornstarch), fresh ginger root, spring onions (scallions), soy sauce and sherry makes the dish a unique experience for the palate. Apart from the Chinese dried mushrooms,* which can be substituted by fresh mushrooms, nothing out of the ordinary is used in the way of ingredients and everything can easily be obtained in any quality grocer or supermarket.

### Cooking Techniques and Preparation

Chinese cooking techniques are quite simple, and one of the most important aspects is the preparation before cooking.

### Cutting

Most Chinese foods are cut into very small pieces before cooking; therefore only a short cooking time is required and this helps to preserve the natural flavours. The Chinese attach great importance to the various methods of cutting.
*Slicing:* The ingredients are cut into thin slices, normally not much larger than a postage stamp, and as thin as cardboard. When slicing meat, always cut across the grain, which makes it more tender when cooked. Vegetables, such as carrots, are often cut on the slant so that the slices have a larger surface area to absorb flavourings.
*Shredding:* The ingredients are first sliced, then stacked like a pack of cards and cut into thin strips about the size of matchsticks.
*Dicing:* The ingredients are first cut into strips as wide as they are thick, then cut at right angles to the same width to make cubes, usually about 1cm/½ inch.
*Mincing (grinding):* The ingredients are very finely chopped in a mincer (grinder).

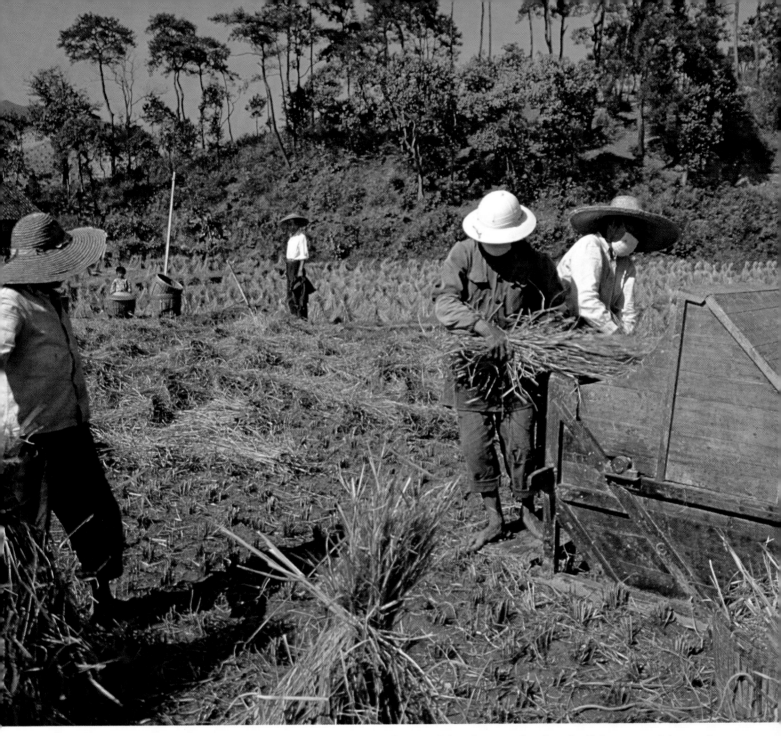

*Diagonal cutting:* This method is normally used for cutting vegetables, such as carrots and celery. A diagonal cut is made straight down, then the vegetable is rolled a half-turn and sliced diagonally again, in order to obtain a diamond-shaped piece.

*Chopping:* A heavy cleaver is used to cut through the bones and flesh of a chicken or duck. The normal method of cutting up a chicken is as follows: (1) Chop off the 'parson's nose' and either discard or, if it is to be served, split in half. (2) Disjoint the two wings. (3) Remove the legs and thighs. (4) Turn the body on its side, then separate the breast from the backbone. (5) Divide the breast into two sections, then cut each half crossways into three or four pieces. (6) Cut each wing into three pieces, and each leg and thigh into five pieces.

## Marinating

After cutting, the next step is to prepare the meat for cooking by marinating it. Salt, egg white and cornflour (cornstarch) are normally used for chicken and fish; soy sauce, sugar, sherry and cornflour (cornstarch) are used for meat.

## Cooking Methods

The various cooking methods can be divided into four basic categories:

*Water cooking:* Boiling and simmering.

*Oil cooking:* Frying and braising.

*Fire cooking:* Roasting and barbecuing.

*Steam cooking:* Steaming.

The most important factor in cooking Chinese food is the degree of heat. The actual timing, although important, is governed by the heat. It is therefore very difficult for most Chinese recipes to give a precise cooking time as so much depends on the size of the ingredients and the type of stove and utensils used. For this reason, cooking times for the recipes in this chapter are intended as a guide, rather than a strict rule.

## Cooking Equipment

The Chinese wok is a most useful utensil. It is cone-shaped with a rounded bottom and is normally made of iron, which keeps an intense, steady heat throughout cooking. The main advantage of the wok is its shape, which enables the heat to spread evenly so only a short cooking time is required. The shape of the wok also encourages ingredients to return to the centre, however vigorously you stir them.

A wok will fit on most gas burners, especially those with a metal ring. Electric cookers are generally less suitable because the heat cannot usually be controlled as easily. If a wok is not available, a deep heavy frying pan (deep-fat fryer) can be used instead.

A wok is ideal for stir-frying, the cooking method most commonly used in China. First heat the wok over high heat, then add a small amount of vegetable oil or lard; never use butter or dripping. Heat until the oil or fat is very hot and smoking, then toss in the ingredients and stir and turn constantly for a short time. Timing is of the utmost importance; overcooking will either burn the food or turn it into a soggy mess. Correctly cooked, Chinese food is crisp and wholesome.

Very little water – or none at all – is added, since the high heat will extract sufficient juices from the meat and vegetables to moisten, particularly if they are fresh. In most cases when two or more ingredients are combined in one dish, each ingredient is partially cooked separately and then mixed together for the final stage of cooking.

After cooking, the wok must always be rinsed thoroughly in very hot water to prevent it retaining flavours. Iron woks should be dried immediately to prevent rusting.

## Regional Cooking Styles

China is a vast country, about the same size as the United States, and its climate and food products are as varied. Each region of China has its own specialities and different methods of cooking. Although many of these different schools have merged into each other in recent years, most regions still retain strong individual characteristics. There are four broadly defined schools of cuisine:

## Eastern School

This school is also known as the *Jiangsi Fujian* style of cooking. It includes the lower Yangtse basin, Shanghai and the provinces of Jiangsi (Kiangsi), and Fujian (Fukien), although the latter is often linked with the southern school. This is one of the most fertile parts of China, known as the 'Land of Fish and Rice'. Besides being famous for its various noodles and dumplings, the main characteristics of its style can be summarized as subtle in flavour, sweet in taste and exquisite in appearance.

## Southern School

Guangdong, with its capital Guangshau (Canton), is the southern school, although it is possible to pick out several different regional styles. Here the climate is subtropical and the land extremely fertile. It can undoubtedly be described as the jewel of Chinese cuisine, although its reputation

has unfortunately been damaged outside China by the so-called 'chop suey house'. Cantonese cuisine prides itself on being able to bring out the best of the natural flavours of any food.

## Western School

Sichuan (Szechuan), in contrast, is the western school of richly flavoured and piquant food. It is a comparatively recent discovery in the West and is sadly less well known than the other styles of cooking. The neighbouring province of Hunan, with its peppery food is generally associated with this school.

## Northern School

This consists of the Beijing (Peking), Shandong and Henan cuisines. Although the northern school may not be the best, it is certainly the oldest of Chinese culinary art, as its origin lies on the basin of the Yellow River – the cradle of Chinese civilization. Because Peking has been the capital of China for many centuries, it has accumulated the best dishes from each region to become the culinary centre of China while, at the same time, developing a cuisine of its own.

## Serving

Harmony is the most important aspect of Chinese food. When planning a menu, it is most important to choose a selection of dishes which complement each other, but give contrast in flavour, texture and colour. A meal composed of three main dishes and one soup will provide adequate contrast and will be sufficient for four to six people. The more people eating a meal, the more variety can be achieved for – not only is the quantity of food increased – a wider selection of dishes can be offered.

The Chinese seldom serve only one dish at a meal, as it offers little variety. If you are dining alone, you should have at least two cooked dishes to provide contrast, or choose one dish with two different ingredients. The cooked dish or dishes form one part of a meal; rice or wheat – cooked either as dumplings or noodles – forms the other part. These cereals are the staple food for most Chinese. The art of Chinese cooking lies in selecting the cooked dishes to accompany the staple food.

Do not serve tea with a Chinese meal – have either soup or wine. Tea is seldom drunk during the meal, it is more frequently served as an aperitif or as a digestif, and is frequently taken at other times of the day but not with food. There is no reason why wine cannot be drunk with Chinese food; let your personal taste be your guide.

Bon appetit! or *Chin-chin* as we say in Chinese.

## Beef and Egg-Flower Soup
### Niurou Danhua Tang

METRIC/IMPERIAL

1.2 litres/2 pints hot chicken stock or
   water
100 g/4 oz beef steak, coarsely
   chopped
2 teaspoons salt
1 celery stick, coarsely chopped
1 egg, beaten
freshly ground black pepper
few spring onions, sliced, to garnish

AMERICAN

5 cups hot chicken stock or water
½ cup coarsely chopped round steak
2 teaspoons salt
1 celery stalk, coarsely chopped
1 egg, beaten
freshly ground black pepper
few scallions, sliced, to garnish

METHOD

Bring the stock or water to the boil in a
pan, then add the beef, salt and celery.
Bring back to the boil, then add the egg, a
little at a time, stirring vigorously to
achieve the 'egg-flower' effect. Add
pepper to taste.

   Sprinkle with spring onions (scallions)
before serving. Serve hot.

## Sliced Carrot and Pork Soup
### Luopu Roupian Tang

METRIC/IMPERIAL

100 g/4 oz boned lean pork, very
   thinly sliced
1 tablespoon soy sauce
1 tablespoon sesame seed oil*
1 teaspoon cornflour
225 g/8 oz carrots, scraped and sliced
1.2 litres/2 pints chicken stock
2 teaspoons salt
chopped coriander leaves* to garnish

AMERICAN

½ cup very thinly sliced boneless
   pork loin
1 tablespoon soy sauce
1 tablespoon sesame seed oil*
1 teaspoon cornstarch
1½ cups sliced carrots
5 cups chicken stock
2 teaspoons salt
chopped coriander leaves* to garnish

METHOD

Put the pork in a bowl with the soy sauce,
oil and cornflour (cornstarch). Stir well,
then leave to marinate for 10 minutes.

   Meanwhile, place the carrots, stock
and salt in a pan, bring to the boil and
simmer for 5 minutes. Add the pork and
simmer for 8 to 10 minutes until the pork
and carrots are tender.

   Pour into a warmed soup tureen and
sprinkle with coriander. Serve hot.

## Pork and Tomato Soup
### Fanqie Roupian Tang

METRIC/IMPERIAL

100 g/4 oz boned lean pork, very
   thinly sliced
1 teaspoon soy sauce
1 teaspoon medium or dry sherry
2 tablespoons vegetable oil
1 small onion, peeled and chopped
2 tomatoes, chopped
1.2 litres/2 pints chicken stock
2 teaspoons salt
freshly ground black pepper
1 egg, beaten
chopped coriander leaves* to garnish

AMERICAN

½ cup very thinly sliced boneless pork
1 teaspoon soy sauce
1 teaspoon medium or pale dry sherry
2 tablespoons vegetable oil
1 small onion, peeled and chopped
2 tomatoes, chopped
5 cups chicken stock
2 teaspoons salt
freshly ground black pepper
1 egg, beaten
chopped coriander leaves* to garnish

METHOD

Put the pork in a bowl with the soy sauce
and sherry. Stir well, then leave to marinate for about 20 minutes.

   Heat the oil in a wok or frying pan
(skillet), add the onion and pork and stir-
fry for 2 minutes. Add the tomatoes and
stock and bring to the boil. Add salt and
pepper to taste and simmer for a few
minutes.

   Stir in the egg, then immediately pour
into a warmed soup tureen and sprinkle
with coriander. Serve hot.

# Sliced Pork and Szechuan Preserved Vegetable Soup

## Zhacai Roupian Tang

### METRIC/IMPERIAL

225 g/8 oz boned lean pork, very
  thinly sliced
1 teaspoon soy sauce
1 teaspoon medium or dry sherry
1 tablespoon cornflour
40 g/1½ oz transparent noodles,*
  soaked in water for 10 minutes
1 tablespoon vegetable oil
1.5 litres/2½ pints hot chicken stock
½ cucumber, sliced into thin strips
1 teaspoon salt
freshly ground black pepper
50 g/2 oz Szechuan preserved
  vegetable,* thinly sliced

### AMERICAN

1 cup very thinly sliced boneless pork
  loin
1 teaspoon soy sauce
1 teaspoon medium or pale dry sherry
1 tablespoon cornstarch
1½ oz cellophane noodles,* soaked in
  water for 10 minutes
1 tablespoon vegetable oil
6¼ cups hot chicken stock
½ cucumber, sliced into thin strips
1 teaspoon salt
freshly ground black pepper
½ cup thinly sliced Szechuan preserved
  vegetable*

### METHOD

Put the pork in a bowl with the soy sauce, sherry and cornflour (cornstarch). Stir well, then leave to marinate for about 20 minutes.

Meanwhile, cut the noodles into manageable lengths with scissors.

Heat the oil in a wok or frying pan (skillet). Add the pork and stir-fry until it changes colour.

Bring the stock to a rolling boil in a separate pan. Add the cucumber, salt and pepper to taste. Return to the boil, then add the pork, preserved vegetable and noodles. Boil for a few seconds, then pour into a warmed soup tureen. Serve hot.

**Sliced Carrot and Pork Soup; Beef and Egg-Flower Soup; Pork and Tomato Soup**

# Meatballs in Soup
## Rouwan Tang

### METRIC/IMPERIAL

*225 g/8 oz boned lean pork, finely
    minced*
*2½ teaspoons salt*
*1 slice fresh root ginger,\* peeled and
    finely chopped*
*½ egg, beaten*
*2 tablespoons cornflour*
*1.5 litres/2½ pints hot chicken stock*
*15 g/½ oz dried wood ears,\* soaked in
    warm water for 20 minutes*
*½ cucumber, cut into diamond-shaped
    chunks*
*1 tablespoon medium or dry sherry*
*freshly ground black pepper*

### AMERICAN

*1 cup finely ground pork loin*
*2½ teaspoons salt*
*1 slice fresh ginger root,\* peeled and
    finely chopped*
*½ egg, beaten*
*2 tablespoons cornstarch*
*6¼ cups hot chicken stock*
*½ cup tree ears,\* soaked in warm water
    for 20 minutes*
*½ cucumber, cut into diamond-shaped
    chunks*
*1 tablespoon medium or pale dry
    sherry*
*freshly ground black pepper*

### METHOD

Mix the pork with ½ teaspoon salt, the
ginger, egg and cornflour (cornstarch).
Form the mixture into about 20 small
meatballs.

Bring the stock to the boil in a pan. Add
the meatballs, wood (tree) ears and the
remaining salt, then add the cucumber
and sherry. Simmer until the meatballs
float to the surface. Pour into a warmed
soup tureen and sprinkle with pepper to
taste. Serve hot.

# Chicken and Mushroom Soup
## Donggu Dun Ji

This soup can be eaten as a complete
meal because the chicken is served
whole in its cooking liquid. The meat
should be very tender so that it can easily
be torn into pieces with chopsticks or a
soup spoon.

### METRIC/IMPERIAL

*25 g/1 oz Chinese dried mushrooms,\*
    soaked in warm water for 30 minutes*
*1 chicken, weighing 1 kg/2–2¼ lb*
*1 tablespoon medium or dry sherry*
*1 spring onion*
*1 slice fresh root ginger,\* peeled*
*1½ teaspoons salt*

### AMERICAN

*8 medium Chinese dried mushrooms,\*
    soaked in warm water for 30 minutes*
*1 chicken, weighing 2–2¼ lb*
*1 tablespoon medium or pale dry
    sherry*
*1 scallion*
*1 slice fresh ginger root,\* peeled*
*1½ teaspoons salt*

### METHOD

Drain the mushrooms, then squeeze dry,
reserving the soaking liquid. Discard the
mushroom stalks.

Put the chicken in a large pan of boiling
water. Boil rapidly for 2 to 3 minutes,
then remove the chicken and rinse
thoroughly under cold running water.

Put the chicken and mushrooms in a
pan or casserole with a tight-fitting lid.
Add just enough water to cover the
chicken, then add the sherry, spring
onion (scallion), ginger and reserved
soaking liquid from the mushrooms.

Bring to the boil, then lower the heat,
cover and simmer gently for at least
2 hours.

Just before serving, remove any im-
purities that float to the surface of the
soup and discard the spring onion (scallion) and ginger if wished. Stir in the salt
and pour into a warmed soup tureen.
Serve hot.

# Cauliflower Gruel

## Caihua Geng

Do not be put off by the term 'gruel'; this is in fact a delicious thick soup and a very colourful dish.

### METRIC/IMPERIAL

1 small cauliflower, finely chopped
100 g/4 oz chicken meat, coarsely chopped
1 litre/1¾ pints chicken stock
2 eggs, beaten
1 teaspoon salt
50 g/2 oz lean ham, finely chopped
chopped coriander leaves* to garnish

### AMERICAN

1 small cauliflower, finely chopped
½ cup coarsely chopped chicken
4¼ cups chicken stock
2 eggs, beaten
1 teaspoon salt
¼ cup finely chopped lean ham
chopped coriander leaves* to garnish

### METHOD

Put the cauliflower, chicken and stock in a pan and cook gently for 15 to 20 minutes.

Pour the eggs into the soup, then stir in the salt. Add the ham, pour into a warmed soup tureen and sprinkle with coriander. Serve hot.

# Duck and Cabbage Soup

## Yagu Baicai Tang

### METRIC/IMPERIAL

1 duck carcass, with giblets
2 slices fresh root ginger,* peeled
450 g/1 lb Chinese cabbage, sliced
salt
freshly ground black pepper

### AMERICAN

1 duck carcass, with giblets
2 slices fresh ginger root,* peeled
1 lb bok choy, sliced
salt
freshly ground black pepper

### METHOD

Break up the carcass, then place in a large pan. Add the giblets and any other meat left over from the duck.

Cover with water, add the ginger, then bring to the boil. Skim, then lower the heat and simmer gently for at least 30 minutes.

Add the cabbage (bok choy) and salt and pepper to taste. Continue cooking for about 20 minutes.

Discard the duck carcass and ginger, taste and adjust the seasoning. Pour into a warmed soup tureen. Serve hot.

# Shredded Pork and Noodles in Soup

## Rousi Tangmian

### METRIC/IMPERIAL

3–4 Chinese dried mushrooms,*
    soaked in warm water for 30 minutes
225 g/8 oz boned lean pork, shredded
1 tablespoon soy sauce
1 tablespoon medium or dry sherry
1 teaspoon sugar
2 teaspoons cornflour
350 g/12 oz egg noodles
3 tablespoons vegetable oil
2 spring onions, cut into 2.5 cm/1 inch lengths
100 g/4 oz bamboo shoot, shredded
salt
600 ml/1 pint boiling chicken stock

### AMERICAN

3–4 Chinese dried mushrooms,*
    soaked in warm water for 30 minutes
1 cup shredded pork loin
1 tablespoon soy sauce
1 tablespoon medium or pale dry sherry
1 teaspoon sugar
2 teaspoons cornstarch
¾ lb egg noodles
3 tablespoons vegetable oil
2 scallions, cut into 1 inch lengths
1 cup shredded bamboo shoot
salt
2½ cups boiling chicken stock

### METHOD

Drain the mushrooms, then squeeze dry, reserving the soaking liquid. Discard the hard stalks, then slice the caps into thin strips.

Put the pork in a bowl with the soy sauce, sherry, sugar and cornflour (cornstarch). Stir well, then leave to marinate for about 20 minutes.

Cook the noodles in boiling water for about 5 minutes, then drain.

Heat half the oil in a wok or frying pan (skillet), add the pork and stir-fry until it changes colour. Remove from the pan with a slotted spoon and drain.

Heat the remaining oil in the pan, add the spring onions (scallions), then the mushrooms and bamboo shoot. Stir, then add a little salt. Return the pork to the pan together with the soaking liquid from the mushrooms.

Place the noodles in a large serving bowl, pour over the boiling stock then add the pork and vegetables. Serve hot.

**Duck and Cabbage Soup; Shredded Pork and Noodles in Soup; Cauliflower Gruel**

# Bean Curd and Spinach Soup

## Bocai Doufu Tang

### METRIC/IMPERIAL

1 cake bean curd*
750 ml/1¾ pints chicken stock
100 g/4 oz fresh spinach leaves, torn
  into pieces
1 spring onion, chopped (optional)
2 teaspoons salt
½ teaspoon monosodium glutamate*
freshly ground black pepper

### AMERICAN

1 cake bean curd*
2 cups chicken stock
¼ lb fresh spinach leaves, torn into
  pieces
1 scallion, chopped (optional)
2 teaspoons salt
½ teaspoon msg*
freshly ground black pepper

### METHOD

Cut the bean curd into 1 cm/½ inch cubes.
Bring the stock to the boil in a saucepan,
add the spinach and spring onion (scallion) if using. Simmer for 5 minutes then
add the bean curd and simmer for 2 to 3
minutes.

Skim the soup, then add the salt, monosodium glutamate (msg) and pepper to
taste. Pour into a warmed soup tureen.
Serve hot.

# Crab Omelet

## Xierou Chao Dan

### METRIC/IMPERIAL

2 spring onions
4 eggs, beaten
salt
3 tablespoons vegetable oil
2 slices of fresh root ginger,* peeled
    and shredded
175 g/6 oz fresh, frozen or canned
    crabmeat
1 tablespoon medium or dry sherry
1½ tablespoons soy sauce
2 teaspoons sugar
**To garnish:**
shredded lettuce
tomato and grape (optional)

### AMERICAN

2 scallions
4 eggs, beaten
salt
3 tablespoons vegetable oil
2 slices of fresh ginger root,* peeled
    and shredded
6 oz fresh, frozen or canned crabmeat
1 tablespoon medium or pale dry
    sherry
1½ tablespoons soy sauce
2 teaspoons sugar
**To garnish:**
shredded lettuce
tomato and grape (optional)

### METHOD

Cut the white part of the spring onions (scallions) into 2.5 cm/1 inch lengths. Chop the green parts finely and beat into the eggs, with salt to taste.

Heat the oil in a wok or frying pan (skillet). Add the white spring onions (scallions) and the ginger, then the crab and sherry.

Stir-fry for a few seconds then add the soy sauce and sugar. Lower the heat, pour in the egg mixture and cook for a further 30 seconds.

Transfer to a serving plate and garnish with shredded lettuce. To finish, place a serrated-cut tomato half and a grape in the centre to resemble a flower head, if liked. Serve immediately.

Stir-Fried Squid with Mixed
Vegetables; Crab Omelet

# Stir-Fried Squid with Mixed Vegetables

## Zajin Chao Xianyou

Do not overcook the squid or it will be tough and chewy.

### METRIC/IMPERIAL

400 g/14 oz squid
2 slices of fresh root ginger,* peeled
    and finely chopped
1 tablespoon medium or dry sherry
1 tablespoon cornflour
15 g/½ oz dried wood ears,* soaked in
    warm water for 20 minutes
4 tablespoons vegetable oil
2 spring onions, white part only, cut
    into 2.5 cm/1 inch lengths
225 g/8 oz cauliflower or broccoli,
    divided into florets
2 medium carrots, peeled and cut into
    diamond-shaped chunks
1 teaspoon salt
1 teaspoon sugar
1 teaspoon sesame seed oil*

### AMERICAN

1 lb squid
2 slices of fresh ginger root,* peeled
    and finely chopped
1 tablespoon medium or pale dry
    sherry
1 tablespoon cornstarch
½ cup tree ears,* soaked in warm water
    for 20 minutes
¼ cup vegetable oil
2 scallions, white part only, cut into
    1 inch lengths
½ lb cauliflower or broccoli, divided
    into florets
2 medium carrots, peeled and cut into
    diamond-shaped chunks
1 teaspoon salt
1 teaspoon sugar
1 teaspoon sesame seed oil*

### METHOD

Clean the squid, discarding the head, transparent backbone and ink bag. Cut the flesh into thin slices or rings. Place in a bowl with half the ginger, the sherry and cornflour (cornstarch). Mix well, then leave to marinate for about 20 minutes.

Meanwhile, drain the wood (tree) ears and break into small pieces, discarding the hard bits.

Heat 2 tablespoons of the oil in a wok or frying pan (skillet). Add the spring onions (scallions) and remaining ginger, then the cauliflower or broccoli, carrots and wood (tree) ears. Stir, then add the salt and sugar and continue cooking until the vegetables are tender, adding a little water if necessary. Remove from the pan with a slotted spoon and drain.

Heat the remaining oil in the pan, add the squid and stir-fry for about 1 minute. Return the vegetables to the pan, add the sesame seed oil and mix all the ingredients well together. Serve hot.

# Steamed Eggs

## Zheng Jidan

Dry the spinach leaves thoroughly after rinsing them.

### METRIC/IMPERIAL

6 eggs, beaten
250 ml/8 fl oz hot water
1 teaspoon salt
2 teaspoons medium or dry sherry
50 g/2 oz fresh spinach leaves
50 g/2 oz cooked ham, chopped
50 g/2 oz peeled prawns
**To garnish:**
1 tablespoon soy sauce
1 teaspoon sesame seed oil*

### AMERICAN

6 eggs, beaten
1 cup hot water
1 teaspoon salt
2 teaspoons medium or pale dry
    sherry
¾ cup fresh spinach leaves
¼ cup chopped cooked ham
1 large shrimp, peeled
**To garnish:**
1 tablespoon soy sauce
1 teaspoon sesame seed oil*

### METHOD

Put the eggs in a heatproof bowl, add the water, salt and sherry and stir well.

Arrange the spinach, ham and prawns (shrimp) on top of the egg mixture, then lower the uncovered bowl into a large pan of boiling water.

Cover the pan, lower the heat so the water in the pan is just simmering and steam the eggs gently for 20 minutes. Sprinkle with the soy sauce and sesame seed oil. Serve hot.

# Abalone in Oyster Sauce

## Haoyou Baoyu

### METRIC/IMPERIAL

3 Chinese dried mushrooms,* soaked
   in warm water for 30 minutes
2 tablespoons vegetable oil
1 × 425 g/15 oz can abalone, sliced
50 g/2 oz bamboo shoot, sliced
1 teaspoon medium or dry sherry
1 tablespoon oyster sauce*
1 teaspoon sugar
½ teaspoon salt
2 teaspoons cornflour, mixed to a paste
   with a little water
1 teaspoon sesame seed oil*

### AMERICAN

3 Chinese dried mushrooms,* soaked
   in warm water for 30 minutes
2 tablespoons vegetable oil
1 × 15 oz can abalone, sliced
½ cup bamboo shoot, sliced
1 teaspoon medium or pale dry sherry
1 tablespoon oyster sauce*
1 teaspoon sugar
½ teaspoon salt
2 teaspoons cornstarch, mixed to a
   paste with a little water
1 teaspoon sesame seed oil*

### METHOD

Squeeze the mushrooms dry, discard the
stalks, then slice the caps.

Heat the vegetable oil in a wok or
frying pan (skillet). Add the abalone with
the juice from the can, the mushrooms,
bamboo shoot, sherry, oyster sauce,
sugar and salt. Stir-fry for about 2 minutes, then add the cornflour (cornstarch) mixture and cook until the sauce
thickens.

Add the sesame seed oil, then serve
hot.

# Bean Curd and Prawns (Shrimp)

## Xiaren Shao Doufu

### METRIC/IMPERIAL

6 cakes bean curd*
50 g/2 oz peeled prawns
3 tablespoons vegetable oil
½ teaspoon salt
1 teaspoon sugar
1 teaspoon medium or dry sherry
2 tablespoons soy sauce
shredded spring onions, green part
   only, to garnish

### AMERICAN

6 cakes bean curd*
⅓ cup shelled shrimp
3 tablespoons vegetable oil
½ teaspoon salt
1 teaspoon sugar
1 teaspoon medium or pale dry sherry
2 tablespoons soy sauce
shredded scallions, green part only, to
   garnish

### METHOD

Cut each bean curd cake into 5 mm/¼ inch
thick slices, then cut each slice into 6 to 8
pieces. Cut any large prawns (shrimp) in
half, leaving the small ones whole.

Heat the oil in a wok or frying pan
(skillet). Add the bean curd and stir-fry
until golden on all sides. Add the salt,
sugar, sherry and soy sauce and stir-fry
for a few seconds.

Add the prawns (shrimp), stir gently
and cook for 1 to 2 minutes.

Serve hot, garnished with shredded
spring onion (scallion).

**Bean Curd and Prawns (Shrimp);
Abalone in Oyster Sauce; Deep-Fried
Prawns (Shrimp) in Shells**

## Deep-Fried Prawns (Shrimp) in Shells
### Youbao Xianxia

METRIC/IMPERIAL

450 g/1 lb fresh prawns in shell
2 slices of fresh root ginger,* peeled
  and finely chopped
1 teaspoon medium or dry sherry
1½ teaspoons cornflour
450 ml/¾ pint vegetable oil for deep-
  frying
1 teaspoon salt
1 teaspoon chilli sauce (optional)
**To garnish:**
coriander leaves*
lemon peel (optional)

AMERICAN

1 lb fresh shrimp, unshelled
2 slices of fresh ginger root,* peeled
  and finely chopped
1 teaspoon medium or pale dry sherry
1½ teaspoons cornstarch
2 cups vegetable oil for deep-frying
1 teaspoon salt
1 teaspoon chili sauce (optional)
**To garnish:**
coriander leaves*
lemon peel (optional)

METHOD

Place the unshelled prawns (shrimp) in a
bowl with the ginger, sherry and cornflour (cornstarch). Stir gently to mix,
then leave to marinate in the refrigerator
for about 20 minutes.

  Heat the oil in a wok or deep-fat fryer to
180°C/350°F. Lower the heat, add the
prawns (shrimp) and deep-fry for about 1
minute. Remove the prawns (shrimp) with
a slotted spoon and drain.

  Pour off the oil, then return the prawns
(shrimp) to the pan. Add the salt and chilli
sauce if using; mix well. Serve hot, garnished with coriander and lemon peel, if
liked.

## Stir-Fried Prawns (Shrimp) and Peas
### Qingdou Xiaren

If fresh peas are unobtainable, frozen
ones may be used for this recipe, but
they should be thawed first and stir-fried
for 1 minute only.

METRIC/IMPERIAL

225 g/8 oz peeled prawns
1 egg white
2 teaspoons cornflour
3 tablespoons vegetable oil
2 spring onions, white part only, finely
  chopped
1 slice of fresh root ginger,* peeled
  and finely chopped
225 g/8 oz shelled peas
1 teaspoon salt
1 tablespoon medium or dry sherry

AMERICAN

1 lb shelled shrimp
1 egg white
2 teaspoons cornstarch
3 tablespoons vegetable oil
2 scallions, white part only, finely
  chopped
1 slice of fresh ginger root,* peeled
  and finely chopped
1½ cups shelled peas
1 teaspoon salt
1 tablespoon medium or pale dry
  sherry

METHOD

Put the prawns (shrimp) in a bowl with
the egg white and cornflour (cornstarch).
Mix well, then leave to marinate in the
refrigerator for about 20 minutes.

  Heat the oil in a wok or frying pan
(skillet), add the prawns (shrimp) and
stir-fry over moderate heat for about 1
minute. Remove from the pan with a
slotted spoon and drain.

  Increase the heat, add the spring
onions (scallions), ginger, peas and salt
and stir-fry for 2 minutes.

  Return the prawns (shrimp) to the pan,
add the sherry and continue cooking for
a further 1 minute. Serve hot.

# Carp with Sweet and Sour Sauce

## Tangcu Liyu

Carp is a symbol of good fortune, so it is served at New Year and other festivities.

### METRIC/IMPERIAL

15 g/½ oz dried wood ears,* soaked in warm water for 20 minutes
1 carp, weighing 750 g–1 kg/1½–2 lb
2 teaspoons salt
3 tablespoons flour
4 tablespoons vegetable oil
2–3 spring onions, shredded
2 slices of fresh root ginger,* peeled and shredded
1 garlic clove, peeled and finely chopped
15 g/½ oz bamboo shoot, thinly sliced
50 g/2 oz water chestnuts,* thinly sliced
1 red pepper, cored, seeded and shredded
3 tablespoons wine vinegar

### Sauce:

3 tablespoons sugar
2 tablespoons soy sauce
2 tablespoons medium or dry sherry
2 teaspoons cornflour
150 ml/¼ pint chicken stock or water
1 teaspoon chilli sauce

### AMERICAN

½ cup tree ears,* soaked in warm water for 20 minutes
1 carp, weighing 1½–2 lb
2 teaspoons salt
3 tablespoons flour
¼ cup vegetable oil
2–3 scallions, shredded
2 slices of fresh ginger root,* peeled and shredded
1 garlic clove, peeled and finely chopped
2 tablespoons thinly sliced bamboo shoot
¼ cup water chestnuts,* thinly sliced
1 red pepper, cored, seeded and shredded
3 tablespoons wine vinegar

### Sauce:

3 tablespoons sugar
2 tablespoons soy sauce
2 tablespoons medium or pale dry sherry
2 teaspoons cornstarch
⅔ cup chicken stock or water
1 teaspoon chili sauce

### METHOD

Drain the wood (tree) ears and slice very thinly, discarding the hard bits.

Clean the fish thoroughly and remove the fins and tail but leave the head on. Make diagonal slashes through to the bone along both sides of the fish at 5 mm/¼ inch intervals. Dry thoroughly, then rub the fish inside and out with 1 teaspoon salt. Coat with the flour from head to tail.

Heat the oil in a large wok or frying pan (skillet) until very hot. Lower the heat a little, add the fish and fry for about 3 to 4 minutes on each side until golden and crisp, turning the fish carefully. Drain, then transfer carefully to a warmed serving dish. Keep hot.

Mix the sauce ingredients together. Add the spring onions (scallions), ginger and garlic to the oil remaining in the pan. Stir in the wood (tree) ears, bamboo shoot, water chestnuts and red pepper, then the remaining salt and the vinegar. Add the sauce mixture and cook, stirring, until thickened. Pour over the fish. Serve immediately.

**Prawn (Shrimp) Balls with Broccoli; Braised Fish with Spring Onions (Scallions) and Ginger**

# Braised Fish with Spring Onions (Scallions) and Ginger
## Jiangcong Shao Yu

The skin of a whole fish must be scored before cooking, to prevent it from bursting and to allow the heat to penetrate more quickly. It will also make it easier for the flesh to absorb the flavours of the seasoning and sauce.

### METRIC/IMPERIAL

1 fish (mullet, bream etc.), weighing
    750 g/1½ lb
1 teaspoon salt
2 tablespoons flour
3 tablespoons vegetable oil
3–4 spring onions, cut into
    2.5 cm/1 inch lengths
2–3 slices of fresh root ginger,* peeled
    and shredded

**Sauce:**
2 tablespoons soy sauce
2 tablespoons medium or dry sherry
150 ml/¼ pint chicken stock or water
1 teaspoon cornflour
freshly ground black pepper

**To garnish:**
tomato halves
coriander leaves*
cherries

### AMERICAN

1 fish (mullet, sea bass etc.), weighing
    1½ lb
1 teaspoon salt
2 tablespoons flour
3 tablespoons vegetable oil
3–4 scallions, cut into 1 inch lengths
2–3 slices of fresh ginger root,* peeled
    and shredded

**Sauce:**
2 tablespoons soy sauce
2 tablespoons medium or pale dry
    sherry
⅔ cup chicken stock or water
1 teaspoon cornstarch
freshly ground black pepper

**To garnish:**
tomato halves
coriander leaves*
cherries

### METHOD

Clean the fish thoroughly, leaving the fins, tail and head on. Slash both sides of the fish diagonally with a sharp knife at 5 mm/¼ inch intervals as far as the bone. Rub the fish inside and out with the salt, then coat with the flour from head to tail.

Heat the oil in a large wok or frying pan (skillet) until very hot. Lower the heat a little, add the fish and fry for about 2 minutes on each side or until golden and crisp, turning the fish carefully. Remove from the pan.

Mix the sauce ingredients together. Increase the heat and add the spring onions (scallions) and ginger to the oil remaining in pan. Stir-fry for a few seconds, then stir in the sauce mixture and return the fish to the pan.

Simmer for a few minutes, then carefully transfer the fish to a warmed serving dish and pour over the sauce.

If liked, garnish the dish with tomato halves, trimmed with coriander leaves and cherries. Serve hot.

# Prawn (Shrimp) Balls with Broccoli
## Jielan Chao Xiaqiu

Do not overcook the prawns (shrimp) or they will lose their delicate flavour.

### METRIC/IMPERIAL

225 g/8 oz Dublin Bay or Pacific (King)
    prawns in shell
1 slice of fresh root ginger,* peeled
    and finely chopped
1 teaspoon medium or dry sherry
1 egg white
1 tablespoon cornflour
3 tablespoons vegetable oil
2 spring onions, finely chopped
225 g/8 oz broccoli, cut into small
    pieces
1 teaspoon salt
1 teaspoon sugar

### AMERICAN

½ lb unshelled jumbo shrimp
1 slice of fresh ginger root,* peeled
    and finely chopped
1 teaspoon medium or pale dry sherry
1 egg white
1 tablespoon cornstarch
3 tablespoons vegetable oil
2 scallions, finely chopped
½ lb broccoli, cut into small pieces
1 teaspoon salt
1 teaspoon sugar

### METHOD

Wash the unshelled prawns (shrimp), dry thoroughly with kitchen paper towels, then use a sharp knife to make a shallow incision down the back of the prawn (shrimp) and pull out the black intestinal vein. Split each prawn (shrimp) in half lengthways, then cut into small pieces so that they become little round balls when cooked.

Put the prawns (shrimp) in a bowl with the ginger, sherry, egg white and cornflour (cornstarch). Stir well, then leave to marinate in the refrigerator for about 20 minutes.

Heat 1 tablespoon of the oil in a wok or frying pan (skillet), add the prawns (shrimp) and stir-fry over moderate heat until they change colour. Remove from the pan with a slotted spoon.

Heat the remaining oil in the pan, add the spring onions (scallions) and broccoli, stir, then add the salt and sugar. Cook until the broccoli is just tender, then add the prawns (shrimp) and stir well. Serve hot.

# White-Cut Chicken
## Baiqie Ji

This famous Cantonese dish is very simple to cook. It makes an ideal starter for a banquet, or it can be served as part of a buffet.

METRIC/IMPERIAL

*1 chicken, weighing 1.5 kg/3–3½ lb*
**Sauce:**
*2–3 spring onions, finely chopped*
*2 slices of fresh root ginger,\* peeled and finely chopped*
*1 teaspoon salt*
*1 tablespoon soy sauce*
*1 tablespoon sesame seed oil\**
*freshly ground black pepper*

AMERICAN

*1 chicken, weighing 3–3½ lb*
**Sauce:**
*2–3 scallions, finely chopped*
*2 slices of fresh ginger root,\* peeled and finely chopped*
*1 teaspoon salt*
*1 tablespoon soy sauce*
*1 tablespoon sesame seed oil\**
*freshly ground black pepper*

METHOD

Put the chicken in a large pan, add cold water to cover, then cover the pan with a tight-fitting lid. Bring to the boil, then lower the heat and simmer for exactly 7 minutes. Turn off the heat and leave the chicken to cook in the hot water for at least 30 minutes, without removing the lid.

About 1 hour before serving, remove the chicken from the water and chop it into small pieces, using a cleaver. Re-assemble the chicken pieces on a serving dish.

Mix together the sauce ingredients and pour over the chicken. Serve warm or cover and leave in the refrigerator for at least 30 minutes before serving chilled.

# Oil-Basted Chicken

## Youlin Ji

### METRIC/IMPERIAL

1 chicken, weighing 1.5 kg/3–3½ lb
2 tablespoons soy sauce
1 tablespoon medium or dry sherry
1.2 litres/2 pints vegetable oil for
    deep-frying
**Sauce:**
2 spring onions, finely chopped
2 slices of fresh root ginger,* peeled
    and finely chopped
1 garlic clove, peeled and finely
    chopped
2 tablespoons vinegar
1½ tablespoons sugar
1 tablespoon yellow bean sauce*

### AMERICAN

1 chicken, weighing 3–3½ lb
2 tablespoons soy sauce
1 tablespoon medium or pale dry
    sherry
5 cups vegetable oil
**Sauce:**
2 scallions, finely chopped
2 slices of fresh ginger root,* peeled
    and finely chopped
1 garlic clove, peeled and finely
    chopped
2 tablespoons vinegar
1½ tablespoons sugar
1 tablespoon bean sauce*

### METHOD

Wash and clean the chicken thoroughly, then plunge into a large pan of boiling water. Boil rapidly for 2 to 3 minutes, then remove and drain.

Mix together the soy sauce and sherry, then brush over the chicken. Leave to marinate for about 20 minutes. Meanwhile, mix together the sauce ingredients in a small pan.

Heat the oil in a large wok or deep-fat fryer. Add the chicken and cook over moderate heat for 20 to 30 minutes until browned on all sides, basting constantly.

Remove the chicken from the pan, chop into small pieces, then arrange neatly on a warmed serving dish. Add any remaining marinade to the sauce mixture, heat through, then pour over the chicken. Serve hot.

# Soy Chicken

## Chiyou Ji

This dish can be served hot as a main course, or cold as a starter. Do not discard the cooking sauce; it can be stored in the refrigerator for future use.

### METRIC/IMPERIAL

1 chicken, weighing 1.5 kg/3–3½ lb
1 teaspoon freshly ground black
    pepper
2 teaspoons finely chopped fresh root
    ginger*
5 tablespoons soy sauce
3 tablespoons medium or dry sherry
1 tablespoon brown sugar
3 tablespoons vegetable oil
300 ml/½ pint chicken stock or water
coriander leaves* to garnish

### AMERICAN

1 chicken, weighing 3–3½ lb
1 teaspoon freshly ground black
    pepper
2 teaspoons finely chopped fresh
    ginger root*
⅓ cup soy sauce
3 tablespoons medium or pale dry
    sherry
1 tablespoon brown sugar
3 tablespoons vegetable oil
1¼ cups chicken stock or water
coriander leaves* to garnish

### METHOD

Wash the chicken, dry thoroughly and rub inside and out with the pepper and ginger. Mix together the soy sauce, sherry and sugar. Spoon over the chicken and leave to marinate for at least 3 hours, turning the chicken occasionally.

Heat the oil in a large pan, add the whole chicken and fry, turning, until lightly browned on all sides.

Dilute the marinade with the stock or water. Add to the pan, bring to the boil, then lower the heat. Cover and simmer for 45 minutes, turning the chicken several times during cooking taking care to avoid breaking the skin.

Chop the chicken into small pieces. Arrange on a serving dish and baste with 2 tablespoons of the sauce. Garnish with coriander leaves. Serve hot.

# Shredded Chicken with Peppers

## Chijiao Chao Jisi

This is a very colourful dish with a piquant taste.

### METRIC/IMPERIAL

225 g/8 oz chicken breast meat,
    skinned and shredded
½ teaspoon salt
1 tablespoon soy sauce
1 egg white
1 tablespoon cornflour
5 tablespoons vegetable oil
2 slices of fresh root ginger,*
    peeled and shredded
2–3 spring onions, shredded
1 hot chilli, shredded
1 green pepper, cored, seeded and
    shredded
1 red pepper, cored, seeded and
    shredded
2–3 celery sticks, shredded
2 tablespoons black bean sauce*

### AMERICAN

1 cup shredded, skinned chicken
    breast meat
½ teaspoon salt
1 tablespoon soy sauce
1 egg white
1 tablespoon cornstarch
⅓ cup vegetable oil
2 slices of fresh ginger root,* peeled
    and shredded
2–3 scallions, shredded
1 hot chili, shredded
1 green pepper, cored, seeded and
    shredded
1 red pepper, cored, seeded and
    shredded
2–3 celery stalks, shredded
2 tablespoons salted black beans*

### METHOD

Put the chicken in a bowl with the salt, soy sauce, egg white and cornflour (cornstarch) and mix well.

Heat the oil in a wok or frying pan (skillet), add the chicken and stir-fry over moderate heat until half-cooked. Remove from the pan with a slotted spoon.

Increase the heat to high. When the oil starts to smoke, add the ginger to the pan with the spring onions (scallions), chilli, peppers and celery. Stir well, then add the black bean sauce (salted black beans) and continue cooking for a few seconds.

Return the chicken to the pan, mix well, then stir-fry for about 1 to 1½ minutes until the meat is tender, but the vegetables are still crisp and crunchy. Serve hot.

**Soy Chicken; Shredded Chicken with Peppers**

## Steamed Chicken with Chinese Dried Mushrooms

### Donggu Zheng Ziji

METRIC/IMPERIAL

*450 g/1 lb boned chicken (breasts and thighs), cut into small pieces*
*1½ tablespoons soy sauce*
*1 tablespoon medium or dry sherry*
*1 teaspoon sugar*
*1 teaspoon cornflour*
*4 Chinese dried mushrooms,\* soaked in warm water for 30 minutes*
*1 tablespoon vegetable oil*
*2 slices of fresh root ginger,\* peeled and shredded*
*freshly ground black pepper*
*1 teaspoon sesame seed oil\**

AMERICAN

*1 lb boneless chicken (breasts and thighs), cut into small pieces*
*1½ tablespoons soy sauce*
*1 tablespoon medium or pale dry sherry*
*1 teaspoon sugar*
*1 teaspoon cornstarch*
*4 Chinese dried mushrooms,\* soaked in warm water for 30 minutes*
*1 tablespoon vegetable oil*
*2 slices of fresh ginger root,\* peeled and shredded*
*freshly ground black pepper*
*1 teaspoon sesame seed oil\**

METHOD

Put the chicken in a bowl with the soy sauce, sherry, sugar and cornflour (cornstarch). Mix well, then leave to marinate for about 20 minutes.

Squeeze the mushrooms dry, discard the stalks, then cut the caps into pieces, roughly the same size as the chicken.

Brush a heatproof plate with the vegetable oil. Place the chicken pieces on the plate, top with the mushrooms, then sprinkle with the ginger, pepper to taste and the sesame seed oil.

Place in a steamer or over a pan of simmering water and cover the plate with a lid. Steam over high heat for 25 to 30 minutes. Serve hot.

## Shredded Chicken with 'Fish Sauce'

### Yuxiang Jisi

Fish is not used in this recipe; the sauce is normally used for cooking fish dishes, hence the name.

Shredded Chicken with 'Fish Sauce'; Golden Flower and Jade Tree Chicken

METRIC/IMPERIAL

*350 g/12 oz chicken breast meat, skinned and shredded*
*½ teaspoon salt*
*½ egg white*
*1 teaspoon cornflour*
*4 tablespoons vegetable oil*
*2 spring onions, cut into 2.5 cm/1 inch lengths*
*1 slice of fresh root ginger,\* peeled and shredded*
*1 small green pepper, cored, seeded and cut into rings*
*1 small red pepper, cored, seeded and cut into rings*
*3 celery sticks, sliced*
*1 tablespoon soy sauce*
*1 teaspoon sugar*
*1 teaspoon vinegar*
*1 teaspoon chilli sauce (optional)*

# Golden Flower and Jade Tree Chicken
## Zinhua Yushu Ji

This is a very colourful dish, as its name implies; 'Golden Flower' refers to the ham from King-hua, 'Jade' is the chicken, and 'Tree' is the greens. It can be served as a starter at formal dinners, or as a main course for an informal dinner.

### METRIC/IMPERIAL

1 chicken, weighing 1.5 kg/3–3½ lb
2 slices of fresh root ginger,* peeled
2 spring onions
3 tablespoons vegetable oil
450 g/1 lb broccoli or other greens, divided into small florets or pieces
2 teaspoons salt
250 ml/8 fl oz chicken stock
225 g/8 oz cooked ham
1 tablespoon cornflour, mixed to a paste with a little water

### AMERICAN

1 chicken, weighing 3–3½ lb
2 slices of fresh ginger root,* peeled
2 scallions
3 tablespoons vegetable oil
1 lb broccoli or other greens, divided into small florets or pieces
2 teaspoons salt
1 cup chicken stock
½ lb cooked ham
1 tablespoon cornstarch, mixed to a paste with a little water

### METHOD

Put the chicken in a large pan and cover with cold water. Add the ginger and spring onions (scallions), cover with a tight-fitting lid and bring to the boil. Lower the heat and simmer for exactly 3 minutes. Turn off the heat and leave the chicken to cook in the hot water for at least 3 hours, without removing the lid.

Heat the oil in a wok or frying pan (skillet). Add the broccoli or greens and 1 teaspoon salt and stir-fry for 3 to 4 minutes, until cooked to taste, moistening with a little of the stock if necessary. Remove from the pan and arrange around the edge of a large serving dish.

Remove the chicken from the pan, then carefully remove the meat from the bones, keeping the skin on the meat. Cut the chicken and ham into thin rectangular slices and arrange in alternating, overlapping layers in the centre of the broccoli.

Just before serving, heat the remaining stock with the remaining salt in a small pan. Add the cornflour (cornstarch) paste and cook, stirring, until thickened. Pour over the chicken and ham to form a thin glaze, resembling jade. Serve hot.

---

### AMERICAN

1½ cups shredded, skinned chicken breast meat
½ teaspoon salt
½ egg white
1 teaspoon cornstarch
¼ cup vegetable oil
2 scallions, cut into 1 inch lengths
1 slice of fresh ginger root,* peeled and shredded
1 small green pepper, cored, seeded and cut into rings
1 small red pepper, cored, seeded and cut into rings
3 celery stalks, sliced
1 tablespoon soy sauce
1 teaspoon sugar
1 teaspoon vinegar
1 teaspoon chili sauce (optional)

### METHOD

Put the chicken in a bowl with the salt, egg white and cornflour (cornstarch). Mix well, then leave to stand for about 20 minutes.

Heat 2 tablespoons oil in a wok or frying pan (skillet), add the chicken and stir-fry over moderate heat for about 2 minutes. Remove from the pan with a slotted spoon and drain.

Heat the remaining oil in the pan and add the spring onions (scallions), ginger, peppers and celery. Stir in the soy sauce, sugar, vinegar and chilli sauce, if using. Return the chicken to the pan and combine all the ingredients together. Serve hot.

# Fried Chicken Legs
## Zha Jitui

**METRIC/IMPERIAL**

6 chicken legs
2 tablespoons soy sauce
1 tablespoon medium or dry sherry
½ teaspoon freshly ground black
   pepper
2 tablespoons cornflour
600 ml/1 pint vegetable oil for deep-
   frying
1 tablespoon finely chopped spring
   onion

**AMERICAN**

6 chicken legs
2 tablespoons soy sauce
1 tablespoon medium or pale dry
   sherry
½ teaspoon freshly ground black
   pepper
2 tablespoons cornstarch
2½ cups vegetable oil for deep-frying
1 tablespoon finely chopped scallion

**METHOD**

Chop each chicken leg into 2 or 3 pieces, then mix with the soy sauce, sherry and pepper. Leave to marinate for about 20 minutes, turning occasionally.

Coat each piece of chicken with cornflour (cornstarch). Heat the oil in a wok or deep-fat fryer to 180°C/350°F. Lower the heat, add the chicken pieces and deep-fry until golden. Remove from the pan with a slotted spoon and drain.

Pour off all but 1 tablespoon oil, then add the spring onion (scallion) to the pan with the drained chicken pieces. Stir-fry over moderate heat for about 2 minutes. Serve hot.

# Chicken in Silver Foil
## Yinxiang Bao Ji

This is a variation of the traditional 'paper-wrapped chicken'. Prawns (shrimp) or other meat can be used instead of chicken.

**METRIC/IMPERIAL**

450 g/1 lb skinned chicken breast meat
3 spring onions, white part only
¼ teaspoon salt
1 tablespoon soy sauce
1 teaspoon sugar
1 teaspoon medium or dry sherry
1 teaspoon sesame seed oil*
4 tablespoons vegetable oil
**To garnish:**
shredded spring onion
finely chopped red pepper

**AMERICAN**

1 lb chicken breast meat, skinned
3 scallions, white part only
¼ teaspoon salt
1 tablespoon soy sauce
1 teaspoon sugar
1 teaspoon medium or pale dry sherry
1 teaspoon sesame seed oil*
¼ cup oil
**To garnish:**
shredded scallion
finely chopped red pepper

**METHOD**

Cut the chicken into 12 roughly equal-sized pieces. Cut each spring onion (scallion) into 4 pieces. Combine the chicken and spring onions (scallions) with the salt, soy sauce, sugar, sherry and sesame seed oil in a bowl. Leave to marinate for about 20 minutes.

Cut 12 squares of foil large enough to wrap around the chicken pieces 4 times. Brush the pieces of foil with oil, then place a piece of chicken on each. Top with a slice of spring onion (scallion), then wrap the foil around the chicken to make a parcel, making sure that no meat is exposed.

Heat the oil in a wok or frying pan (skillet). Add the chicken parcels and fry over moderate heat for about 2 minutes on each side. Remove and leave to drain on a wok rack or in a strainer for a few minutes; turn off the heat.

Reheat the oil. When it is very hot, return the chicken parcels to the pan and fry for 1 minute only. Serve hot in the silver foil, garnished with shredded spring onion (scallion) and red pepper.

Chicken in Silver Foil; Fried Chicken Legs; Lotus-White Chicken

# Lotus-White Chicken
## Furong Ji

METRIC/IMPERIAL

5 egg whites
120 ml/4 fl oz chicken stock
1 teaspoon salt
1 teaspoon medium or dry sherry
2 teaspoons cornflour
100 g/4 oz chicken breast meat,
 skinned and finely chopped
oil for deep-frying
**To garnish:**
1–2 tablespoons cooked green peas
25 g/1 oz cooked ham, shredded

AMERICAN

5 egg whites
½ cup chicken stock
1 teaspoon salt
1 teaspoon medium or pale dry sherry
2 teaspoons cornstarch
½ cup finely chopped, skinned chicken
 breast meat
oil for deep-frying
**To garnish:**
1–2 tablespoons cooked green peas
1 slice cooked ham, shredded

METHOD

Put the egg whites in a bowl. Stir in 3 tablespoons of the chicken stock, the salt, sherry and half the cornflour (cornstarch). Add the chicken and mix well.

Heat the oil in a wok or deep-fat fryer to 180°C/350°F, then gently pour in about one third of the egg and chicken mixture. Deep-fry for 10 seconds until the mixture begins to rise to the surface, then carefully turn over. Deep-fry until golden, then remove from the pan with a slotted spoon, drain and place on a warmed serving dish. Keep hot while cooking the remaining chicken mixture in the same way.

Heat the remaining stock in a small pan. Mix the remaining cornflour (cornstarch) to a paste with a little cold water add to the stock and simmer, stirring, until thickened. Pour over the chicken.

Garnish with the peas and ham. Serve hot.

# Onion Duck

## Congyou Ya

### METRIC/IMPERIAL

4 Chinese dried mushrooms,* soaked
  in warm water for 30 minutes
1 duckling, weighing 2–2.25 kg/4½–5¼ lb
120 ml/4 fl oz soy sauce
3 tablespoons sugar
100 g/4 oz bamboo shoot, sliced
25 g/1 oz lard
3 spring onions, finely chopped

### AMERICAN

4 Chinese dried mushrooms,* soaked
  in warm water for 30 minutes
1 duckling, weighing 4½–5¼ lb
½ cup soy sauce
3 tablespoons sugar
1 cup sliced bamboo shoot
2 tablespoons lard
3 scallions, finely chopped

### METHOD

Squeeze the mushrooms dry, then discard the stalks.

Put the duckling in a large pan, cover with cold water and bring to the boil. Remove the duckling from the pan and rinse under cold running water. Skim the surface of the cooking water, then return the duckling to the pan. Add more fresh water to cover the duckling if necessary and bring back to the boil.

Add the soy sauce, sugar and mushrooms to the pan. Cover and cook gently for 2½ hours, turning the duckling halfway through cooking. Add the bamboo shoot and simmer for 30 minutes. Transfer the duckling to a warmed serving dish. Drain the mushrooms and bamboo shoot and arrange around the duckling.

Heat the lard in a separate pan, add the spring onions (scallions) and fry for 1 to 2 minutes. Pour over the duckling and serve hot.

**Pan-Fried Chicken Breast; Diced
Chicken with Celery**

## Diced Chicken with Celery

### Jiecai Chao Jiding

METRIC/IMPERIAL

3–4 Chinese dried mushrooms,*
   soaked in warm water for 30 minutes
225 g/8 oz chicken breast meat,
   skinned and diced
½ teaspoon salt
1 egg white
1 tablespoon cornflour
5 tablespoons vegetable oil
2 slices of fresh root ginger,* peeled
   and finely chopped
2–3 spring onions, finely chopped
1 small head celery, diced
100 g/4 oz bamboo shoot, diced
1 red pepper, cored, seeded and
   diced
3 tablespoons soy sauce
1 teaspoon medium or dry sherry
chopped coriander leaves* or parsley
   to garnish

AMERICAN

3–4 Chinese dried mushrooms,*
   soaked in warm water for 30 minutes
1 cup diced, skinned chicken breast
   meat
½ teaspoon salt
1 egg white
1 tablespoon cornstarch
⅓ cup vegetable oil
2 slices of fresh ginger root,* peeled
   and finely chopped
2–3 scallions, finely chopped
1 small bunch celery, diced
1 cup diced bamboo shoot
1 red pepper, cored, seeded and
   diced
3 tablespoons soy sauce
1 teaspoon medium or pale dry sherry
chopped coriander leaves* or parsley
   to garnish

METHOD

Squeeze the mushrooms dry, discard the stalks then dice the caps.

Sprinkle the chicken with the salt, dip into the egg white, then coat with the cornflour (cornstarch).

Heat the oil in a wok or frying pan (skillet). Add the chicken and stir-fry over moderate heat until half-cooked, then remove with a slotted spoon.

Increase the heat to high and add the ginger and spring onions (scallions) to the pan. Add the mushrooms and remaining vegetables and stir-fry for 1 minute.

Return the chicken to the pan, add the soy sauce and sherry and cook for a further 1 minute until the liquid thickens, stirring constantly. Serve hot, garnished with chopped coriander or parsley.

## Pan-Fried Chicken Breast

### Ganjian Jipu

METRIC/IMPERIAL

1 large chicken breast, skinned and
   boned
1–2 spring onions, chopped
1 slice of fresh root ginger,* peeled
   and finely chopped
1 tablespoon medium or dry sherry
2 teaspoons salt
1 egg, beaten
2 teaspoons cornflour
3 tablespoons vegetable oil
1 small lettuce
**Sauce:**
1 tablespoon tomato purée
1 teaspoon sugar
1 teaspoon sesame seed oil*
1 tablespoon water

AMERICAN

1 large chicken breast, skinned and
   boned
1–2 scallions, chopped
1 slice of fresh ginger root,* peeled
   and finely chopped
1 tablespoon medium or pale dry
   sherry
2 teaspoons salt
1 egg, beaten
2 teaspoons cornstarch
3 tablespoons vegetable oil
1 small head of lettuce
**Sauce:**
1 tablespoon tomato paste
1 teaspoon sugar
1 teaspoon sesame seed oil*
1 tablespoon water

METHOD

Cut the chicken into thin rectangular slices and place in a bowl. Add the spring onion (scallion), ginger, sherry and salt and mix well. Leave to marinate for about 20 minutes.

Stir the egg into the marinated chicken, then sprinkle with the cornflour (cornstarch) and toss to coat thoroughly. Heat the oil in a wok or frying pan (skillet). Add the chicken mixture and fry until tender and golden on all sides. Remove from the pan with a slotted spoon and arrange on a bed of lettuce.

Mix together the sauce ingredients. Add to the pan in which the chicken was cooked and heat through, then either pour over the chicken, or serve as a dip. Serve hot.

# Roast Duck Peking-Style

## Beijing Kao Ya

Peking-style duck is unique in Chinese cuisine, not only for the way in which it is cooked, but also for the specially reared species of duck used. The ducks are brought to exactly the right degree of plumpness and tenderness by several stages of force-feeding and care.

If liked, the sauce given here may be replaced by 6 tablespoons commercially prepared hoi sin sauce.*

Spring onion (scallion) flowers are the traditional garnish for Peking-style duck. To prepare these: Make several cuts from top to bottom along each spring onion (scallion), without cutting right through the base. Leave in a bowl of iced water to open.

The traditional way to serve this dish is to arrange all the separate dishes of food on the table and allow the guests to help themselves.

### METRIC/IMPERIAL

*1 duckling, weighing*
 *1.5–1.75 kg/3–4¼ lb*
*1 tablespoon sugar*
*1 teaspoon salt*
*300 ml/½ pint water*
**Sauce:**
*3 tablespoons yellow bean sauce\**
*2 tablespoons sugar*
*1 tablespoon sesame seed oil\**
**To serve:**
*24 Mandarin Pancakes (see opposite)*
*10–12 spring onion flowers*
*4 leeks, cut into 7.5 cm/3 inch strips*
*½ cucumber, cut into 7.5 cm/3 inch*
 *strips*
*½ red pepper, cored, seeded and*
 *shredded*

### AMERICAN

*1 duckling, weighing 3–4¼ lb*
*1 tablespoon sugar*
*1 teaspoon salt*
*1¼ cups water*
**Sauce:**
*3 tablespoons bean sauce\**
*2 tablespoons sugar*
*1 tablespoon sesame seed oil\**
**To serve:**
*24 Mandarin Pancakes (see opposite)*
*10–12 scallion flowers*
*4 leeks, cut into 3 inch strips*
*½ cucumber, cut into 3 inch strips*
*½ red pepper, cored, seeded and*
 *shredded*

**Roast Duck Peking-Style, served with traditional accompaniments: Mandarin Pancakes, dipping sauce and raw vegetables**

## METHOD

Clean the duck and hang it up to dry thoroughly, preferably overnight in a cool, well-ventilated room.

The next day, dissolve the sugar and salt in the water and rub all over the duck. Leave for several hours until dry.

Place the duck on a rack in a roasting pan and roast in the centre of a preheated moderately hot oven (200°C/400°F, Gas Mark 6) for 1 hour.

Place the sauce ingredients in a pan and heat gently for 2 to 3 minutes, stirring constantly, then pour into a serving bowl.

Carve the duck into neat slices and arrange on a serving dish. Arrange the Mandarin pancakes on a separate dish and garnish both dishes with spring onion (scallion) flowers. Put the leeks, cucumber, and pepper on another dish.

To eat: Spread each pancake with a little sauce, then place a little leek and cucumber in the middle. Top with 1 or 2 slices of duck. Roll up the pancake.

# Oil-Braised Duck
## Yashao Ya

### METRIC/IMPERIAL

1 duckling, weighing 1.75–2 kg/4–4¾ lb
4 tablespoons orange juice
2 tablespoons sugar
4 tablespoons soy sauce
4 teaspoons salt
4 tablespoons medium or dry sherry
1 tablespoon vinegar
½ teaspoon five spice powder*
1 slice of fresh root ginger,* peeled
600 ml/1 pint chicken stock
1.2 litres/2 pints vegetable oil for deep-frying

### AMERICAN

1 duckling, weighing 4–4¾ lb
¼ cup orange juice
2 tablespoons sugar
¼ cup soy sauce
4 teaspoons salt
¼ cup medium or pale dry sherry
1 tablespoon vinegar
½ teaspoon five spice powder*
1 slice of fresh ginger root,* peeled
2½ cups chicken stock
5 cups vegetable oil for deep-frying

### METHOD

Plunge the duckling into a pan of boiling water. Leave for a few minutes, then drain and place in a clean pan with all the remaining ingredients. Bring to the boil, then lower the heat. Cover with a tight-fitting lid and simmer gently for 45 minutes, turning the duckling at least twice during cooking. Remove the duckling from the pan, drain and dry thoroughly. Leave the cooking liquid simmering over low heat to reduce and thicken.

Heat the oil in a wok or deep-fat fryer. Add the duckling to the oil and cook over moderate heat until browned on all sides.

Return the duckling to the simmering liquid and turn it several times to coat with the sauce.

Remove from the pan and cut into small pieces. Re-arrange the duckling on a warmed serving dish and pour the remaining sauce over the top. Serve hot.

# Mandarin Pancakes
## Bo Bing

### METRIC/IMPERIAL

450 g/1 lb plain flour
300 ml/½ pint boiling water
little vegetable oil

### AMERICAN

4 cups all-purpose flour
1¼ cups boiling water
little vegetable oil

### METHOD

Sift the flour into a bowl. Mix the water with 1 teaspoon oil, then slowly stir into the flour, using chopsticks or a wooden spoon.

Knead the mixture into a firm dough, then divide into 3 equal portions. Roll each portion into a long 'sausage', then cut each sausage into 8 equal pieces.

Press each piece into a flat pancake with the palm of the hand. Brush one pancake with a little oil, then place another on top to form a 'sandwich'; repeat with the remaining dough to make 12 sandwiches.

Flatten each 'sandwich' on a lightly floured surface with a rolling-pin into a 15 cm/6 inch circle.

Place an ungreased frying pan (skillet) over moderate heat. When it is very hot, fry the 'sandwiches', one at a time. Turn the pancakes as soon as air bubbles appear on the surface. Cook the other side until little brown spots appear underneath. Remove the 'sandwich' from the pan and peel the 2 layers apart very gently. Fold each pancake into four to serve.

MAKES 24 PANCAKES

**Note:** Cold pancakes can be reheated in a steamer or hot oven for 5 to 10 minutes.

# Stir-Fried 'Three Whites'

## Chao Sanbai

### METRIC/IMPERIAL

100 g/4 oz chicken breast meat,
  skinned and diced
100 g/4 oz pork fillet, diced
1 teaspoon salt
1 egg white
1 tablespoon cornflour
3 tablespoons vegetable oil
2 spring onions, white part only, finely
  chopped
2 garlic cloves, peeled and finely
  chopped
100 g/4 oz bamboo shoot, diced
1 tablespoon medium or dry sherry
1 tablespoon yellow bean sauce*

### AMERICAN

½ cup diced, skinned chicken breast
  meat
½ cup diced pork loin
1 teaspoon salt
1 egg white
1 tablespoon cornstarch
3 tablespoons vegetable oil
2 scallions, white part only, finely
  chopped
2 garlic cloves, peeled and finely
  chopped
1 cup diced bamboo shoot
1 tablespoon medium or pale dry
  sherry
1 tablespoon bean sauce*

### METHOD

Put the chicken and pork in separate
bowls. Mix together the salt, egg white
and cornflour (cornstarch); divide equally
between the chicken and pork and
mix well.

Heat 1 tablespoon oil in a wok or frying
pan (skillet), add the chicken and stir-fry
until half-cooked. Remove from the pan
with a slotted spoon and drain. Add
another tablespoon oil to the pan and stir-fry
the pork until half-cooked. Remove
and drain.

Increase the heat and add the remaining
oil to the pan. Add the spring onions
(scallions), garlic and bamboo shoot,
then return the chicken and pork to the
pan. Stir in the sherry and bean sauce,
then add a little stock or water to moisten
if necessary.

Cook, stirring, until the meats and
bamboo shoot are well coated with sauce
and most of the liquid has been absorbed.
Serve hot.

# Braised Eggs with Pork

## Lu Jidan Zhurou

If you happen to have any sauce left
over from *Soy Chicken* (see page 99),
add it to the sauce with the pork and
eggs, as it will greatly improve the
flavour of this dish.

### METRIC/IMPERIAL

6 eggs
225 g/8 oz boned lean pork, in one
  piece
**Sauce:**
4 tablespoons soy sauce
2 tablespoons sugar
1 teaspoon salt
1 teaspoon five spice powder*
1.2 litres/2 pints water

### AMERICAN

6 eggs
½ lb boneless pork loin, in one piece
**Sauce:**
¼ cup soy sauce
2 tablespoons sugar
1 teaspoon salt
1 teaspoon five spice powder*
5 cups water

### METHOD

Cook the unshelled eggs in boiling water
for 5 minutes, plunge into cold water,
then carefully remove the shells.

Add the pork to a pan of boiling water.
Remove when it changes colour, drain
and dry on kitchen paper towels.

To make the sauce: Put all the ingredients
in a pan, bring to the boil,
stirring, then lower the heat and simmer
for about 1 hour. Add the pork and eggs
and simmer for 15 minutes, then turn off
the heat and leave the eggs and pork to
cool in the sauce for at least 50 minutes.

Remove the eggs and pork from the
sauce. Cut the eggs into halves or quarters
and thinly slice the pork. Arrange
the eggs around the edge of a serving
plate and place the pork in the centre.
Serve cold.

**Note:** Keep the sauce in the
refrigerator for
future use.

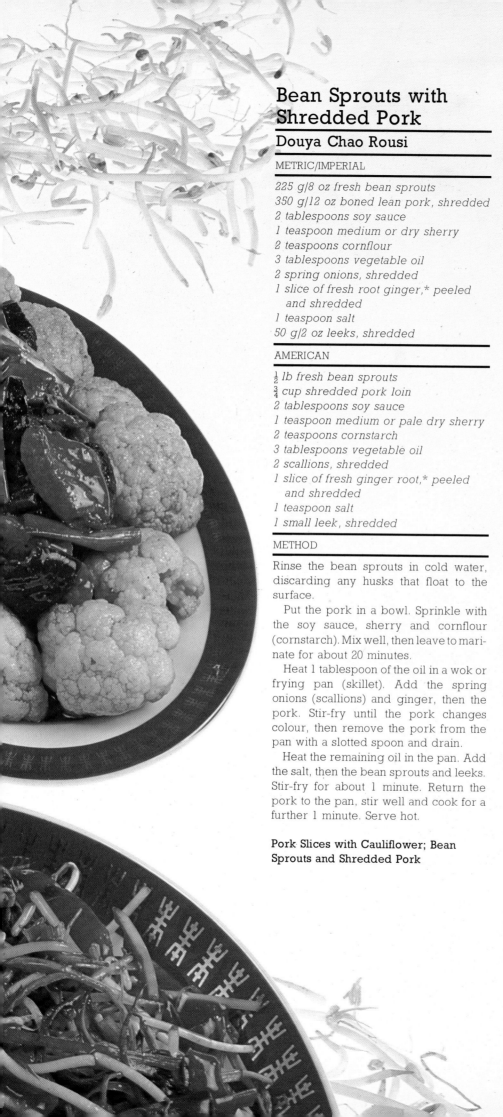

## Bean Sprouts with Shredded Pork
### Douya Chao Rousi

METRIC/IMPERIAL

225 g/8 oz fresh bean sprouts
350 g/12 oz boned lean pork, shredded
2 tablespoons soy sauce
1 teaspoon medium or dry sherry
2 teaspoons cornflour
3 tablespoons vegetable oil
2 spring onions, shredded
1 slice of fresh root ginger,* peeled and shredded
1 teaspoon salt
50 g/2 oz leeks, shredded

AMERICAN

½ lb fresh bean sprouts
¾ cup shredded pork loin
2 tablespoons soy sauce
1 teaspoon medium or pale dry sherry
2 teaspoons cornstarch
3 tablespoons vegetable oil
2 scallions, shredded
1 slice of fresh ginger root,* peeled and shredded
1 teaspoon salt
1 small leek, shredded

METHOD

Rinse the bean sprouts in cold water, discarding any husks that float to the surface.

Put the pork in a bowl. Sprinkle with the soy sauce, sherry and cornflour (cornstarch). Mix well, then leave to marinate for about 20 minutes.

Heat 1 tablespoon of the oil in a wok or frying pan (skillet). Add the spring onions (scallions) and ginger, then the pork. Stir-fry until the pork changes colour, then remove the pork from the pan with a slotted spoon and drain.

Heat the remaining oil in the pan. Add the salt, then the bean sprouts and leeks. Stir-fry for about 1 minute. Return the pork to the pan, stir well and cook for a further 1 minute. Serve hot.

**Pork Slices with Cauliflower; Bean Sprouts and Shredded Pork**

## Pork Slices with Cauliflower
### Caihua Chao Roupian

METRIC/IMPERIAL

4 Chinese dried mushrooms,* soaked in warm water for 30 minutes
225 g/8 oz boned lean pork, sliced
2 tablespoons soy sauce
1 tablespoon medium or dry sherry
1 tablespoon cornflour
1 medium cauliflower, divided into florets
salt
3 tablespoons vegetable oil
2 spring onions, cut into 2.5 cm/1 inch lengths
1 slice of fresh root ginger,* peeled and cut into strips

AMERICAN

4 Chinese dried mushrooms,* soaked in warm water for 30 minutes
½ lb pork loin, sliced
2 tablespoons soy sauce
1 tablespoon medium or pale dry sherry
1 tablespoon cornstarch
1 medium cauliflower, divided into florets
salt
3 tablespoons vegetable oil
2 scallions, cut into 1 inch lengths
1 slice of fresh ginger root,* peeled and cut into strips

METHOD

Squeeze the mushrooms dry, discard the stalks, then cut the mushroom caps into halves or quarters, according to size.

Put the pork in a bowl and sprinkle with the soy sauce, sherry and 1 teaspoon of the cornflour (cornstarch). Mix well, then leave to marinate for about 20 minutes.

Meanwhile, blanch the cauliflower in boiling salted water for 1 to 2 minutes, then drain and set aside.

Heat the oil in a large wok or frying pan (skillet). Add the spring onions (scallions) and ginger, then the pork. Stir-fry until the pork changes colour, then add the mushrooms and 1 teaspoon salt. Stir-fry for a further 1 minute, then add the cauliflower and stir well.

Mix the remaining cornflour (cornstarch) to a paste with a little water, add to the pan and cook, stirring, until thickened.

Arrange the cauliflower around the edge of a serving dish and pile the pork mixture into the centre. Serve hot.

# Red-Cooked Pork Leg or Shoulder

## Hongshao Zhuti

Red-cooked pork should be so tender that it can easily be pulled off the bone with chopsticks or a fork.

### METRIC/IMPERIAL

4 Chinese dried mushrooms,* soaked in warm water for 30 minutes
1 leg or shoulder of pork, weighing 1.5 kg/3–3½ lb
1 garlic clove, peeled and crushed
6 tablespoons soy sauce
3 tablespoons medium or dry sherry
3 tablespoons crystallized or brown sugar
1 teaspoon five spice powder*

**To garnish:**
1 carrot, thinly sliced into rounds
shredded spring onion

### AMERICAN

4 Chinese dried mushrooms,* soaked in warm water for 30 minutes
1 pork leg or shoulder, weighing 3–3½ lb
1 garlic clove, peeled and crushed
6 tablespoons soy sauce
3 tablespoons medium or pale dry sherry
3 tablespoons rock or brown sugar
1 teaspoon five spice powder*

**To garnish:**
1 carrot, thinly sliced into rounds
shredded scallion

### METHOD

Squeeze the mushrooms dry, then discard the stalks.

Put the pork in a large pan of cold water. Bring to the boil, boil for a few minutes, then drain. Rinse the pork under cold running water, then drain again.

Return the pork to the cleaned pan. Add the mushrooms, garlic, soy sauce, sherry, sugar and five spice powder. Cover with a tight-fitting lid and bring to the boil.

Lower the heat and simmer gently for 2 to 3 hours, turning the pork several times during cooking. There should be very little liquid left at the end of the cooking time; if necessary, increase the heat and simmer, uncovered, until the liquid has reduced and thickened.

Serve the pork hot or cold, garnished with carrot slices and shredded spring onion (scallion).

# Steamed Spareribs in Black Bean Sauce

## Chizhi Zheng Paigu

### METRIC/IMPERIAL

450 g/1 lb pork spareribs, chopped into small pieces
1 garlic clove, peeled and crushed
1 slice of fresh root ginger,* peeled and finely chopped
1 tablespoon vegetable oil

**Sauce:**
2 tablespoons black bean sauce*
1 tablespoon soy sauce
1 teaspoon sugar
1 teaspoon medium or dry sherry
1 teaspoon cornflour

**To garnish:**
1 small green or red pepper, cored, seeded and shredded
1 teaspoon sesame seed oil* (optional)

### AMERICAN

1 lb pork spareribs, chopped into small pieces
1 garlic clove, peeled and crushed
1 slice of fresh ginger root,* peeled and finely chopped
1 tablespoon vegetable oil

**Sauce:**
2 tablespoons salted black beans*
1 tablespoon soy sauce
1 teaspoon sugar
1 teaspoon medium or pale dry sherry
1 teaspoon cornstarch

**To garnish:**
1 small green or red pepper, cored, seeded and shredded
1 teaspoon sesame seed oil* (optional)

### METHOD

Put the spareribs in a bowl with the garlic, ginger and sauce ingredients. Mix well, then leave to marinate for about 20 minutes.

Brush a heatproof plate with the vegetable oil, then put the sparerib mixture on the plate. Place in a steamer, or over a pan of boiling water and cover with a lid. Steam over high heat for 30 minutes. Sprinkle with the green or red pepper and sesame seed oil, if using. Serve hot.

## Braised Meatballs
### Hongshao Rouwan

METRIC/IMPERIAL

3 Chinese dried mushrooms,* soaked
  in warm water for 30 minutes
225 g/8 oz boned pork, finely
  minced
1 egg white
2 tablespoons soy sauce
1 tablespoon medium or dry sherry
1 teaspoon sugar
1 tablespoon cornflour
3 tablespoons vegetable oil
1 slice of fresh root ginger,* peeled
  and finely chopped
2 spring onions, white part only, finely
  chopped
225 g/8 oz Chinese cabbage,
  shredded
1 teaspoon salt
450 ml/¾ pint chicken stock
  (approximately)
50 g/2 oz transparent noodles,* soaked
  in water for 10 minutes and drained

AMERICAN

3 Chinese dried mushrooms,* soaked
  in warm water for 30 minutes
1 cup ground pork
1 egg white
2 tablespoons soy sauce
1 tablespoon medium or pale dry
  sherry
1 teaspoon sugar
1 tablespoon cornstarch
3 tablespoons vegetable oil
1 slice of fresh ginger root,* peeled
  and finely chopped
2 scallions, white part only, finely
  chopped
½ lb bok choy, shredded
1 teaspoon salt
2 cups chicken stock (approximately)
2 oz cellophane noodles, soaked in
  water for 10 minutes and drained

METHOD

Squeeze the mushrooms dry, then discard the hard stalks.

Mix the pork with the egg white, soy sauce, sherry, sugar and cornflour (cornstarch). Form the mixture into about 8 meatballs.

Heat the oil in a pan, add the meatballs and fry until golden. Remove from the pan with a slotted spoon. Add the ginger and spring onions (scallions) to the pan, then stir in the cabbage (bok choy), mushrooms and salt. Return the meatballs to the pan and pour in just enough stock to cover. Bring to the boil, then lower the heat and simmer for 25 minutes.

Stir in the noodles and simmer for about 3 minutes. Serve hot.

## Stir-Fried Pork with Bamboo Shoot
### Dongsun Chao Rousi

METRIC/IMPERIAL

225 g/8 oz boned lean pork, thinly
  sliced
1 teaspoon dry sherry
2 tablespoons soy sauce
3 tablespoons vegetable oil
1 garlic clove, peeled and chopped
275 g/10 oz bamboo shoot, thinly sliced
2 teaspoons vinegar
shredded spring onion and tomato to
  garnish

AMERICAN

1 cup thinly sliced pork loin
1 teaspoon pale dry sherry
2 tablespoons soy sauce
3 tablespoons vegetable oil
1 garlic clove, peeled and chopped
2½ cups thinly sliced bamboo shoot
2 teaspoons vinegar
shredded scallion and tomato to
  garnish

METHOD

Put the pork in a bowl with the sherry and ½ tablespoon of the soy sauce. Mix well, then leave to marinate for about 20 minutes.

Heat the oil in a wok or frying pan (skillet), add the garlic and fry until golden brown. Remove from the pan with a slotted spoon and discard.

Add the pork to the pan and stir-fry until it changes colour. Add the bamboo shoot, the remaining soy sauce and the vinegar. Stir-fry for about 30 seconds. Serve hot, garnished with shredded spring onion (scallion) and tomato.

Red-Cooked Pork Leg; Stir-Fried Pork with Bamboo Shoot

111

# Stir-Fried Kidney Flowers

## Chao Yaohua

### METRIC/IMPERIAL

15 g/½ oz wood ears,* soaked in warm
    water for 20 minutes
225 g/8 oz pigs' kidney
1½ teaspoons salt
2 teaspoons cornflour
6 tablespoons vegetable oil
1 garlic clove, peeled and crushed
1 slice of fresh root ginger,* peeled
    and finely chopped
1 spring onion, finely chopped
50 g/2 oz water chestnuts,* sliced
50 g/2 oz bamboo shoot, sliced
100 g/4 oz seasonal green vegetables
    (lettuce, cabbage or spinach),
    blanched in boiling water and
    drained
1 tablespoon vinegar
1 tablespoon soy sauce

### AMERICAN

½ cup tree ears,* soaked in warm water
    for 20 minutes
½ lb pork kidney
1½ teaspoons salt
2 teaspoons cornstarch
6 tablespoons vegetable oil
1 garlic clove, peeled and crushed
1 slice of fresh ginger root,* peeled
    and finely chopped
1 scallion, finely chopped
¼ cup water chestnuts,* sliced
½ cup sliced bamboo shoot
¼ lb seasonal green vegetables (lettuce,
    cabbage or spinach), blanched in
    boiling water and drained
1 tablespoon vinegar
1 tablespoon soy sauce

### METHOD

Drain the wood (tree) ears and discard
the hard parts. Split the kidneys in half
lengthways and discard the fat and white
core. Score the surface of the kidneys in a
criss-cross pattern, then cut into pieces.
Sprinkle with ½ teaspoon salt and 1 teaspoon cornflour (cornstarch).

Heat the oil in a pan until it reaches
smoking point. Add the kidneys and stir-
fry until evenly browned. Remove from
the pan with a slotted spoon and drain.

Pour off all but 2 tablespoons oil, then
add the garlic, ginger and spring onion
(scallion) to the pan. Stir-fry for a few
seconds, then add the wood (tree) ears,
water chestnuts, bamboo shoot and
green vegetables.

Stir in the vinegar and remaining salt,
then return the kidneys to the pan. Mix
the remaining cornflour (cornstarch) to a
paste with a little water, then add to the
pan with the soy sauce and cook, stirring,
for 1 minute. Serve hot.

Stir-Fried Kidney Flowers (above); Stir-Fried Beef with Green Peppers (below)

## Stir-Fried Beef with Green Peppers
### Qing Jiao Niurou Pian

METRIC/IMPERIAL

225 g/8 oz beef steak, thinly sliced
2 teaspoons salt
2 teaspoons sugar
1 tablespoon medium or dry sherry
1 tablespoon cornflour
½ teaspoon chilli sauce (optional)
freshly ground black pepper
3 tablespoons vegetable oil
1 large green pepper, cored, seeded
   and thinly sliced
1 large tomato, cut into 6 pieces
2 spring onions, chopped
1 slice of fresh root ginger,* peeled
   and finely chopped
1 tablespoon soy sauce

AMERICAN

1 cup thinly sliced flank or round steak
2 teaspoons salt
2 teaspoons sugar
1 tablespoon medium or pale dry
   sherry
1 tablespoon cornstarch
½ teaspoon chili sauce (optional)
freshly ground black pepper
3 tablespoons vegetable oil
1 large green pepper, cored, seeded
   and thinly sliced
1 large tomato, cut into 6 pieces
2 scallions, chopped
1 slice of fresh ginger root,* peeled
   and finely chopped
1 tablespoon soy sauce

METHOD

Put the steak in a bowl with ½ teaspoon salt, the sugar, sherry, cornflour (cornstarch), chilli sauce if using, and black pepper to taste. Mix well, then leave to marinate for about 20 minutes.

Heat 1 tablespoon of the oil in a wok or frying pan (skillet). Add the green pepper, tomato and remaining salt and stir-fry for a few seconds over high heat. Remove from the pan with a slotted spoon and drain.

Heat the remaining oil in the pan. Add the spring onions (scallions) and ginger, then the meat. Stir-fry for a few seconds, then add the soy sauce. Return the green pepper mixture to the pan and stir well. Serve hot.

## Red-Cooked Beef
### Hongshao Niurou

METRIC/IMPERIAL

750 g/1½ lb stewing beef, in one piece
4 slices of fresh root ginger,* peeled
2 tablespoons medium or dry sherry
2 tablespoons vegetable oil
5 tablespoons soy sauce
1 tablespoon sugar
1 tablespoon sesame seed oil*
   (optional)

AMERICAN

1½ lb stewing beef, in one piece
4 slices of fresh ginger root,* peeled
2 tablespoons medium or pale dry
   sherry
2 tablespoons vegetable oil
⅓ cup soy sauce
1 tablespoon sugar
1 tablespoon sesame seed oil*
   (optional)

METHOD

Put the beef, ginger and sherry in a large pan. Add just enough water to cover and bring to the boil. Skim the surface, then lower the heat, cover and simmer gently for about 1 hour.

Remove the beef from the pan, reserving the cooking liquid, drain and cut into 2.5 cm/1 inch chunks.

Heat the vegetable oil in a clean pan, add the beef and stir-fry for about 30 seconds, then add the soy sauce, sugar and reserved cooking liquid.

Cover and simmer for about 40 minutes or until the beef is tender. Sprinkle with the sesame oil if using. Serve hot.

113

## Mange-Tout (Snow Peas) and Beef
### Xuedo Niurou

#### METRIC/IMPERIAL

225 g/8 oz beef steak, thinly sliced
2 tablespoons oyster sauce*
1 tablespoon medium or dry sherry
1 teaspoon cornflour
4 tablespoons vegetable oil
2 spring onions, cut into 2.5 cm/1 inch
   lengths
1 slice of fresh root ginger,* peeled
   and cut into strips
225 g/8 oz mange-tout, topped and
   tailed
1 tablespoon salt
1 teaspoon sugar

#### AMERICAN

1 cup thinly sliced flank or round steak
2 tablespoons oyster sauce*
1 tablespoon medium or pale dry
   sherry
1 teaspoon cornstarch
¼ cup vegetable oil
2 scallions, cut into 1 inch lengths
1 slice of fresh ginger root,* peeled
   and cut into strips
½ lb snow peas, topped and tailed
1 tablespoon salt
1 teaspoon sugar

#### METHOD

Put the beef in a bowl with the oyster sauce, sherry and cornflour (cornstarch). Mix well, then leave to marinate for about 20 minutes.

Heat half the oil in a wok or frying pan (skillet). Add the spring onions (scallions) and ginger. Stir-fry for a few seconds, then add the beef. Stir-fry until evenly browned, then transfer to the mixture to a warmed serving dish and keep hot.

Heat the remaining oil in the pan. Add the mange-tout (snow peas), salt and sugar and stir-fry for about 2 minutes. (Do not overcook, or the mange-tout (snow peas) will lose their texture and colour.)

Add the mange-tout (snow peas) to the beef and mix well. Serve hot.

## Stir-Fried Beef with Broccoli
### Jielan Chao Niurou

#### METRIC/IMPERIAL

225 g/8 oz lean beef steak, thinly sliced
2 teaspoons salt
1 teaspoon medium or dry sherry
1 tablespoon cornflour
4 tablespoons vegetable oil
225 g/8 oz broccoli, divided into small
   florets
little chicken stock or water (optional)
2 spring onions, cut into 2.5 cm/1 inch
   lengths
100 g/4 oz button mushrooms, sliced
1 tablespoon soy sauce

#### AMERICAN

½ lb flank or round steak, thinly sliced
2 teaspoons salt
1 teaspoon medium or pale dry sherry
1 tablespoon cornstarch
¼ cup vegetable oil
½ lb broccoli, divided into small florets
little chicken stock or water (optional)
2 scallions, cut into 1 inch lengths
1 cup button mushrooms, sliced
1 tablespoon soy sauce

#### METHOD

Put the steak in a bowl with ½ teaspoon salt, the sherry and cornflour (cornstarch); mix well. Leave for 20 minutes.

Heat 2 tablespoons of the oil in a wok or frying pan (skillet). Add the broccoli and remaining salt and stir-fry for a few minutes, adding a little stock or water to moisten if necessary. Remove from the pan with a slotted spoon and drain.

Heat the remaining oil in the pan. Add the spring onions (scallions) and fry for a few seconds. Add the steak and stir-fry until evenly browned. Stir in the mushrooms, soy sauce and broccoli. Serve hot.

# Beef and Carrot Stew

## Luopu Men Niunan

### METRIC/IMPERIAL

2 tablespoons vegetable oil
1 garlic clove, peeled and crushed
1 slice of fresh root ginger,* peeled
    and chopped
1 spring onion, chopped
750 g/1½ lb stewing beef, cut into
    1 cm/½ inch squares
4 tablespoons soy sauce
1 tablespoon sugar
1 tablespoon medium or dry sherry
½ teaspoon five spice powder*
450 g/1 lb carrots, peeled

### AMERICAN

2 tablespoons vegetable oil
1 garlic clove, peeled and crushed
1 slice of fresh ginger root,* peeled
    and chopped
1 scallion, chopped
1½ lb stewing beef, cut into ½ inch
    squares
¼ cup soy sauce
1 tablespoon sugar
1 tablespoon medium or dry sherry
½ teaspoon five spice powder*
1 lb carrots, peeled

### METHOD

Heat the oil in a heavy pan or flameproof casserole. Add the garlic, ginger and spring onion (scallion) and fry until golden brown. Add the beef and the remaining ingredients, except the carrots. Add just enough cold water to cover. Bring to the boil, lower the heat and simmer for about 1½ hours.

Cut the carrots diagonally into diamond shapes. Add to the beef and simmer for 30 minutes or until the beef and carrots are tender. Serve hot.

Beef and Carrot Stew; Mange-Tout (Snow Peas) and Beef; Stir-Fried Beef with Broccoli

115

# Mongolian Lamb Hot Pot

## Shua Yangrou

This is the famous Peking dish that ranks almost as high as Roast Duck. It is not quite as popular because the Chinese generally prefer pork, beef or poultry to lamb; this is particularly true in the South.

If the meat is sliced when half-frozen, it will be much easier to obtain the very thin slices required.

The Hot Pot – sometimes known as a Mongolian Fire Pot or Chafing Pot – is placed in the centre of the table with the other ingredients arranged around it. A fondue set can be used instead.

### METRIC/IMPERIAL

1 boned shoulder, loin or leg of lamb, weighing 1.5 kg/3–3½ lb
450 g/1 lb fresh spinach leaves, cut into large pieces
1 kg/2 lb Chinese cabbage, cut into large pieces
3 cakes bean curd,* each cut into 8–10 slices
100 g/4 oz transparent noodles,* soaked in water for 10 minutes and drained

**Sauces:**
3 tablespoons hoi sin sauce*
3 tablespoons chilli sauce
2 tablespoons soy sauce
1 tablespoon sesame seed oil*
2 tablespoons chopped spring onions
1 tablespoon chopped fresh root ginger*
2–3 garlic cloves, peeled and finely chopped

**To serve:**
2.25 litres/4 pints chicken stock or water

### AMERICAN

1 boned shoulder, loin or leg of lamb, weighing 3–3½ lb
1 lb fresh spinach leaves, cut into large pieces
2 lb bok choy, cut into large pieces
3 cakes bean curd,* each cut into 8–10 slices
¼ lb cellophane noodles,* soaked in water for 10 minutes and drained

**Sauces:**
3 tablespoons hoi sin sauce*
3 tablespoons chili sauce
2 tablespoons soy sauce
1 tablespoon sesame seed oil*
2 tablespoons chopped scallions
1 tablespoon chopped fresh ginger root*
2–3 garlic cloves, peeled and finely chopped

**To serve:**
5 pints chicken stock or water

## METHOD

Cut the lamb into fairly large, very thin slices and arrange on a serving plate. Arrange the spinach, cabbage (bok choy), bean curd and noodles on another serving plate.

Put the hoi sin sauce and chilli sauce in separate bowls. Combine the soy sauce and sesame seed oil in a third bowl. Mix the spring onions (scallions), ginger and garlic in another bowl.

Place the meat, vegetables and sauces on the table. Stand the Hot Pot in the middle and pour in the stock or water.

When the diners are seated, bring the stock to the boil. Meanwhile, allow guests to prepare their own sauces by mixing the different ingredients together according to taste.

When the stock is boiling vigorously, each guest should pick up a piece of lamb with chopsticks and cook it in the stock until just tender; this should take no longer than 20 to 30 seconds, depending on the thickness of the meat. The meat is then dipped into a sauce before eating.

The vegetables can be cooked and eaten in the same way, adding more stock or water to the Hot Pot as necessary. When all the meat is eaten, put the remaining vegetables in the pot. Boil vigorously for a few minutes, then serve as a soup in individual bowls.

**Mongolian Lamb Hot Pot**

# Ten-Variety Fried Rice

## Shijin Chaofan

### METRIC/IMPERIAL

*3 Chinese dried mushrooms,\* soaked*
  *in warm water for 30 minutes*
*225 g/8 oz long-grain rice*
*3 eggs*
*salt*
*3 tablespoons vegetable oil*
*4–5 spring onions, finely chopped*
*100 g/4 oz peeled prawns*
*50 g/2 oz cooked ham, diced*
*50 g/2 oz cooked chicken or pork,*
  *diced*
*50 g/2 oz bamboo shoot, diced*
*25 g/1 oz shelled peas*
*2 tablespoons soy sauce*

### AMERICAN

*3 Chinese dried mushrooms,\* soaked*
  *in warm water for 30 minutes*
*1 cup long-grain rice*
*3 eggs*
*salt*
*3 tablespoons vegetable oil*
*4–5 scallions, finely chopped*
*2 large shrimp, shelled*
*¼ cup diced cooked ham*
*¼ cup diced cooked chicken or pork*
*½ cup diced bamboo shoot*
*¼ cup shelled peas*
*2 tablespoons soy sauce*

### METHOD

Squeeze the mushrooms dry, discard the hard stalks, then dice the caps.

Wash the rice in cold water once only, then place in a saucepan and cover with enough cold water to come about 2.5 cm/1 inch above the surface of the rice.

Bring to the boil, then stir once with a spoon to prevent the rice sticking to the bottom of the pan during cooking. Cover with a tight-fitting lid, reduce the heat to as low as possible and cook for 15 to 20 minutes.

Meanwhile, beat the eggs with a little salt. Heat 1 tablespoon of the oil in a frying pan (skillet) over low heat. Add the eggs and cook to make an omelet. Remove from the pan and leave to cool.

Heat the remaining oil in the pan, add the spring onions (scallions), then stir in the prawns (shrimp), ham, chicken or pork, mushrooms, bamboo shoot and peas. Add the soy sauce and cooked rice. Cook, stirring, for about 1 minute. Break the omelet into pieces and fold into the rice mixture. Serve hot.

# Bean Sprout·Salad

## Laingban Douyar

### METRIC/IMPERIAL

450 g/1 lb fresh bean sprouts
salt
2 eggs
1 tablespoon vegetable oil
100 g/4 oz cooked ham, cut into thin
  strips
**Sauce:**
2 tablespoons soy sauce
2 tablespoons vinegar
1 tablespoon sesame seed oil*
freshly ground black pepper
**To garnish:**
thinly pared strip of red pepper
parsley sprig

### AMERICAN

1 lb fresh bean sprouts
salt
2 eggs
1 tablespoon vegetable oil
½ cup thinly sliced cooked ham
**Sauce:**
2 tablespoons soy sauce
2 tablespoons vinegar
1 tablespoon sesame seed oil*
freshly ground black pepper
**To garnish:**
thinly pared strip of red pepper
parsley sprig

### METHOD

Wash and rinse the bean sprouts in cold water, discarding any husks that float to the surface. Cook in boiling salted water for 3 minutes. Drain, rinse in cold water, then drain again and set aside.

Beat the eggs with a little salt. Heat the oil in a frying pan (skillet) over low heat. Add the eggs and cook to make a thin omelet. Remove from the pan, leave to cool, then cut into thin strips.

Combine all the sauce ingredients together, then mix with the bean sprouts. Transfer to a serving plate and arrange the ham and omelet strips on top. Garnish with the red pepper, coiled to resemble a flower head, with the parsley in the middle. Serve cold.

# Kidney-Flower Salad
## Liangban Yaohua

The kidneys are scored and cut before cooking so that they will open up – hence the name kidney flowers.

### METRIC/IMPERIAL

*350 g/12 oz pigs' kidneys, skinned and split in half lengthways*
*1 medium head celery, sliced diagonally*
*2 slices of fresh root ginger,\* peeled and finely shredded*
*2 spring onions, finely chopped*
**Sauce:**
*2 tablespoons soy sauce*
*1 tablespoon vinegar*
*1 tablespoon sesame seed oil\**
*1 teaspoon chilli sauce*
*½ teaspoon sugar*
**To garnish:** *(optional)*
*pineapple chunks*
*radish slices*
*grapes*

### AMERICAN

*¾ lb pork kidney, skinned and split in half lengthways*
*1 medium bunch celery, sliced diagonally*
*2 slices of fresh ginger root,\* peeled and finely shredded*
*2 scallions, finely chopped*
**Sauce:**
*2 tablespoons soy sauce*
*1 tablespoon vinegar*
*1 tablespoon sesame seed oil\**
*1 teaspoon chili sauce*
*½ teaspoon sugar*
**To garnish:** *(optional)*
*pineapple chunks*
*radish slices*
*grapes*

### METHOD

Score the surface of the kidneys in a criss-cross pattern, then cut them into pieces.

Cook the kidneys in boiling water for 2 minutes. Drain, rinse in cold water then drain again and transfer to a serving plate. Arrange the celery around the kidneys.

Combine all the sauce ingredients together, then mix with half the ginger and the spring onions (scallions). Pour the sauce over the kidneys, then leave to marinate for about 30 minutes before serving.

Top with the remaining ginger. Garnish with pineapple, radish and grapes, if liked. Serve cold.

Kidney Flower Salad; Bean Sprout Salad

# Celery and Giblet Salad
## Qincai Ban Zhengan

Gizzards need thorough cleaning before cooking. Make sure the dark green gall bladder is not broken when removing it from the liver or it will give a sharp, bitter taste to the salad.

### METRIC/IMPERIAL

*giblets (gizzard and liver) from 2 chickens, cut into small pieces*
*1 teaspoon dry or medium sherry*
*½ teaspoon salt*
*½ teaspoon cornflour*
*25 g/1 oz wood ears,\* soaked in warm water for 20 minutes*
*1 slice of fresh root ginger,\* peeled and finely shredded*
*1 small head celery, sliced diagonally*
**Sauce:**
*2 tablespoons soy sauce*
*2 tablespoons vinegar*
*1 tablespoon sesame seed oil\**
*freshly ground black pepper*

### AMERICAN

*giblets (gizzard and liver) from 2 chickens, cut into small pieces*
*1 teaspoon pale dry or medium sherry*
*½ teaspoon salt*
*½ teaspoon cornstarch*
*1 cup tree ears,\* soaked in warm water for 20 minutes*
*1 slice of fresh ginger root,\* peeled and finely shredded*
*1 small bunch celery, sliced diagonally*
**Sauce:**
*2 tablespoons soy sauce*
*2 tablespoons vinegar*
*1 tablespoon sesame seed oil\**
*freshly ground black pepper*

### METHOD

Put the giblets in a bowl and sprinkle with the sherry, salt and cornflour (cornstarch). Mix well, then leave to marinate for 30 minutes.

Drain the wood (tree) ears, discard the hard parts and cook in boiling water for 1 minute. Drain, rinse under cold running water and drain again.

Cook the giblets in boiling water for 2 minutes, then drain. Combine all the sauce ingredients together and mix with half the ginger.

Arrange the giblets, celery and wood (tree) ears on a serving plate and pour over the sauce. Garnish with the remaining ginger. Serve cold.

# Ten-Variety Fried Noodles (Chow Mein)
## Shijin Chaomian

### METRIC/IMPERIAL

*175 g/6 oz boned lean pork, shredded*
*1 tablespoon soy sauce*
*1 teaspoon sugar*
*2 teaspoons cornflour*
*350 g/12 oz egg noodles*
*2 eggs*
*salt*
*4 tablespoons vegetable oil*
*2 spring onions, cut into 2.5 cm/1 inch lengths*
*100 g/4 oz bamboo shoot, shredded*
*100 g/4 oz fresh spinach leaves or other green vegetable, shredded*
*100 g/4 oz peeled prawns*
*little chicken stock or water (optional)*

### AMERICAN

*¾ cup shredded pork loin*
*1 tablespoon soy sauce*
*1 teaspoon sugar*
*2 teaspoons cornstarch*
*¾ lb egg noodles*
*2 eggs*
*salt*
*¼ cup vegetable oil*
*2 scallions, cut into 1 inch lengths*
*1 cup shredded bamboo shoot*
*1½ cups shredded fresh spinach leaves or other green vegetable*
*2 large shrimp, shelled*
*little chicken stock or water (optional)*

### METHOD

Put the pork in a bowl with the soy sauce, sugar and cornflour (cornstarch). Mix well, then leave to marinate for about 20 minutes.

Cook the noodles in boiling water for about 5 minutes, drain and rinse under cold running water, then drain again.

Beat the eggs with a little salt. Heat a little of the oil in a frying pan (skillet) over low heat. Add the eggs and cook to make a thin omelet. Remove from the pan and cut into thin strips.

Heat a little more oil in the pan, add the pork and stir-fry until it changes colour. Remove from the pan with a slotted spoon and drain.

Heat the remaining oil in the pan. Add the spring onions (scallions), then the bamboo shoot, spinach and a little salt. Stir, then add the prawns (shrimp) and return the pork to the pan with the egg strips.

Mix the ingredients thoroughly, adding a little chicken stock or water to moisten if necessary. Stir in the noodles, heat through and stir-fry until there is no liquid remaining in the pan. Serve hot.

# Non-Stick Three Ways

## San Buzhan

This dessert is so called because it should not stick to the pan, nor the chopsticks, nor the teeth!

### METRIC/IMPERIAL

5 egg yolks
175 g/6 oz sugar
2 tablespoons cornflour
150 ml/¼ pint water
5 tablespoons vegetable oil or 65 g/ 2½ oz lard

### AMERICAN

5 egg yolks
¾ cup sugar
2 tablespoons cornstarch
⅔ cup water
5 tablespoons vegetable oil or lard

### METHOD

Put the egg yolks in a bowl, add the sugar, cornflour (cornstarch) and water and mix well.

Heat the oil or lard in a frying pan (skillet) until it reaches smoking point. Pour about half into a cup and reserve. Add the egg mixture to the pan, tilting the pan in order to hold the mixture together. Stir continuously for 2 minutes, adding the reserved oil or lard little by little around the edges. Cook until golden. Serve immediately.

**Steamed Dumplings with Sweet Filling**

# Sweet Bean Paste Pancakes (Crêpes)

## Dousha Shao Bing

Sweet red bean paste – also called sweet soy bean paste – is a thick bean paste sold in cans in Chinese foodstores. It is often used as a base for sweet sauces.

### METRIC/IMPERIAL

100 g/4 oz plain flour
1 egg, beaten
150 ml/¼ pint water
6–8 tablespoons sweet red bean paste or finely chopped dates
vegetable oil for deep-frying

### AMERICAN

1 cup all-purpose flour
1 egg, beaten
⅔ cup water
6–8 tablespoons sweet red bean paste or ground dates
vegetable oil for deep-frying

### METHOD

Put the flour into a large bowl, make a well in the centre and add the egg. Add the water gradually, beating constantly, to make a smooth batter.

Lightly oil an 18 cm/7 inch frying pan (skillet) and place over moderate heat. When the pan is very hot, pour in just enough batter to cover the bottom thinly, tilting the pan to spread it evenly. Cook for 30 seconds or until the underside is just firm, then carefully remove from the pan. Repeat with the remaining batter.

Divide the sweet red bean paste or dates equally between the pancakes (crêpes), placing it in the centre of the uncooked side of each one. Fold the bottom edge over the filling, then fold the sides towards the centre, to form an envelope. Brush the edge of the top flap with a little water, fold down and press the edges together firmly to seal.

Heat the oil in a deep-fat fryer and fry the pancakes (crêpes) for 1 minute or until crisp and golden. Remove and drain on kitchen paper towels.

Cut each pancake (crêpe) into 6 or 8 slices. Serve hot, with Chinese tea.

# Steamed Dumplings with Sweet Filling

## Dousha Bao

If liked, you can make these dumplings with a cooked savoury filling, such as finely chopped pork and mushrooms.

### METRIC/IMPERIAL

**Pastry:**
1½ tablespoons dried yeast
2½ teaspoons sugar
3 tablespoons lukewarm water
450 g/1 lb plain flour
300 ml/½ pint lukewarm milk

**Filling:**
1 × 225 g/8 oz can sweetened chestnut purée, or yellow bean sauce*

### AMERICAN

**Pastry:**
1½ tablespoons active dry yeast
2½ teaspoons sugar
3 tablespoons lukewarm water
4 cups all-purpose flour
1¼ cups lukewarm milk

**Filling:**
1 × ½ lb can chestnut purée, or bean sauce*

### METHOD

To make the pastry: Dissolve the yeast and sugar in the water. Sift the flour into a large bowl, then gradually stir in the yeast mixture and the milk. Mix to a firm dough.

Turn the dough out onto a lightly floured surface and knead well for at least 5 minutes. Transfer to a bowl, cover with a damp cloth and leave in a warm place for 1½ to 2 hours or until doubled in bulk.

To make the dumplings: Knead the dough on a lightly floured surface for about 5 minutes, then roll into a long 'sausage' about 5 cm/2 inches in diameter. Slice the 'sausage' with a sharp knife into 2.5 cm/1 inch rounds. Flatten each round with the palm of the hand, then roll out until 10 cm/4 inches in diameter.

Place 1 teaspoon chestnut purée or bean sauce in the centre of each round, then gather up the dough around the filling to meet at the top. Twist the top of the dough to enclose the filling tightly. Leave to rest for at least 20 minutes.

Place the dumplings on a damp cloth in the bottom of a steamer, leaving 2.5 cm/1 inch space between each one. Steam for 15 to 20 minutes. Serve hot.
MAKES ABOUT 24 DUMPLINGS

# Plum-Blossom and Snow Competing for Spring

## Meixue Zhengchun

### METRIC/IMPERIAL

2 dessert apples
2 bananas
juice of ½ lemon
2 eggs, separated
100 g/4 oz sugar
3 tablespoons milk
3 tablespoons water
3 tablespoons cornflour

### AMERICAN

2 dessert apples
2 bananas
juice of ½ lemon
2 eggs, separated
½ cup sugar
3 tablespoons milk
3 tablespoons water
3 tablespoons cornstarch

### METHOD

Peel and core the apples and slice thinly. Peel the bananas and slice thinly. Arrange the apple and banana slices in alternate layers on an ovenproof dish, sprinkling each layer with lemon juice.

Put the egg yolks in a pan with the sugar, milk, water and cornflour (cornstarch). Heat very gently, stirring, until smooth, then pour over the fruit.

Beat the egg whites until stiff, then spoon over the top. Bake in a preheated hot oven (220°C/425°F, Gas Mark 7) for about 5 minutes until the top is crisp and golden. Serve hot or cold.

# Japan

## Kay Shimizu

---

Under the cherry-trees,
On soup, and fish-salad and all,
Flower petals.

Basho

---

This Japanese *haiku* (poem) is most appropriate as an introduction to Japanese cuisine. Even in poetry, food is given dignity and beauty.

Japan is a country with a very small area, but because of its length it encompasses a wide range of climatic conditions and geographic differences. There is an endless assortment of foods, but this does not mean that the food is so plentiful that it is inexpensive!

For centuries, Japan was a closed port and was not subject to foreign influence until quite recently, which is most probably why this country developed such a unique, elegant style of cooking. Despite the proximity to China and the use of many similar ingredients, the Japanese approach to cooking, and the flavours, are entirely different from the Chinese.

Japanese cuisine is exquisite, aesthetic and sophisticated. Visual feasting is part of the traditional Japanese meal – you feed your eyes as well as your stomach. Japanese food is made pleasing by the artistic way in which the food is arranged and garnished on beautiful ceramic plates or bowls. The Japanese have a strong sensitivity and awareness for natural colour, symmetry and general appearance of each prepared food. Indeed, there is probably no other cuisine in the world which practises 'culinary art' to the same extent as the Japanese. Hand-crafted serving dishes and bowls, often specially created by a potter, are carefully selected for each food. The Japanese have a talent of arranging the food and garnish to display contrast of colour, shapes and textures. Seasonal fresh flowers and leaves are a common garnish.

Each food is prepared separately and thus, even when served together, the individual flavours and colourings are retained. Seasonings are delicate and fragrant. The Japanese have a great reverence for food; they appreciate Nature for her ability to produce such a fabulous array of edibles according to season. Japan is probably one of the few countries in the world where people will pay any price to savour the very 'first' sweet strawberry, fragrant *matsutake* (pine mushroom) or juicy melon of the season. These are often packed individually in special boxes,

with elaborate cushioning, and sold as gifts. A great deal of time and effort goes into producing these gourmet delights.

Certain holidays are celebrated in grand style: New Year is probably the most important. Food is prepared and placed in beautiful tiered, lacquered boxes. Friends, relatives and neighbours come to greet each other and food and drink are served. A rice patty made from glutinous (sweet) rice* is dropped into *ozoni* (a special New Year's soup). So sacred is this holiday that the 'o' is put before the word '*zoni*' to

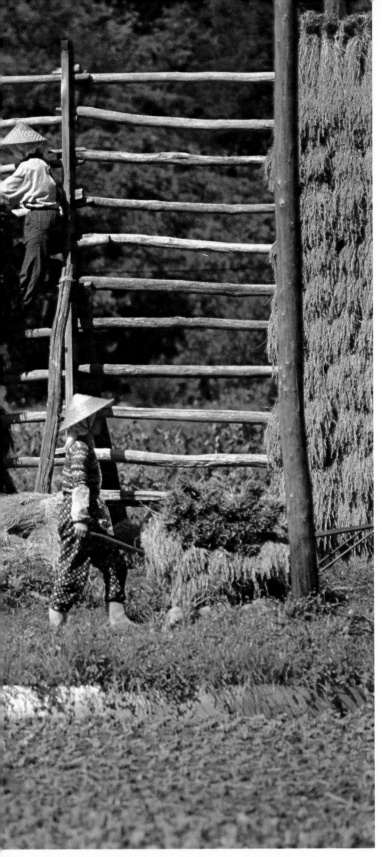

for only the freshest marine life; in hand massaging their cattle and feeding them beer to produce the world's most expensive and beautifully marbled tender beef. The average housewife makes a daily trip to the market to buy the choicest fresh foods for her table, even if she has a refrigerator. Menus are kept fairly simple with an entrée, a few side dishes, pickles, soup and always rice and green tea.

The traditional Japanese meal is served on a low table with the diners sitting on cushions placed on the *tatami* (straw mat) floor. In the entrance of every home, shoes are removed and slippers put on, so dining at floor level is a very clean custom. In many homes, however, meals are now served at normal table height and chairs are used.

There are no matching place settings in Japan; after a traditional dinner there is a mountain of little dishes and plates to be cleared. Knives are not used for eating; the food is cut into small pieces during preparation and eaten with chopsticks, unless it is something like a whole fish which can be separated easily with chopsticks when cooked.

Japanese cooking is relatively simple. Most dishes are cooked in advance and served at room temperature, since sometimes there are only two burners on the gas stove. In the past, few Japanese kitchens had ovens, but, in recent years, portable ones have become available. In fact, Japan was the first country to introduce microwave ovens for domestic use.

Medium-grain rice is served at all meals. So valued is this 'staff of life' grain, that the Japanese have an old saying, '*Tsukiyo ni kome no meshi*'. Translated, this is 'Moonlight and boiled rice' – one never tires of eating even a simple meal of boiled rice by moonlight. When you have become acquainted with the delights of Japanese cuisine you will appreciate the full meaning of this ancient proverb. Plain boiled rice does have a special satisfying flavour, and is delicious by itself.

Be sure to use *shoyu* (Japanese light soy sauce)* in these recipes; to use Chinese soy sauce instead would ruin the flavour of the dish. The same applies to *miso* (Japanese soy bean paste),* which is entirely different from Chinese soy bean paste.*

*Sake* (rice wine)* is the traditional accompaniment to Japanese food. It is served warm and enjoyed throughout the meal. Green tea is a national 'habit'; it is served frequently during the day and at meal times in fragile ceramic tea cups without handles. Green tea has a very delicate flavour, and is therefore most suited to Japanese cuisine.

This chapter provides a selection of the more popular Japanese recipes; essentially they are simple, light, delicious and beautifully presented – truly representative of an exquisite cuisine.

specify the honorific form of the word. *Osechi ryori* is a carefully planned combination of foods for the New Year feast. During this period, of almost one week's celebrating, the shops are closed and virtually all of Japan is at a standstill.

Children's Day in May (formerly Boy's Day) is celebrated with fragrant cherry leaves wrapped around special rice cakes. The Japanese still observe these ancient traditions, despite the influences of the Western world in recent years.

The Japanese take extreme care and pride in growing the best fruit and vegetables; in fishing

# Harusame Soup
## Spring Rain Soup

This light soup has a wonderful aroma and a chewy texture. It can be prepared at the table if wished, in which case each guest has a bowl of stock and adds ingredients to taste.

### METRIC/IMPERIAL

100 g/4 oz dehydrated mung bean threads* or harusame,* soaked in boiling water for 30 minutes
2–3 shiitake,* soaked in boiling water for 20 minutes
1 litre/1¾ pints dashi (see opposite) or chicken stock
pinch of monosodium glutamate* (optional)
1 tablespoon sake*
salt
100 g/4 oz peeled prawns
6–8 mange tout
1 gobo*, par-boiled (optional)
4–6 spring onions
2 carrots
few cucumber strips
100 g/4 oz napa*
few spinach leaves

**To garnish:**
1 teaspoon grated fresh root ginger*
1 spring onion, finely shredded
2 teaspoons puréed daikon*

### AMERICAN

1 cup dehydrated mung bean threads* or harusame,* soaked in boiling water for 30 minutes
2–3 shiitake,* soaked in boiling water for 20 minutes
4 cups dashi (see opposite) or chicken stock
pinch of msg* (optional)
1 tablespoon sake*
salt
⅔ cup shelled shrimp
6–8 snow peas
1 gobo*, par-boiled (optional)
4–6 scallions
2 carrots
few cucumber strips
¼ lb napa*
few spinach leaves

**To garnish:**
1 teaspoon grated fresh ginger root*
1 scallion, finely shredded
2 teaspoons grated daikon*

### METHOD

Drain the mung bean threads and cut into 5 cm/2 inch lengths. Drain the mushrooms, reserving the liquid, and discard the stems.

Put the stock in a pan. Carefully pour in the reserved mushroom liquid, leaving any sandy sediment at the bottom – this should be discarded. Bring to the boil, then lower the heat and simmer for about 2 minutes. Add the monosodium glutamate (msg) if using, the sake and salt to taste.

Divide the stock between 4 warmed individual soup bowls. Arrange the other ingredients attractively on a serving dish, cutting the vegetables to make interesting shapes, if liked. Place the garnish ingredients on separate dishes. Serve immediately.
SERVES 4

# Miso Shiru
## Bean Soup

This is a traditional thick bean soup which can be served at any meal. Years ago it was the basic hot soup that was served for breakfast as a mainstay, but nowadays more and more people are turning to the Western-style breakfast and giving up the Japanese-style meal. Made with soya beans, this soup is very nutritious, especially when served with rice. For a stronger flavour, substitute akamiso* for the shiromiso* and adjust the quantity according to taste.

### METRIC/IMPERIAL

225 g/8 oz shiromiso*
1.2 litres/2 pints dashi (see page 125)
1 block tofu,* cut into bite-sized pieces
pinch of monosodium glutamate* (optional)
finely shredded spring onion, green part only, to garnish

### AMERICAN

½ cup shiromiso*
5 cups dashi (see page 125)
1 block tofu,* cut into bite-sized pieces
pinch of msg* (optional)
finely shredded scallion, green part only, to garnish

### METHOD

Put the shiromiso and dashi in a pan and heat gently until dissolved, stirring constantly. Bring to the boil, add the tofu and heat through, then stir in the monosodium glutamate (msg) if using.

Pour into warmed individual soup bowls and garnish with the spring onion (scallion). Serve hot.
SERVES 4

Harusame Soup (above); Miso Shiru (below)

# Dashi
## Japanese Basic Stock

Dashi is indispensable in Japanese cooking. Chicken stock or broth occasionally makes a suitable substitute, but to cook truly 'Japanese', one should always use dashi where stock or broth is called for in a recipe. Dashi is a light fish and seaweed stock. It is usually made as a 'first dashi' and generally used for the delicate flavouring of soups. The same basic ingredients are saved for making a 'second dashi', to which *katsoubushi** (dried bonito fish) and water are added. This second type of dashi is used for sauces and pan-fried dishes.

To save time, you may use one of the many excellent instant dashi powders which are available in foil packets.

### METRIC/IMPERIAL

1 × 10 cm/4 inch square kombu*
1.2 litres/2 pints water
15 g/½ oz flaked katsuobushi*
1½ teaspoons salt
1 teaspoon shoyu*
pinch of monosodium glutamate*
  (optional)

### AMERICAN

1 × 4 inch square kombu*
5 cups water
½ cup flaked katsuobushi*
1½ teaspoons salt
1 teaspoon shoyu*
pinch of msg* (optional)

### METHOD

Rinse the kombu and wipe with a damp cloth. Put the kombu and water in a pan and bring to the boil. Remove the kombu, add the katsuobushi to the pan and remove from the heat; leave to stand for 2 minutes. Strain, then add the remaining ingredients.
MAKES 1.2 litres/2 pints/5 cups
**Note:** The seaweed need not be wasted; cook it with a little shoyu and sugar, then slice and serve as a 'nibble'.

# Tempura
## Assorted Fritters

Japanese deep-fried foods are noted for their delicacy, and extreme care is taken to use the lightest vegetable oils. The crisp batter is almost as thin as gauze, so the colour and texture of the ingredients show through faintly and look most attractive. Best results are obtained if all the ingredients for the batter are ice cold and the batter should be made just before using.

Fish fillets, strips of carrot, shiitake,* asparagus stalks, parsley and slices of yellow courgette (baking squash) can be substituted for the prawns (shrimp) and vegetables suggested here. The dipping sauce reduces the oiliness of the tempura and adds a delicate seasoning to the crispy coating.

METRIC/IMPERIAL

450 g/1 lb prawns
1 medium sweet potato, peeled and
　sliced into 5 mm/¼ inch rounds
1 small aubergine, cut lengthways into
　5 mm/¼ inch slices
8 mange tout
12 mushrooms, whole or sliced
1 onion, peeled and thinly sliced into
　rings
12 French or runner beans, cut into
　5 cm/2 inch lengths
vegetable oil for deep-frying
**Tentsuyu (Dipping sauce):**
450 ml/¾ pint dashi (see page 125)
2 tablespoons shoyu*
3 tablespoons mirin*
pinch of salt
pinch of monosodium glutamate*
　(optional)
**Batter:**
50 g/2 oz plain flour
50 g/2 oz cornflour
1½ teaspoons baking powder
½ teaspoon salt
1 teaspoon monosodium glutamate
　(optional)
1 egg, lightly beaten
200 ml/⅓ pint iced water
1 ice cube
**To garnish:**
4 tablespoons puréed daikon*
3 tablespoons grated fresh root
　ginger*

AMERICAN

1 lb shrimp
1 medium sweet potato, peeled and
　sliced into ¼ inch rounds
1 small eggplant, cut lengthways into
　¼ inch slices
8 snow peas
12 mushrooms, whole or sliced
1 onion, peeled and thinly sliced into
　rings
12 string beans, cut into 2 inch lengths
vegetable oil for deep-frying
**Tentsuyu (Dipping sauce):**
2 cups Dashi (see page 125)
2 tablespoons shoyu*
3 tablespoons mirin*
pinch of salt
pinch of msg* (optional)
**Batter:**
½ cup flour
½ cup cornstarch
1½ teaspoons baking powder
½ teaspoon salt
1 teaspoon msg* (optional)
1 egg, lightly beaten
1 cup ice water
1 ice cube
**To garnish:**
¼ cup puréed daikon*
3 tablespoons grated fresh ginger
　root*

METHOD

Peel (shell) and devein the prawns (shrimp), leaving the last segment of the shell and tail intact. Pat the prawns (shrimp) and vegetables dry with kitchen paper towels. Arrange on a large serving dish, cover with plastic wrap and chill in the refrigerator until required.

To make the tentsuyu: Put all the ingredients in a pan and stir well to combine. Heat through, then keep hot while making the batter.

To make the batter: Put the dry ingredients in a chilled bowl and stir well. Mix together the beaten egg and water, then stir gently into the dry ingredients, taking care not to overmix. Add the ice cube.

Heat the oil in a deep-fat fryer to 180°C/350°F. Dip the prawns (shrimp) and vegetables into the batter, a piece at a time, then fry a few pieces at a time in the hot oil until light golden. Drain on kitchen paper towels, then serve immediately in a folded napkin.

Pour the hot sauce into individual bowls and arrange the garnish on individual plates. Diners should then mix together the sauce and garnish according to taste, using it as a dip for the fritters. Serve hot.
SERVES 4

# Nuta Negi
## Spring Onions (Scallions) with Miso

Spring onions (scallions) make a delectable cooked vegetable – not pungent and piquant-flavoured as in their raw state.

METRIC/IMPERIAL

2 bunches of spring onions, root ends
　removed
3 tablespoons shiromiso*
3 tablespoons dashi (see page 125)
1 tablespoon su*
**Sauce:**
3 tablespoons shiromiso*
3 tablespoons dashi (see page 179)
1 tablespoon su*
1 tablespoon water
1 teaspoon dry mustard

AMERICAN

2 bunches of scallions, root ends
　removed
3 strips of wakame* (optional)
15 fresh scallops, boiled and chopped
　into large pieces
**Sauce:**
3 tablespoons shiromiso*
3 tablespoons dashi (see page 125)
1 tablespoon su*
1 tablespoon water
1 teaspoon dry mustard

METHOD

Drop the spring onions (scallions) into a pan of boiling water. Boil for 2½ minutes, then drain and squeeze out the excess moisture. Cut into 5 cm/2 inch lengths.

Soak the wakame in water to cover for 10 minutes. Drain, rinse under cold running water, then drain and cut into thin strips.

To make the sauce: Put all the ingredients in a pan and stir well. Cook for 3 minutes until quite thick, stirring constantly.

Put the spring onions (scallions), wakame and prepared scallops in a bowl, pour over the sauce, then fold gently to mix. Transfer to individual serving dishes and serve at room temperature.
SERVES 4

Sashimi

# Kyuri To Kani No Sunomono

## Crab and Cucumber with Vinegar Sauce

This is an ideal dish for a buffet because it will keep well for several hours. If liked, prawns (shrimp) or abalone can be used instead of crab. Score the cucumber using a canelling knife, or fork, to give an attractive serrated edge.

### METRIC/IMPERIAL

*1 small cucumber, 18–20 cm/7–8 inches long*
*¼ teaspoon salt*
*100 g/4 oz fresh crabmeat*
**Sauce:**
*5 tablespoons su\**
*4 tablespoons sugar*
*½ teaspoon salt*
*pinch of monosodium glutamate\* (optional)*
**To garnish:**
*1 tablespoon sesame seeds,\* toasted*
*few strips of lemon rind*

### AMERICAN

*1 small cucumber, 7–8 inches long*
*¼ teaspoon salt*
*½ cup fresh crabmeat*
**Sauce:**
*5 tablespoons su\**
*¼ cup sugar*
*½ teaspoon salt*
*pinch of msg\* (optional)*
**To garnish:**
*1 tablespoon sesame seeds,\* toasted*
*few strips of lemon rind*

### METHOD

Score the cucumber lengthwise, slice into paper-thin rounds and sprinkle with the salt. Leave for 20 minutes.

Meanwhile, to make the sauce: Put all the ingredients in a bowl and stir well.

Squeeze the cucumber slices and discard the juice. Pour the sauce over the cucumber, add the crab and toss lightly.

Transfer to individual serving bowls and garnish with the sesame seeds and lemon rind. Serve cold.
SERVES 4

# Sashimi
## Sliced Raw Fish

Sashimi is a culinary miracle – raw fish without a fishy smell or taste! Always use absolutely fresh fish; check for firm flesh, clear, bright eyes if the head is still attached, and no odour.

Octopus (parboiled), squid, abalone, sea bass, bream, sea urchin, cuttlefish, red clam, striped bass, prawns and shrimps are some of the raw seafoods which can be prepared in this way; raw chicken breasts, sprinkled with lemon juice, can be treated in the same way.

### METRIC/IMPERIAL

*750 g/1½ lb sea bass, tuna or other saltwater fish, filleted*
*175 g/6 oz daikon,\* shredded*
*1 carrot, shredded*
*4–5 spring onions, shredded*
*few mange tout*
*few cooked, unshelled giant prawns*
*1 tablespoon wasabi\**
*few lemon wedges*
*1 tablespoon freshly grated root ginger\**
*shoyu\* to taste*

### AMERICAN

*1½ lb sea bass, tuna or other saltwater fish, filleted*
*2 cups shredded daikon\**
*1 carrot, shredded*
*4–5 scallions, shredded*
*few snow peas*
*few cooked, unshelled king shrimp*
*1 tablespoon wasabi\**
*few lemon wedges*
*1 tablespoon freshly grated ginger root\**
*shoyu\* to taste*

### METHOD

Remove any skin, blood and dark sections from the fish. Cut the flesh diagonally with a sharp knife into slices about 2.5 cm/1 inch long and 5 mm/¼ inch thick.

Arrange the shredded daikon, carrot and spring onions (scallions) in mounds on a serving platter, together with the mange tout (snow peas). Arrange the raw fish slices and cooked shrimp (prawns) on the platter.

Mix the wasabi to a thick paste with a little water. Place on the platter, with the lemon wedges and ginger.

To serve: Pour shoyu into individual bowls, then allow each diner to add wasabi and ginger to his own bowl of shoyu according to taste. The fish and vegetables are then dipped into the sauce before eating. Serve with Japanese-style medium-grain rice.
SERVES 4

## Shake No Kasuzuke

### Salmon with Sake Lees

When fresh salmon is plentiful, this is an excellent way to preserve some for later use. This dish makes a quick entrée and will keep for several months in the refrigerator. The flavour of *kasu** goes well with salmon, but it is strongly flavoured and should therefore be eaten in small quantities – until you acquire a taste for it, that is!

METRIC/IMPERIAL

*4 fresh salmon steaks*
*1½ tablespoons salt*
**Marinade:**
*450 ml/¾ pint kasu**
*225 g/8 oz sugar*
**To serve:**
*1 small lettuce, shredded*
*½ small daikon,* puréed*

AMERICAN

*4 fresh salmon steaks*
*1½ tablespoons salt*
**Marinade:**
*2 cups kasu**
*1 cup sugar*
**To serve:**
*1 small head of lettuce, shredded*
*½ small daikon,* puréed*

METHOD

Put the salmon in a bowl and sprinkle both sides with the salt. Cover with plastic wrap or foil and leave in the refrigerator for 4 days to allow the flesh of the salmon to become firm.

Drain the fish well, then pat dry with kitchen paper towels. Mix together the marinade ingredients and use to coat both sides of the salmon. Place in a dish, cover and keep in the refrigerator for 7 days before serving.

Remove most of the marinade from the salmon, then grill (broil) for about 7 minutes on one side only until the fish flakes easily when tested with a fork. Take care not to overcook as the marinade causes the fish to char easily.

Serve hot, with small mounds of shredded lettuce and puréed daikon.
SERVES 4

## Shio Yaki

### Salt Grilled (Broiled) Fish

This method of preparing protein-rich fish is surprisingly simple – the fat in the skin of the fish oozes out during cooking and the salt creates moisture so that the flesh is deliciously moist. Hot steamed rice and green tea make good accompaniments.

METRIC/IMPERIAL

*1 mackerel or red snapper, weighing*
*750 g/1½ lb*
*salt*
**To serve:**
*few lemon wedges*
*shoyu* (optional)*

AMERICAN

*1 mackerel or red snapper, weighing*
*1½ lb*
*salt*
**To serve:**
*few lemon wedges*
*shoyu* (optional)*

METHOD

Remove the scales from the fish, leaving the skin intact. Clean the fish thoroughly and remove the head if wished, then sprinkle lightly inside and out with salt. Leave to stand for about 30 minutes.

Make 3 diagonal slashes on the surface of the fish. Grill (broil) under a preheated grill (broiler) for about 5 minutes on each side, until the fish flakes easily when tested with a fork; do not overcook.

Serve hot with lemon wedges and shoyu. Hand shoyu separately, if liked.
SERVES 4

## Nizakana

### Braised Fish

This dish makes a quick, simple meal with plenty of flavour. Serve with rice and a green vegetable, with *shichimi** and *sansho** as condiments, if liked.

METRIC/IMPERIAL

*1 tablespoon vegetable oil*
*1 kg/2–2¼ lb fresh salmon, cut into*
*serving pieces*
*1 medium onion, peeled, halved and*
*cut into 1 cm/½ inch thick slices*
*1½ tablespoons sake**
*2 tablespoons water*
*4 tablespoons shoyu**
*2½ tablespoons sugar*
*1 teaspoon freshly grated root*
*ginger**
*pinch of monosodium glutamate**
*(optional)*

AMERICAN

*1 tablespoon vegetable oil*
*2 lb fresh salmon, butterfish or*
*yellowtail, cut into serving pieces*
*1 medium onion, peeled, halved and*
*cut into ½ inch thick slices*
*1½ tablespoons sake**
*2 tablespoons water*
*¼ cup shoyu**
*2½ tablespoons sugar*
*1 teaspoon freshly grated ginger root**
*pinch of msg* (optional)*

METHOD

Place a frying pan (skillet), over moderate heat, add the oil, then the fish and onion. Mix the remaining ingredients

# Chiri Nabe

## Fish Stew

This dish can be prepared at the table like a fondue, if wished. Guests should eat from the pan, dipping the cooked morsels into the sauce.

### METRIC/IMPERIAL

15 cm/6 inch piece of kombu*
1.75 litres/3 pints water
225 g/8 oz filleted red snapper, cod or
    other white fish, cut into serving
    pieces
1 bunch of spring onions, sliced
    diagonally.
4 fresh shiitake,* stems removed, or
    button mushrooms
1 block tofu,* cut into 2.5 cm/1 inch
    chunks
4 large napa* leaves, cut into
    5 cm/2 inch pieces

**Dipping sauce:**
120 ml/4 fl oz shoyu*
175 ml/6 fl oz lemon juice
seasoning suggestions: minced spring
    onions, toasted sesame seeds,*
    freshly grated root ginger,* grated
    white daikon,* shichimi*

### AMERICAN

6 inch piece of kombu*
7½ cups water
½ lb filleted red snapper, cod or other
    white fish, cut into serving pieces
1 bunch of scallions, sliced diagonally
4 fresh shiitake,* stems removed, or
    button mushrooms
1 block tofu,* cut into 1 inch chunks
4 large napa* leaves, cut into 2 inch
    pieces

**Dipping sauce:**
½ cup shoyu*
¾ cup lemon juice
seasoning suggestions: ground
    scallions, toasted sesame seeds,*
    freshly grated ginger root,* grated
    white daikon,* shichimi*

### METHOD

Rinse the kombu, wipe with a damp cloth and place in a fondue pan or electric frying pan (skillet). Add the water, bring to the boil, then add the fish. Bring back to the boil and add the spring onions (scallions), mushrooms, tofu and napa. Bring back to the boil, stirring constantly. The vegetables should then be crisp and tender and the fish cooked through.

To make the dipping sauce: Mix together the shoyu and lemon juice, then add suggested seasonings according to taste. Divide between individual dishes.

Serve the fish stew hot, with the dipping sauce and steamed rice.
SERVES 4

together, then pour into the pan. Cover and simmer for about 10 minutes until the fish flakes easily when tested with a fork. Serve hot.
SERVES 4 to 6

Shio Yaki, Shake No Kasuzuke

# Yakitori

## Grilled (Broiled) Chicken

This is one of the most popular of all Japanese grilled (broiled) dishes. A charcoal grill (broiler) imparts a flavour which is unsurpassed, but the dish can be cooked under an ordinary grill (broiler). Use bamboo skewers if possible; these should be soaked in water for about 15 minutes before using.

### METRIC/IMPERIAL

1 kg/2–2¼ lb boned chicken, cut into
   chunks
1 bunch of spring onions, cut into
   5 cm/2 inch lengths
2 green peppers, cored, seeded and
   cut into 5 cm/2 inch chunks
**Marinade:**
175 ml/6 fl oz shoyu*
50 g/2 oz sugar
175 ml/6 fl oz sake*
pinch of monosodium glutamate*
   (optional)
**To serve:**
pinch of powdered sansho*

### AMERICAN

2–2¼ lb boneless chicken, cut into
   chunks
1 bunch of scallions, cut into 2 inch
   lengths
2 green peppers, cored, seeded and
   cut into 2 inch chunks
**Marinade:**
¾ cup shoyu*
¼ cup sugar
¾ cup sake*
pinch of msg* (optional)
**To serve:**
pinch of powdered sansho*

### METHOD

Thread the chicken, spring onions (scallions) and green peppers alternately on 4 skewers. Mix together the marinade ingredients and brush over the skewers. Leave to marinate for 30 minutes, basting occasionally.

Grill (broil) for 3 minutes, then dip the skewers in the marinade again, turn and grill (broil) for 2 minutes; do not overcook.

Serve hot with a pinch of sansho pepper.
SERVES 4

# Buta Teriyaki

## Pork on Skewers

Pork marinated in Teriyaki sauce has an exquisite flavour, especially if cooked over a charcoal grill (broiler). If this is not available, an ordinary grill (broiler) may be used, although the flavour will not be quite so good.

If liked, spring onions (scallions), mushroom caps and strips of green pepper can be added to the skewers, alternating with the pork. Use bamboo skewers if possible; these should be soaked in water for about 15 minutes before use.

As a variation, chicken, beef, prawns (shrimp) or fish may be used instead of pork.

### METRIC/IMPERIAL

1 kg/2–2¼ lb pork fillet, thinly sliced
1 teaspoon grated fresh root ginger*
1 medium onion, peeled and finely
   chopped
½ teaspoon monosodium glutamate*
   (optional)
5 tablespoons shoyu*
4 tablespoons sugar
4 tablespoons sake*

### AMERICAN

2–2¼ lb pork loin, thinly sliced
1 teaspoon grated fresh ginger root*
1 medium onion, peeled and finely
   chopped
½ teaspoon msg* (optional)
⅓ cup shoyu*
¼ cup sugar
¼ cup sake*

### METHOD

Put all the ingredients in a bowl, mix well, then leave to marinate for at least 1 hour.

Thread the pork on 4 skewers, reserving the marinade. Grill (broil) for 3 minutes on each side, basting frequently with the marinade. Serve immediately.
SERVES 4

# Tonkatsu

## Pork Cutlets

This dish was probably introduced to the Japanese by foreign traders some centuries ago. It is very popular and most suitable for anyone trying Japanese food for the first time, since it is similar to Western dishes. It is equally good served cold, or in sandwiches.

### METRIC/IMPERIAL

4–6 boned loin or chump pork chops,
   or fillet steaks
salt
freshly ground black pepper
flour for coating
2 eggs, beaten
panko* or breadcrumbs for coating
vegetable oil for deep-frying
**To serve:**
175 g/6 oz cabbage, finely shredded
few parsley sprigs
tonkatsu sauce* (optional)

### AMERICAN

4–6 boneless loin or butterfly pork
   chops or tenderloin steaks
salt
freshly ground black pepper
flour for coating
2 eggs, beaten
panko* or breadcrumbs for coating
vegetable oil for deep-frying
**To serve:**
2 cups finely shredded cabbage
few parsley sprigs
tonkatsu sauce* (optional)

### METHOD

Pound the pork with a mallet to flatten it slightly, then sprinkle lightly with salt and pepper. Coat with flour, dip in the egg, then coat with panko or breadcrumbs.

Heat the oil in a deep-fat fryer to 180°C/350°F. Deep-fry the pork for 10 minutes, turning down the heat a little so that the pork cooks thoroughly; turn the pork once during frying to brown both sides.

Test the pork to make sure the meat is no longer pink, then remove from the pan with a slotted spoon and drain on kitchen paper towels. Cut each piece of pork into 3 to 4 slices, then re-shape on a warmed serving dish.

Arrange the cabbage around the pork and garnish with parsley. Serve hot with tonkatsu sauce, if liked.
SERVES 4 to 6

# Niku No Miso Yaki

## Meat with Miso

*Akamiso\* is Japanese red soybean paste. It gives meat an entirely different flavour. Served with hot steamed rice and salad, this dish makes a quick family meal.*

### METRIC/IMPERIAL

*750 g/1½ lb beef flank steak, in one piece*

**Marinade:**

*4 tablespoons akamiso\**
*2 tablespoons shoyu\**
*1½ tablespoons sugar*
*1 teaspoon grated fresh root ginger\**
*1 spring onion, chopped*
*2 tablespoons vegetable oil*
*toasted sesame seeds\* to garnish*

### AMERICAN

*1½ lb beef flank steak, in one piece*
**Marinade:**
*¼ cup akamiso\**
*2 tablespoons shoyu\**
*1½ tablespoons sugar*
*1 teaspoon grated fresh ginger root\**
*1 scallion, chopped*
*2 tablespoons vegetable oil*
*toasted sesame seeds\* to garnish*

### METHOD

Cut the meat lengthways through the middle, then cut into thin slices across the grain. Place the slices in a bowl with the akamiso, shoyu, sugar, ginger and spring onion (scallion). Mix well, then leave to marinate for 10 minutes.

Place a frying pan (skillet) over high heat. Add the oil, then the meat and marinade. Stir-fry for about 2 minutes. Serve hot, sprinkled with toasted sesame seeds.

SERVES 4

Buta Teriyaki

# Teppanyaki
## Mixed Grill

*Teppan* means 'iron', and *yaki* means 'to fry'. Any combination of meat, seafood or poultry can be used with vegetables in season for this dish. As illustrated, vegetables, such as radishes, chopped fresh spinach leaves, sliced green or red peppers, mange tout (snow peas), French (green) beans and spring onions (scallions) are all suitable. Traditionally, a heavy iron griddle is used at the table, but an electric frying pan (skillet) may be used instead.

At Japanese speciality restaurants, talented cooks bow before the diners and act out a 'show', waving sharp knives in the air while they prepare this scrumptious meal before your very eyes.

### METRIC/IMPERIAL

*4 sirloin or fillet steaks, or 4 boned chicken breasts, cut into chunks*
*8 cooked, unshelled prawns*
*2 medium courgettes, sliced into julienne strips*
*2 medium onions, peeled and finely sliced*
*225 g/8 oz fresh bean sprouts*
*225 g/8 oz button mushrooms*
*1 tablespoon vegetable oil*

**Ponzu (Tart sauce):**
*120 ml/4 fl oz shoyu\**
*120 ml/4 fl oz lime or lemon juice*
*4 tablespoons mirin\**

**Karashi jyoyu (Mustard sauce):**
*2 teaspoons dry mustard*
*2 teaspoons hot water*
*3 tablespoons shoyu\**
*2 tablespoons su\**
*1 teaspoon sesame seed oil\**
*pinch of monosodium glutamate\* (optional)*

### AMERICAN

*4 top sirloin or fillet beef steaks, or 4 boned chicken breasts, cut into chunks*
*8 cooked, unshelled shrimp*
*2 medium zucchini, sliced into julienne strips*
*2 medium onions, peeled and finely sliced*
*4 cups fresh bean sprouts*
*2 cups button mushrooms*
*1 tablespoon vegetable oil*

**Ponzu (Tart sauce):**
*½ cup shoyu\**
*½ cup lime or lemon juice*
*¼ cup mirin\**

**Karashi jyoyu (Mustard sauce):**
*2 teaspoons dry mustard*
*2 teaspoons hot water*
*3 tablespoons shoyu\**
*2 tablespoons su\**
*1 teaspoon sesame seed oil\**
*pinch of msg\* (optional)*

### METHOD

Arrange the beef or chicken, prawns (shrimp) and vegetables artistically on a large serving plate.

To make the ponzu sauce: Mix together all the ingredients and pour into individual dishes. To make the karashi jyoyu sauce: Mix the mustard and water to a paste, then add the remaining ingredients. Pour into individual dishes.

Heat a griddle or electric frying pan (skillet) at the table. Add the oil, then some of the meat and prawns (shrimp). As the meat becomes tender, add a few vegetables to the pan and cook until they are tender but still crisp.

Serve the meat, prawns (shrimp) and vegetables as they are ready, letting the guests dip them into their sauces while more teppanyaki is cooking.
SERVES 4

# Sukiyaki
## Meat with Vegetables

This extraordinary combination of ingredients with its tasty sauce is a delectable meal-in-one. It is especially good prepared at the table – the guests eat it little by little as it cooks, and more ingredients are added to the pan. Towards the end, as the juices blend together, the flavour is unsurpassed.

Be sure to serve Sukiyaki with hot steamed rice. Vary the vegetables, according to season and taste.

### METRIC/IMPERIAL

*100 g/4 oz dried shiitake,\* soaked in warm water for 20 minutes, or button mushrooms*
*1 × 75 g/3 oz can shirataki,\* or 100 g/ 4 oz mung bean threads,\* soaked in boiling water for 30 minutes*
*few pieces of beef suet*
*1 kg/2–2¼ lb sirloin or fillet steak, thinly sliced*
*1 medium onion, peeled and sliced into rings*
*2 bunches of spring onions, cut into 5 cm/2 inch lengths*
*1 carrot, thinly sliced into squares*
*150 g/5 oz water chestnuts\* or bamboo shoot, sliced*
*few spinach and/or napa\* leaves, cut into 3.5 cm/1½ inch slices*
*1 block tofu,\* diced*

**Sauce:**
*120 ml/4 fl oz shoyu\**
*4 tablespoons sugar*
*120 ml/4 fl oz dashi (see page 125)*
*¾ teaspoon monosodium glutamate\* (optional)*
*120 ml/4 fl oz mirin\**

**To serve:**
*4 eggs (optional)*
*shoyu,\* to taste (optional)*

1 cup shiitake,* soaked in warm water
    for 20 minutes, or button mushrooms
1 × 3 oz can shirataki,* or 1 cup mung
    bean threads,* soaked in boiling
    water for 30 minutes
few pieces of beef suet
2–2¼ lb top sirloin, fillet or rib eye
    beef, thinly sliced
1 medium onion, peeled and sliced
    into rings
2 bunches of scallions, cut into 2 inch
    lengths
1 carrot, thinly sliced into squares
1 cup water chestnuts* or bamboo
    shoot, sliced
few spinach and/or napa* leaves, cut
    into 1½ inch slices
1 block tofu,* diced

**Sauce:**
½ cup shoyu*
¼ cup sugar
½ cup dashi (see page 125)
¾ teaspoon msg* (optional)
½ cup mirin*

**To serve:**
4 eggs (optional)
shoyu,* to taste (optional)

## METHOD

If using shiitake, drain, squeeze dry, then discard the stems and slice the caps. If using mung bean threads, drain, then cut into 5 cm/2 inch lengths.

Heat an electric frying pan (skillet) at the table. Add the suet and render some of the fat, then remove. Add half the meat and cook for a few minutes.

Mix together the sauce ingredients, then add a little sauce to the pan and mix with the meat. Push this mixture to one side of the pan, then arrange half the remaining ingredients in the other side of the pan. Pour over half the remaining sauce.

Cook over high heat for 3 to 4 minutes, turning the ingredients gently to cook both the top and bottom; do not overstir as the ingredients should still remain whole after cooking.

Push the cooked ingredients carefully to one side of the pan, then continue adding more ingredients and sauce to the pan while the guests are helping themselves to the cooked half.

If liked, provide each diner with an individual bowl into which he may crack an egg. The diner then mixes the egg with shoyu according to taste and dips morsels of hot food into this mixture; the heat of the food will cook the egg slightly.
SERVES 4 to 6

# Hijiki To Aburage

## Seaweed with Fried Bean Cake

Japan is surrounded by water, so it is hardly surprising that seaweeds have become one of the major foodstuffs to the Japanese. These seaweeds are high in protein, starch, sugar, fat, vitamins A, $B_1$, $B_2$, calcium, phosphorus, iron and trace elements.

### METRIC/IMPERIAL

5 tablespoons dry hijiki*
2 aburage*
1 teaspoon vegetable oil
150 ml/¼ pint dashi (see page 125)
1 tablespoon mirin*
2½ teaspoons sugar
2 tablespoons shoyu*

### AMERICAN

5 tablespoons dry hijiki*
2 aburage*
1 teaspoon vegetable oil
⅔ cup dashi (see page 125)
1 tablespoon mirin*
2½ teaspoons sugar
2 tablespoons shoyu*

## METHOD

Pick out as much sediment as possible from the hijiki, then wash and soak in cold water for 1 hour. Drain, then rinse thoroughly under cold running water to remove the sand. Strain in a fine sieve (strainer).

Wash the aburage in boiling water to remove excess oil then cut lengthways into 5 mm/¼ inch slices.

Heat a frying pan (skillet), add the oil, then the hijiki. Fry for about 2 minutes, then add the aburage and dashi. Simmer, uncovered, for 5 minutes.

Add the remaining ingredients, stir well and cook for 7 minutes or until all the liquid has evaporated. Serve hot in warmed individual serving dishes.
SERVES 4

**Above: Teppanyaki**
**Left: Sukiyaki**

# Shiitake No Amanie
## Sweet Black Mushrooms

*Shiitake** is the legendary Black Forest mushroom so favoured by the Japanese and Chinese for its health-giving vitamins.

*Shiitake* is available in dehydrated form in speciality shops and markets and, although it is possible to buy fresh *shiitake*, it is the dehydrated form that should be used in this recipe. Chew the succulent pieces slowly to appreciate their fabulous taste!

### METRIC/IMPERIAL

15 dried shiitake,* with large caps,
    soaked in warm water for 20 minutes
450 ml/¾ pint water
1½ teaspoons sugar
1–2 tablespoons mirin*
pinch of salt
2 teaspoons shoyu*
pinch of monosodium glutamate*
    (optional)
shredded spring onion and carrot
    slices to garnish

### AMERICAN

15 dried shiitake,* with large caps,
    soaked in warm water for 20 minutes
2 cups water
1½ teaspoons sugar
1–2 tablespoons mirin*
pinch of salt
2 teaspoons shoyu*
pinch of msg* (optional)
shredded scallion and carrot slices to
    garnish

### METHOD

Drain the mushrooms, reserving the soaking liquid, then discard the mushroom stems. Leave the caps whole or slice each one into 5 pieces.

Pour the mushroom liquid slowly into a pan, taking care to avoid including the sandy sediment at the bottom which should be discarded. Add the mushrooms and boil for 5 minutes. Add the remaining ingredients and cook for 5 minutes. If liked, sprinkle in a little more mirin.

Remove from the heat, then leave to stand for 10 minutes. Arrange the mushrooms in an attractive pattern on a serving plate. Garnish with the spring onion (scallion) and carrot slices, placed in the centre to resemble a flower head. Serve at room temperature, as an appetizer or side dish.
SERVES 4

# Kimpira
## Chilli-Flavoured Burdock

This can be served as an appetizer or as an accompaniment to any meal. Burdock is considered a nuisance weed in the West, but in Japan *gobo*,* the root, is used as a vegetable. It is an acquired taste, however, and you may have to try it several times before you like it. The chilli pepper gives the dish its name and zip.

### METRIC/IMPERIAL

3 long gobo,* skinned
1 small carrot, peeled
1 tablespoon vegetable oil
1 tablespoon shoyu*
1 tablespoon sugar
pinch of salt
pinch of monosodium glutamate*
    (optional)
pinch of dried chilli pepper flakes

### AMERICAN

3 long gobo,* skinned
1 small carrot, peeled
1 tablespoon vegetable oil
1 tablespoon shoyu*
1 tablespoon sugar
pinch of salt
pinch of msg* (optional)
pinch of dried chili pepper flakes

### METHOD

Cut the gobo and carrot into paper-thin 1 cm/½ inch wide strips, using a vegetable peeler. Place in a bowl of cold water until ready for use, then drain and pat dry with kitchen paper towels.

Heat a frying pan (skillet). When hot, add the oil, then the vegetables and stir-fry for about 2 minutes until tender but still crisp.

Add the remaining ingredients and stir-fry for 2 minutes. Serve hot or at room temperature.
SERVES 4

Shitake No Amanie; Shira Ae

# Shimeji
## Tree Oyster Mushrooms

The *shimeji** (tree oyster) mushroom has been cultivated in Japan for years as a fresh fungi 'vegetable'. It is now becoming more widely available because it can be grown easily under controlled conditions. In damp woods, one can find the wild species of *shimeji** – *Pleurotus ostreatus*; this mushroom is occasionally referred to as the 'shellfish of the forest' since it has a slight shellfish flavour.

### METRIC/IMPERIAL

*225 g/8 oz fresh shimeji**
*1½ teaspoons butter*
*1 garlic clove, peeled and crushed*
*1 teaspoon sake**
*3 tablespoons chicken stock*
*salt*
*freshly ground black pepper*
*pinch of monosodium glutamate**
  *(optional)*

### AMERICAN

*½ lb fresh shimeji**
*1½ teaspoons butter*
*1 garlic clove, peeled and ground*
*1 teaspoon sake**
*3 tablespoons chicken stock*
*salt*
*freshly ground black pepper*
*pinch of msg* (optional)*

### METHOD

Tear the shimeji into bite-sized pieces. Melt the butter in a frying pan (skillet) over low heat. Add the garlic and stir-fry for 30 seconds, then add the shimeji and sake. Stir-fry for 1 minute, then add the remaining ingredients and cook for 2 minutes. Serve immediately, as a side dish.
SERVES 4

# Shira Ae
## Vegetables with Tofu Sauce

This is a most interesting tangy white dressing for cooked vegetables.

### METRIC/IMPERIAL

*6 aburage**
*2 pieces konnyaku,* cut into*
  *5 cm/2 inch strips*
*3 small carrots, peeled and cut into*
  *5 cm/2 inch strips*
*250 ml/8 fl oz dashi (see page 125)*
*1 block tofu**
*5 tablespoons white sesame seeds,**
  *toasted and crushed*
*2 tablespoons shiromiso**
*3 tablespoons sugar*
*1 teaspoon salt*
*pinch of monosodium glutamate**
  *(optional)*
*cucumber strips and carrot slice to*
  *garnish*

### AMERICAN

*6 aburage**
*2 pieces konnyaku,* cut into 2 inch*
  *strips*
*3 small carrots, peeled and cut into*
  *2 inch strips*
*1 cup dashi (see page 125)*
*1 block tofu**
*5 tablespoons white sesame seeds,**
  *toasted and crushed*
*2 tablespoons shiromiso**
*3 tablespoons sugar*
*1 teaspoon salt*
*pinch of msg* (optional)*
*cucumber strips and carrot slice to*
  *garnish*

### METHOD

Wash the aburage in boiling water to remove the excess oil, then cut lengthways into 5 mm/¼ inch slices. Cook the konnyaku in boiling salted water for 2 minutes, then drain.

Cook the aburage, konnyaku and carrots in the dashi for about 5 minutes until the carrots are tender but still crisp and most of the dashi has evaporated. Leave to cool, then cut the vegetables into small pieces and place in a large serving bowl.

Wrap the tofu in a cloth and press down to squeeze out as much water as possible. Crush the tofu. Add the remaining ingredients, mix well, then pour the tofu dressing over the vegetables. Mix together, taking care not to crush the vegetables.

Garnish with cucumber strips and a carrot slice. Serve at room temperature, as a side dish.
SERVES 4

# Gyoza Yaki
## Fried Dumplings

### METRIC/IMPERIAL

3 napa* leaves
225 g/½ lb boned lean pork, minced
2 spring onions, chopped
1 garlic clove, peeled and crushed
½ teaspoon grated fresh root ginger*
2 tablespoons shoyu*
½ teaspoon salt
1 tablespoon sesame seed oil*
½ packet round gyoza skins*
2 tablespoons vegetable oil
**Dipping sauce:**
2 tablespoons su*
2 tablespoons dry mustard
2 tablespoons shoyu*
pinch of monosodium glutamate*
 (optional)

### AMERICAN

3 napa* leaves
1 cup lean ground pork
2 scallions, chopped
1 garlic clove, peeled and ground
½ teaspoon grated fresh ginger root*
2 tablespoons shoyu*
½ teaspoon salt
1 tablespoon sesame seed oil*
½ package round gyoza skins*
2 tablespoons vegetable oil
**Dipping sauce:**
2 tablespoons su*
2 tablespoons dry mustard
2 tablespoons shoyu*
pinch of msg* (optional)

### METHOD

Blanch the napa quickly in boiling water, drain, then squeeze out excess moisture. Mince (grind) coarsely, then combine with the remaining ingredients, except the gyoza skins and vegetable oil.

Put 1 spoonful of the mixture on one half of a gyoza skin. Fold in half, enclosing the filling. Brush the inside edges with water and press together to seal. (For an authentic finish, pleat the top side as you seal the skin.) Repeat with the remaining filling mixture and skins.

Heat a frying pan (skillet), add the vegetable oil, then the gyoza, overlapping them slightly in a neat pattern, with the pleated sides on top. Cover and cook over moderate heat for about 5 minutes.

Add just enough hot water to cover the gyoza, then cover with a lid and cook until all the water has evaporated.

To make the dipping sauce: Combine all the ingredients together and divide between individual dishes.

Serve the gyoza hot, with the dipping sauce.
SERVES 4

# Gohan
## Plain Steamed Rice

The Japanese prefer medium- or short-grain rice because it cooks into a fluffy mass that clings together but is not sticky. This type of rice has an entirely different texture from long-grain rice, which has a tendency to be drier with separate grains.

In Japan, a bowl of rice is usually eaten with every meal. It is generally served plain, with the entrée and side dishes. However, there are speciality dishes using rice with various combinations of meat, fish, poultry and vegetables.

The amount of water required to cook the rice will vary according to its origin and the length of time it has been stored since the harvest; the quantity given in this recipe is therefore only an approximate guide. If you are lucky enough to have an electric rice steamer, it will produce perfect rice every time you use it! No salt is added to plain rice in the cooking stage.

### METRIC/IMPERIAL

575 g/1¼ lb short- or medium-grain rice
750 ml/1¼ pints water

### AMERICAN

3 cups short- or medium-grain rice
3 cups water

### METHOD

Wash the rice thoroughly under cold running water, rubbing it well between the palms of the hands. Drain and repeat this process about 3 times until the rinsing water is clear. Leave to drain in a colander for about 20 minutes.

Put the rice in a heavy pan, add the water, then cover and bring quickly to the boil. Lower the heat and simmer for 20 minutes, by which time most of the water will have been absorbed; do not remove the lid at any stage. Increase the heat and cook for about 20 seconds, then remove the pan from the heat. Leave to stand for 10 minutes, without removing the lid.

Fluff up the rice with a wet rice paddle or a fork. Serve hot in individual rice bowls or on a large serving plate.
SERVES 4 to 6

Nigiri Zushi; Shushi

# Sushi
## Basic Vinegared Rice

The basic recipe for making all kinds of sushi is to combine medium-grain rice with a vinegared sauce, but the variations are endless. It can be made into *Nigiri Zushi* (see opposite), or *Chirashi Zushi*, a kind of rice salad in which the sushi is tossed with salad ingredients. Another variation is *Makizushi*, a rice roll covered with *nori** and filled with layers of different seasoned ingredients.

When making sushi, add a 15 cm/6 inch piece of *kombu** – if available – to the pan of rice. Cook for 3 minutes, then remove. This will impart a more traditional flavour.

METRIC/IMPERIAL

575 g/1¼ lb medium-grain rice
750 ml/1¼ pints water
**Vinegar sauce:**
6 tablespoons su*
4½ tablespoons sugar
2 teaspoons salt
1 teaspoon monosodium glutamate*
   (optional)
**To garnish:**
1–2 tablespoons toasted sesame seeds*
beni-shoga* or sansho* (optional)

AMERICAN

3 cups medium-grain rice
3 cups water
**Vinegar sauce:**
6 tablespoons su*
4½ tablespoons sugar
2 teaspoons salt
1 teaspoon msg* (optional)
**To garnish:**
1–2 tablespoons toasted sesame seeds*
beni-shoga* or sansho* (optional)

METHOD

Wash the rice thoroughly under cold running water, rubbing it well between the palms of the hands. Drain and repeat this process about 3 times until the rinsing water is clear. Drain.

Put the rice in a heavy pan, add the water and leave to soak for 1 hour. Cover the pan and bring quickly to the boil, then reduce the heat to very low and simmer for 15 minutes; do not remove the lid at any stage.

Turn off the heat and leave the rice to steam in its own heat for 10 minutes, then remove from the heat and leave to stand for 10 minutes.

Meanwhile, make the vinegar sauce: Put the sauce ingredients in a small pan (not aluminium) and heat until the sugar has dissolved, stirring constantly. Set aside until required.

Fluff up the rice with a wet rice paddle or fork, then transfer to a large stainless steel or ceramic bowl. Pour the vinegar sauce over the hot rice. Toss lightly, lifting the rice from the bottom up with the wet rice paddle or fork to produce the desired lustre.

Serve hot, sprinkled with toasted sesame seeds and garnished with beni-shoga or sansho, if liked.
SERVES 4 to 6

# Nigiri Zushi
## Rice Balls with Topping

This is the Japanese snack which is prepared at the popular *sushi* bars.

The tuna or sea bass topping given here can be replaced with shrimps. These should be peeled, deveined and boiled briefly, with a toothpick inserted along the underside to prevent them curling. Cut them in half, keeping the back side intact, then place on top of the *wasabi.**

Another variation is to serve the rice ovals topped with rectangular pieces of thin omelet. These make marvellous hors d'oeuvre.

METRIC/IMPERIAL

1 tablespoon su* (approximately)
575 g/1¼ lb sushi (see left)
1 tablespoon wasabi* (approximately),
   mixed to a paste with water
30 small slices of raw fresh tuna or sea
   bass (approximately)
**To serve:**
few parsley sprigs
few slices beni-shoga*
shoyu* to taste

AMERICAN

1 tablespoon su* (approximately)
3 cups sushi (see left)
1 tablespoon wasabi* (approximately),
   mixed to a paste with water
30 small slices of raw fresh tuna or sea
   bass (approximately)
**To serve:**
few parsley sprigs
few slices beni-shoga*
shoyu* to taste

METHOD

Moisten the hands with a little su. Scoop up 2 tablespoons rice in one hand then, with the other hand, squeeze the rice into an egg-shaped oval, about 5 cm/2 inches long. Dab the top with wasabi paste, then cover with a slice of fish, pressing it down firmly. Repeat with the remaining rice, wasabi paste and fish, to make about 30 rice ovals.

Arrange the rice ovals on a tray and garnish with the parsley and beni-shoga. Hand shoyu separately as a dip for the fish. Serve cold with plenty of green tea.
MAKES ABOUT 30

Sekiyan; Hiyashi Somen; Tsukimi Udon

# Hiyashi Somen

## Chilled Noodles

This is a most unusual way to eat noodles;
it is very refreshing in the summer and
looks most attractive. Guests help themselves to the somen, then use individual
bowls of sauce as a dip. If liked, you can
top the somen with boiled fresh shrimps
or seasoned *shiitake.** Grated fresh root
ginger* or *wasabi** can also be served as
an accompaniment.

### METRIC/IMPERIAL

*450 g/1 lb somen**
**Sauce:**
*450 ml/¾ pint dashi (see page 125)*
*120 ml/4 fl oz shoyu**
*4 tablespoons sake**
*1 tablespoon sugar*
**To garnish:**
*few ice cubes*
*few small tomatoes, quartered*
*few spring onions, shredded*

### AMERICAN

*1 lb somen**
**Sauce:**
*2 cups dashi (see page 125)*
*½ cup shoyu**
*¼ cup sake**
*1 tablespoon sugar*
**To garnish:**
*few ice cubes*
*few cherry tomatoes, quartered*
*few scallions, shredded*

### METHOD

Cook the somen in plenty of boiling
water for about 5 minutes until *al dente*.
Drain, rinse thoroughly under cold running water and drain again. Place in a
large shallow glass serving bowl and
chill in the refrigerator.

Put the sauce ingredients in a pan and
stir well. Bring to the boil, then lower the
heat and simmer for 2 minutes. Leave to
cool, then pour into individual glass
bowls and chill in the refrigerator.

Garnish the chilled somen with ice
cubes, tomatoes and spring onions (scallions). Serve the sauce separately.
SERVES 4

## Tsukimi Udon
### Noodles with Broth

Noodles are consumed in large quantities, and with great relish, in Japan. 'Slurping' is good etiquette and everyone eats noodles with their meals or as a snack. There are many varieties of noodle in Japan – thick and wide ones, coloured ones and ones made from buckwheat. This recipe uses the traditional thick, wide *udon,** and the egg on top is like a full moon – the title literally translated means 'seeing the moon noodles'.

METRIC/IMPERIAL

*450 g/1 lb udon\**
*900 ml/1½ pints dashi (see page 125)*
*1 tablespoon sugar*
*1½ teaspoons salt*
*1 tablespoon shoyu\**
*4 eggs*
**To garnish:**
*2 spring onions, thinly sliced*
*13 cm/5 inch square piece of nori,\* toasted and finely shredded*

AMERICAN

*1 lb udon\**
*3¾ cups dashi (see page 125)*
*1 tablespoon sugar*
*1½ teaspoons salt*
*1 tablespoon shoyu\**
*4 eggs*
**To garnish:**
*2 scallions, thinly sliced*
*5 inch square piece of nori,\* toasted and finely shredded*

METHOD

Add the noodles to a large pan of boiling water, stirring constantly. Bring back to the boil, then add 250 ml/8 fl oz/1 cup cold water. Bring back to the boil again, then cook the noodles for 10 to 12 minutes until *al dente*. Drain, then rinse thoroughly under cold running water and drain again.

Put the dashi, sugar, salt and shoyu in a large pan and stir well. Bring to the boil over high heat, then add the noodles. Bring back to the boil, stirring constantly, then cook until the noodles are heated through.

Pour into warmed individual bowls, then break 1 egg over each bowl. Cover the bowls with lids and the heat from the noodles will cook the eggs. Garnish with spring onions (scallions) and nori shreds. Serve hot.
SERVES 4

## Sekihan
### Steamed Pink Rice with Beans

This pale pink rice is a celebration dish, prepared for special occasions such as birthdays. For the rice to acquire a pink colour, preparation must be started the day before the dish is required.

METRIC/IMPERIAL

*200 g/7 oz azuki\**
*750 g/1¾ lb mochigome\**
*goma jio,\* made with 1 teaspoon black sesame seeds\* and 2 teaspoons salt*

AMERICAN

*¾ cup azuki\**
*4 cups mochigome\**
*goma jio,\* made with 1 teaspoon black sesame seeds\* and 2 teaspoons salt*

METHOD

Pick over and wash the azuki, then put them in a pan and cover with water. Bring to the boil, then drain, cover with fresh cold water and bring to the boil again. Lower the heat, cover with a lid and simmer gently for about 40 minutes, adding more water to keep the beans covered during cooking. Drain and reserve the cooking liquid.

Wash the mochigome thoroughly, drain and place in a bowl. Cover with the reserved azuki liquid and leave to stand overnight to allow the rice to acquire a pinkish colour.

Drain the rice and reserve the liquid. Mix the mochigome and azuki together, taking care not to crush the beans. Line a steamer plate, or other heatproof plate, with a piece of cheesecloth (muslin). Bring the water in the steamer to the boil, then spread the rice and bean mixture on the cloth, patting it smooth and making a few vent holes in it. Steam over high heat for about 50 minutes until the rice is cooked, basting every 12 minutes with the reserved azuki liquid.

Divide between warmed individual serving bowls and sprinkle with goma jio. Serve hot or at room temperature.
SERVES 8 to 10

# Zenzai or Shiruko

## Red Bean Soup with Rice Dumplings

This soup is served as a sweet snack, rather than as a dessert. The rice used in these little dumplings is glutinous rice* – sticky and satisfying – for true rice eaters!

### METRIC/IMPERIAL

*225 g/8 oz azuki\**
*275 g/10 oz sugar*
*½ teaspoon salt*
**Dango (dumplings):**
*½ package mochiko\**

### AMERICAN

*1 cup azuki\**
*1¼ cups sugar*
*½ teaspoon salt*
**Dango (dumplings):**
*½ package mochiko\**

### METHOD

Pick over and wash the azuki, then put them in a pan with 1.5 litres/2½ pints/6¼ cups water. Bring to the boil, then lower the heat and simmer for 2 hours until the beans are soft.

Add more water to the pan to make the liquid up to 1.2 litres/2 pints/5 cups (some of the water will have evaporated during cooking). Add the sugar and salt and cook for 15 minutes, stirring occasionally.

Meanwhile, make the dumplings: Mix the mochiko with enough water to make a stiff dough. Knead well, then pinch off tiny portions to form small balls, about the size of marbles. Make a small indentation in the side of each dumpling.

Bring the azuki soup back to the boil, then drop the dumplings into the soup. Cook until the dumplings rise to the surface. Divide between warmed individual bowls. Serve hot.
SERVES 4

# Kasutera

## Sponge Cake

This light cake is not normally baked in Japanese kitchens – it is usually purchased from one of the many pastry shops in Japan. It was originally introduced several centuries ago by the Dutch traders who came to the port of Nagasaki. In recent years, small electric ovens have become part of the Japanese kitchen, and these have made it possible for cakes such as this one to be baked at home.

### METRIC/IMPERIAL

*5 eggs, beaten*
*150 g/5 oz sugar*
*75 g/3 oz honey*
*75 g/3 oz plain flour*
*¾ teaspoon baking powder*
*2 tablespoons icing sugar to decorate*

### AMERICAN

*5 eggs, beaten*
*⅔ cup sugar*
*¼ cup honey*
*¾ cup all-purpose flour*
*¾ teaspoon baking powder*
*2 tablespoons confectioners' sugar to decorate*

### METHOD

Put the eggs in a bowl, then gradually beat in the sugar and honey. Beat for about 10 minutes until thick and pale, using an electric beater if possible. Sift the flour and baking powder together, then fold gently into the egg mixture.

Pour the mixture into a greased and floured 23 cm/9 inch square cake tin (pan). Bake in a preheated moderate oven (180°C/350°F, Gas Mark 4) for 30 minutes. Leave the cake in the tin (pan) for 10 minutes, then transfer to a wire rack and leave to cool completely.

Sprinkle with icing (confectioners') sugar. Cut into squares before serving.
MAKES ONE 23 cm/9 inch CAKE

**Matcha Ice Cream; Momo No Kanten**

## Momo No Kanten
### Peach 'Gelatin'

Serve with tea, either as a snack or a dessert. Unsweetened crushed pineapple may be substituted for the peach pulp, if liked.

METRIC/IMPERIAL

*1 long block kanten\**
*450 ml/¾ pint water*
*350 g/12 oz sugar*
*120 ml/4 fl oz fresh peach pulp*
*juice of ½ lemon*
*2 egg whites*

AMERICAN

*1 long block kanten\**
*2 cups water*
*1½ cups sugar*
*½ cup fresh peach pulp*
*juice of ½ lemon*
*2 egg whites*

METHOD

Wash the kanten under cold running water, then put in a pan, cover with the water and leave to soak for 20 to 30 minutes. Bring to the boil over moderate heat until completely melted, then add the sugar and stir until dissolved. Strain through a very fine sieve (strainer), then stir in the peach pulp and lemon juice and leave to cool.

Beat the egg whites until stiff, then gradually fold in the cooled liquid. Pour into a shallow tin (pan) and chill in the refrigerator until set. Cut into 2.5 cm/ 1 inch squares or diamond shapes. Serve chilled.
MAKES ABOUT 24

## Matcha Ice Cream
### Green Tea Ice Cream

This ice cream, with its pale, minty colour, makes a beautiful ending to a Japanese meal.

METRIC/IMPERIAL

*600 ml/1 pint vanilla ice cream,*
    *softened*
*1 tablespoon matcha\**
*1 can sweetened azuki beans\* (optional)*

AMERICAN

*2½ cups vanilla ice cream, softened*
*1 tablespoon matcha\**
*1 can sweetened azuki beans\* (optional)*

METHOD

Blend together the ice cream and matcha, then freeze until required. Scoop into individual serving dishes and top with sweetened azuki beans, if liked.
SERVES 4

# Korea

## Jan Leeming

The name of Korea or *Koryo* means 'high and clear', and is symbolic of the country's rugged mountains, rushing shallow streams and clear blue skies which have earned it the nickname of the 'Switzerland of Asia'. Korea is roughly the size of Great Britain. It extends southwards from eastern Siberia and Manchuria and lies between Japan on the east and China on the west.

The Koreans are descended from several Mongol tribes dating back to prehistoric times. Despite the proximity to Japan and China and repeated invasions by these two countries, the Koreans have clung to one language, one culture and their own ancient traditions. In the past, the West thought of Korea as a cultural bridge between Japan and China, yet it is now known that many traditions of these countries were directly influenced by Korean culture.

Korea has a temperate climate of four distinct seasons. The summer is hot and humid, the winter is cold, springtime is mild with a proliferation of flowers and blossom, and the autumn is mild and wet. This climate, and the rich soil, provide good agricultural land. Traditionally, the Koreans enjoy the autumn best because it is at this time that the crops have been harvested and food is plentiful.

Korean food consists of staple grains, subsidiary dishes and special foods. The grains are rice, barley and millet, either prepared singly or mixed, but almost always cooked simply by boiling. Special foods are usually highly seasoned with red pepper, garlic, spring onions (scallions), fresh root ginger,* soy sauce, salt, sesame seed oil* and baked sesame seeds,* then served with plain boiled rice and subsidiary dishes such as the peppery-hot, fermented pickled cabbage called *Kim Chee* (see page 145). This is a unique Korean dish and one without which no Korean home would be complete. During the late autumn, making winter Kim Chee is a family event in which all activity centres around preparing and chopping the vegetables and filling the earthenware pickle pots. There is a saying in Korea that, 'When the *Kim Chee* is prepared for the winter, half the harvest is done'. So essential is this pickled cabbage to a Korean's diet, that during the Korean war the soldiers used to take tins of it into battle with them – whatever else they went without, it would not be their *Kim Chee*!

If one had to liken the taste of Korean food to any other, the choice would be Indonesian rather than Japanese or Chinese as might be expected.

Korean food has many different flavours, from chilli-hot to delicately subtle, but the overall impression for the newcomer to the Korean table is one of sweetness, found in such dishes as *Bulgogi* (see page 151) and *Thak Tuigim Jang* (see page 150). The taste of Korean food is unique, but not so remote from Western dishes which combine sweet foods, such as fruit, with meat and poultry. This sweetness, or maybe the sheer satisfaction of eating Korean food, may be the reason why desserts as we know them do not feature in a Korean meal. In fact, Koreans will often eat fruit and rice cakes before a meal, and will finish with a plate of decoratively cut fruit.

The Korean has three meals a day; these are similar in that they all usually consist of soup, rice, fish or beef and the ubiquitous *Kim Chee*. The Korean breakfast is becoming Westernized, but it used to be the main meal of the day and it was usual for guests to be invited to breakfast. Lunch is usually the leftovers from breakfast.

With the advent of the smaller Western breakfast, dinner is fast becoming the main meal of the day. For dinner, each person has a bowl of rice and a bowl of soup; in addition, there are at least five different side dishes, plus soy sauce for dipping, and *Kim Chee*. At a special dinner, at least fifteen different dishes could be offered. The food is eaten with chopsticks and a spoon and in no specific order; soup may well appear on the table halfway through the meal, for example.

There is no fixed dining room in a traditional Korean home; the meal table, small and low, is taken to whichever room is convenient. Traditionally, the men will eat first, then the women, rather like a first and second sitting. However, in some homes today you will find the family almost eating together. The men occupy shapes from a peeled carrot, wielding a massive sharp knife, is an experience to be remembered!

More time is often spent preparing ingredients (chopping, slicing and marinating), than cooking. In many cases, particularly vegetables, the ingredients are literally 'shown' to the pan and taken out again. The Koreans like to eat their vegetables almost raw and their meat and fish are usually so finely sliced that these too, take very little time to cook. Most cooking is over high heat for a short time, otherwise the dishes are steamed.

Nothing is ever wasted in a Korean kitchen. Beef and poultry bones are always boiled to provide stock for soup or a base for a marinade. Remains of cooked meat are sliced and added to soup dishes, such as *Neng Myun* (see page 148) and *Yuk Ke Jang* (see page 146), or form the basis of the 'dish of kings' *Shin-Sol-Lo* (see page 149).

## Festive Cooking

*Shin-Sol-Lo* is time-consuming to prepare, but it is a special dish for special occasions such as *Hansik*, which falls during February or March and is the day on which rites to worship ancestors are observed, or on *Sol* which is New Year's Day.

Although traditional dress is rarely worn by the younger men nowadays, at New Year the women might well wear their beautifully feminine *Chima Chogori*. This comprises a long, full skirt coming up to the bust line and a very short jacket which ends just below the top of the skirt; it is usually brightly coloured and often heavily embroidered.

## Ginseng

Wine or *sake*\* can be drunk with Korean food, but it is more usual to serve the meal with Korean tea made from barley, often with a little Ginseng added. Ginseng, or *insam* as it is called in Korea, is the best known and most firmly credited of all Oriental herb medicines. It can be grown in any temperate climate, but Korean Ginseng is acknowledged as the finest.

A glass of Ginseng brandy at the end of your Korean meal will complement and complete a unique experience.

one table, the children another, and the women's table is placed closest to the kitchen!

In the past, and still found today, in the country regions, the kitchen contained a fire fuelled by logs from the mountains. This provided heat for cooking and, by means of a system of pipes under the floor, warmth for the house. This *ondol* system of heating is so much a part of Korean life, that even the most modern Western-style houses have rooms with concrete floors under which there is a heat-radiating network of pipes.

## Cooking Equipment and Utensils

The basic items in a Korean kitchen are a rice kettle and a soup kettle, which are heavy lidded pots made of pig iron. Other cooking takes place in a *Sot*, which is similar to the Chinese wok, curved at the bottom so that it sits in an aperture over the flame. The Korean housewife would also have a *Shin-Sol-Lo* pot for special occasion cooking. She might also have a *Bulgogi* pan, although this is, in Korean terms, a fairly recent invention having only been around for about 60 years. (The pan almost defies description, being a conical-shaped piece of metal with lipped apertures cut into it to allow the heat through and the meat juices to drip down into a collecting rim.) Without a *Bulgogi* pan, the cook would use a special *Bulgogi* grill (broiler) (see page 151).

Other basic utensils include a chopper and several extremely sharp knives.

## Preparation and Cooking

In Korean cookery, great emphasis is placed on very fine cutting. This art, coupled with the decorative cutting of vegetables for garnish and fresh fruit for pure beauty, is the first element of cuisine learned by a Korean girl. Watching a Korean cook preparing a plate of fresh fruit for the table, or making a garnish of flower-like

# Hobak Chun

## Savoury Battered Courgettes (Zucchini)

This delicate-tasting hors d'oeuvre can be eaten hot or cold.

### METRIC/IMPERIAL

400 g/14 oz large courgettes, thinly
    sliced into rounds
salt
100 g/4 oz bean curd* (optional)
100 g/4 oz beef topside, minced
2 teaspoons sesame seeds*
2 teaspoons sesame seed oil*
4 teaspoons chopped spring onions
1 teaspoon crushed garlic
pinch of monosodium glutamate*
½ teaspoon freshly ground black
    pepper
100 g/4 oz plain flour
3 small eggs, beaten
4 tablespoons vegetable oil
**To serve:**
boo* (optional)
parsley sprig (optional)
Korean soy sauce (see opposite)

### AMERICAN

¾–1 lb zucchini, thinly sliced into
    rounds
salt
1 cake bean curd*
½ cup ground top round beef
2 teaspoons sesame seeds*
2 teaspoons sesame seed oil*
4 teaspoons chopped scallions
1 teaspoon crushed garlic
pinch of msg*
½ teaspoon freshly ground black
    pepper
1 cup all-purpose flour
3 small eggs, beaten
¼ cup vegetable oil
**To serve:**
boo* (optional)
parsley sprig (optional)
Korean soy sauce (see opposite)

### METHOD

Put the courgettes (zucchini) in a single layer on a plate, sprinkle with salt, then set aside.

Mash the bean curd, then squeeze out the water until the bean curd is dry. Place in a bowl with the beef, sesame seeds, sesame seed oil, spring onions (scallions), garlic, monosodium glutamate (msg), pepper and salt to taste. Mix well.

Dip one side of each courgette (zucchini) slice in flour. Spread a little beef mixture on the floured side, pressing it down well and spreading it out to cover. Dip both sides of each courgette (zucchini) slice in more flour, then in the egg.

Heat the oil in a frying pan (skillet), add the courgettes (zucchini), meat side down, and fry for 2 to 3 minutes until brown. Turn the slices over and fry until the underside is golden. Remove with a slotted spoon and drain on kitchen paper towels.

Arrange on a serving dish. Garnish, if liked, with flower shapes, cut from boo, and parsley. Serve hot or cold with Korean soy sauce handed separately as a dip.

SERVES 4

# Koon Mandoo

## Pan-fried Meat Dumplings

These are not the type of dumplings normally found in stews – they look rather like miniature Cornish pasties and are wrapped in a very thin dough. The Koreans often pinch the *wun tun skins** decoratively, or pull the edges of the crescent down and twist them together to form a shape like a hat with a brim. Serve hot as part of a main meal, or cold as part of an hors d'oeuvre.

### METRIC/IMPERIAL

225 g/8 oz beef topside, minced
½ teaspoon sesame seeds*
1 teaspoon sesame seed oil*
2 teaspoons chopped spring onions
1 teaspoon crushed garlic
½ teaspoon salt
2 pinches of monosodium glutamate*
30 wun tun skins*
4 tablespoons vegetable oil
**To serve:**
carrot (optional)
parsley sprig (optional)
Korean soy sauce (see opposite)

### AMERICAN

1 cup ground beef top round
½ teaspoon sesame seeds*
1 teaspoon sesame seed oil*
2 teaspoons chopped scallions
1 teaspoon crushed garlic
½ teaspoon salt
2 pinches of msg*
30 wun tun skins*
¼ cup vegetable oil
**To serve:**
carrot (optional)
parsley sprig (optional)
Korean soy sauce (see opposite)

### METHOD

Put all the ingredients in a bowl, except the wun tun skins and vegetable oil. Mix well, then put a small teaspoon of the mixture in the middle of each wun tun skin. Fold the skin over and pinch together to form a semi-circle.

Drop the dumplings into a pan of boiling water and boil for 3 minutes. Heat the vegetable oil in a frying pan (skillet). Remove the dumplings from the water with a slotted spoon, drain, then transfer to the oil. Fry until golden, turning constantly. Remove and drain.

Arrange on a serving dish. Garnish, if liked, with flower shapes, cut from carrot, and parsley. Serve hot or cold, with Korean soy sauce as a dip.

SERVES 4

**Koon Mandoo, served with Korean Soy Sauce; Hobak Chun**

# Kim Chee

## Pickled Chinese Cabbage (Bok Choy)

This famous hot pickled cabbage, made by the jarful, is something no self-respecting Korean would be without!

### METRIC/IMPERIAL

*1 head Chinese leaves, chopped*
*3 tablespoons salt*
*2 teaspoons hot chilli powder*
*2 teaspoons crushed garlic*
*4 spring onions, finely chopped*
*1 tablespoon sugar*
*1 hard pear, peeled, cored and grated*
*½ teaspoon monosodium glutamate\**

### AMERICAN

*1 head bok choy, chopped*
*3 tablespoons salt*
*2 teaspoons hot chili powder*
*2 teaspoons crushed garlic*
*4 scallions, finely chopped*
*1 tablespoon sugar*
*1 hard pear, peeled, cored and grated*
*½ teaspoon msg\**

### METHOD

Put the Chinese leaves (bok choy) in a bowl, add the salt and leave overnight.

Remove the cabbage from the bowl and rinse under cold running water. Drain, then pat dry. Place in a large jar and stir in the remaining ingredients.

Cover with a heavy weight and leave for 1 to 2 days before using.

# Korean Soy Sauce

This is a basic soy sauce which is enhanced by additional ingredients. It is served in individual bowls as a dip to accompany many of the Korean dishes in this chapter.

### METRIC/IMPERIAL

*3 tablespoons soy sauce*
*1 tablespoon chopped spring onions*
*1 teaspoon sesame seeds\**
*1 teaspoon sesame seed oil\**
*1 teaspoon crushed garlic*
*½ teaspoon sugar*
*1 teaspoon vinegar*
*pinch of chilli powder*
*pinch of monosodium glutamate\**

### AMERICAN

*3 tablespoons soy sauce*
*1 tablespoon chopped scallions*
*1 teaspoon sesame seeds\**
*1 teaspoon sesame seed oil\**
*1 teaspoon crushed garlic*
*½ teaspoon sugar*
*1 teaspoon vinegar*
*pinch of chili powder*
*pinch of msg\**

### METHOD

Mix all the ingredients together, then divide equally between 4 individual shallow dishes.
SERVES 4

# Bintatok

## Korean Pizza

This dish is a cross between a pizza and a pancake (crêpe). It should be made with ground mung beans\*; if these are not available, use split peas instead.

### METRIC/IMPERIAL

*225 g/8 oz mung beans\**
*4 tablespoons vegetable oil*
*1 large onion, peeled and finely chopped*
*4 spring onions, green part only, finely chopped*
*1 carrot, peeled and finely chopped*
*1 small red pepper, cored, seeded and thinly sliced*
*50 g/2 oz minced beef*
*salt*
*freshly ground black pepper*
*Korean soy sauce (see left) to serve*

### AMERICAN

*1⅓ cups mung beans\**
*¼ cup vegetable oil*
*1 large onion, peeled and finely chopped*
*4 scallions, green part only, finely chopped*
*1 carrot, peeled and finely chopped*
*1 small red pepper, cored, seeded and thinly sliced*
*¼ cup ground beef, firmly packed*
*salt*
*freshly ground black pepper*
*Korean soy sauce (see left) to serve*

### METHOD

Put the beans in a bowl, cover with warm water and leave to soak for at least 3 hours, preferably overnight.

Transfer the beans and any remaining liquid to an electric blender and work to a thick, smooth batter. Alternatively, pound the mixture until smooth using a pestle and mortar.

Heat a quarter of the oil in a small omelet pan (about 15 cm/6 inches in diameter). Add a quarter of the batter and tilt the pan to spread the batter evenly over the base.

Sprinkle a quarter of the remaining ingredients over the top of the bintatok and fry for at least 3 minutes until the edges begin to curl. Turn the bintatok over carefully and fry the other side for 3 minutes until golden brown underneath. Transfer to a warmed serving dish and keep hot while cooking the remaining ingredients in the same way to make 4 bintatok.

Serve hot with Korean soy sauce handed separately as a dip.
SERVES 4

## Solong Tang
### Beef Soup with Noodles and Ginger

#### METRIC/IMPERIAL

100 g/4 oz fine noodles
350 g/12 oz cooked beef brisket or
   topside
900 ml/1½ pints beef stock
50 g/2 oz spring onions, finely chopped
2 teaspoons crushed fresh root ginger*
1 teaspoon sugar
2 teaspoons freshly ground black
   pepper
2–3 teaspoons salt
1 teaspoon monosodium glutamate*

#### AMERICAN

¼ lb fresh wheat noodles
¾ lb cooked beef brisket or top round
3¾ cups beef stock
¾ cup finely chopped scallions
2 teaspoons crushed fresh ginger root*
1 teaspoon sugar
2 teaspoons freshly ground black
   pepper
2–3 teaspoons salt
1 teaspoon msg*

#### METHOD

Cook the noodles in boiling water for 3 to 5 minutes then drain and set aside.

Cut the meat into very thin slices, then cut each slice into strips, about 5 cm/ 2 inches long and 1 cm/½ inch wide.

Put all the ingredients in a pan, except the noodles and beef. Bring to the boil, then add the beef and simmer for 5 minutes. Hold the noodles in a sieve (strainer) over the pan and spoon the liquid over them to reheat, allowing the liquid to strain through into the pan.

Divide the noodles equally between 4 warmed individual soup bowls, then pour over the soup, distributing the strips of beef evenly. Serve hot.
SERVES 4

## Yuk Ke Jang
### Spicy Hot Beef Soup with Bean Sprouts

#### METRIC/IMPERIAL

3 tablespoons vegetable oil
1 teaspoon chilli powder
2 teaspoons crushed garlic
1 teaspoon crushed fresh root ginger*
900 ml/1½ pints beef stock
275 g/10 oz cooked beef topside, thinly
   sliced
2 tablespoons chopped spring onions
100 g/4 oz fresh bean sprouts
1 teaspoon monosodium glutamate*
¼–½ teaspoon salt

#### AMERICAN

3 tablespoons vegetable oil
1 teaspoon chili powder
2 teaspoons crushed garlic
1 teaspoon crushed fresh ginger root*
3¾ cups beef stock
1¼ cups thinly sliced cooked beef top
   round
2 tablespoons chopped scallions
1 cup fresh bean sprouts
1 teaspoon msg*
¼–½ teaspoon salt

#### METHOD

Heat the oil in a frying pan (skillet). Add the chilli powder, garlic and ginger and stir-fry over moderate heat for 1 minute. Remove from the heat.

Put the stock in a pan and bring to the boil. Add the chilli mixture and the remaining ingredients and simmer for 10 minutes. Serve hot.
SERVES 4

## Shikumchee-Taeng-Jang-Kuk
### Spinach Soup with Bean Curd and Squid

Despite its lengthy name, this soup is very easy to make.

#### METRIC/IMPERIAL

600 ml/1 pint well-flavoured beef
   stock
100 g/4 oz bean curd,* diced
50 g/2 oz cleaned squid, cut into thin
   strips (optional)
100 g/4 oz fresh young spinach leaves,
   cut into thin strips
2 teaspoons crushed garlic
1 tablespoon soy bean paste*
4 tablespoons sliced spring onions
1 teaspoon monosodium glutamate*
salt

#### AMERICAN

2½ cups well-flavored beef stock
1 cake bean curd,* diced
¼ cup cleaned squid, cut into thin strips
   (optional)
¼ lb fresh young spinach leaves, cut
   into thin strips
2 teaspoons crushed garlic
1 tablespoon soy bean paste*
¼ cup sliced scallions
1 teaspoon msg*
salt

#### METHOD

Put the stock in a pan and bring to the boil. Add the remaining ingredients and boil for 2 minutes. Serve hot in warmed individual soup bowls.
SERVES 4

# Maeum Tang

## Spiced Fish Soup

This is a dish for those who love spicy hot food.

### METRIC/IMPERIAL

*750 g/1½ lb cod fillets, skinned and cut
into large chunks*
*600 ml/1 pint water*
*2 tablespoons vegetable oil*
*1 medium onion, peeled and finely
chopped*
*2 tablespoons chopped spring onions*
*2 teaspoons crushed garlic*
*1 teaspoon crushed fresh root ginger\**
*2–6 teaspoons chilli powder, according
to taste*
*2–3 teaspoons salt*
*100 g/4 oz courgettes, thinly sliced*
*1 medium green pepper, cored,
seeded and finely sliced*

### AMERICAN

*1½ lb cod fillets, skinned and cut into
large chunks*
*2½ cups water*
*2 tablespoons vegetable oil*
*1 medium onion, peeled and finely
chopped*
*2 tablespoons chopped scallions*
*2 teaspoons crushed garlic*
*1 teaspoon crushed fresh ginger root\**
*2–6 teaspoons chili powder, according
to taste*
*2–3 teaspoons salt*
*1 cup thinly sliced zucchini*
*1 medium green pepper, cored,
seeded and finely sliced*

### METHOD

Put the cod in a pan with the water. Bring to the boil, then lower the heat and simmer gently for 5 minutes. Remove from the heat and set aside.

Heat the oil in a frying pan (skillet). Add the onion, spring onions (scallions), garlic. ginger and chilli powder and salt to taste. Stir-fry over moderate heat for 1 minute, then add the courgettes (zucchini) and pepper and stir-fry for 1 minute. Add to the fish and simmer gently until heated through. Serve hot.
SERVES 4

**Shin-Sol-Lo (see page 149), served in a
traditional cook pot; Shikumchee-
Taeng-Jang-Kuk**

# Neng Myun
## Cold Noodle Soup

### METRIC/IMPERIAL

450 g/1 lb fine noodles
225 g/8 oz cooked beef brisket or
   topside
900 ml/1½ pints chicken stock
8 whole black peppercorns
5 cm/2 inch piece of fresh root
   ginger,* peeled
½ teaspoon monosodium glutamate*
1–2 teaspoons salt
1 teaspoon soy sauce
4 dried chillis
**To serve:**
24 cucumber slices
1 large hard pear, peeled, cored and
   thinly sliced
2 hard-boiled eggs, shelled and halved
   lengthways
prepared mustard and vinegar to taste
   (optional)

### AMERICAN

1 lb fresh wheat noodles
½ lb cooked beef brisket or top round
3¾ cups chicken stock
8 whole black peppercorns
2 inch piece of fresh ginger root,*
   peeled
½ teaspoon msg*
1–2 teaspoons salt
1 teaspoon soy sauce
4 dried chilis
**To serve:**
24 cucumber slices
1 large hard pear, peeled, cored and
   thinly sliced
2 hard-cooked eggs, shelled and
   halved lengthways
prepared mustard and vinegar, to taste
   (optional)

### METHOD

Cook the noodles in boiling water for 3 to 5 minutes, then drain and leave to cool.

Cut the meat into very thin slices, then cut each slice into strips, about 5 cm/ 2 inches long and 1 cm/½ inch wide.

Put all the ingredients in a pan, except the noodles. Bring to the boil, then simmer for 5 minutes. Remove from the heat, leave until cold, then remove the peppercorns, ginger and chillis.

Divide the noodles between 4 to 6 individual soup bowls. Divide the cucumber and pear slices between the bowls, alternating the slices in layers on top of the noodles. Top each bowl with an egg half, then gently pour over the cold soup, taking care not to disturb the layers. Add a little mustard and vinegar before serving, if liked. Serve cold.
SERVES 4 to 6

# Ojingo Pokum
## Squid with Vegetables in Chilli-Hot Sweet Sauce

The squid should be scored crossways to help tenderize it during cooking.

### METRIC/IMPERIAL

450 g/1 lb fresh squid
2 tablespoons vegetable oil
1 small green pepper, cored, seeded
   and thinly sliced into rings
1 small red pepper, cored, seeded and
   thinly sliced into rings
1 medium onion, peeled and finely
   chopped
2 teaspoons crushed garlic
2 teaspoons sugar
1 teaspoon monosodium glutamate*
1 tablespoon kochujang*

### AMERICAN

1 lb fresh squid
2 tablespoons vegetable oil
1 small green pepper, cored, seeded
   and thinly sliced into rings
1 small red pepper, cored, seeded and
   thinly sliced into rings
1 medium onion, peeled and finely
   chopped
2 teaspoons crushed garlic
2 teaspoons sugar
1 teaspoon msg*
1 tablespoon kochujang*

Ojingo Pokum

## METHOD

Clean the squid, discarding the head, transparent backbone and ink bag. Cut the flesh into 2.5 cm/1 inch squares and score crossways.

Heat the oil in a frying pan (skillet). Add the vegetables and fry over brisk heat for 2 minutes, shaking the pan constantly. Remove from the heat, then add the squid, garlic, sugar and monosodium glutamate (msg).

Return to the heat and fry briskly for 2 minutes, stirring and shaking the pan constantly. Stir in the kochujang and fry for 1 minute over high heat, stirring all the time. Serve hot.

SERVES 4

# Shin-Sol-Lo

### Korean Celebration Firepot

Shin-Sol-Lo was once the dish of 'kings', because only the royal household could afford to eat it. Originally it would have been served in traditional Korean Royal Palace style in a Shin-Sol-Lo cook pot, and it would have contained crabs, prawns (shrimp) and many different meats. This recipe is a much simplified version, although it is still fairly time-consuming to make. Special Shin-Sol-Lo cook pots are difficult to obtain, but a fondue pot makes an acceptable substitute.

## METRIC/IMPERIAL

450 g/1 lb boo*
2 tablespoons sesame seed oil*
4 medium onions, peeled and finely chopped
2 teaspoons crushed garlic
2 teaspoons sesame seeds*
175 g/6 oz liver, thinly sliced
4 tablespoons vegetable oil
175 g/6 oz cod or other firm white fish fillets, sliced
400 g/14 oz minced beef
2 eggs, beaten
salt
freshly ground black pepper
900 ml/1½ pints beef stock
1 teaspoon monosodium glutamate*
225 g/8 oz cooked beef brisket or topside, cut into thin strips
1 medium cucumber, sliced diagonally
4 mushrooms, finely sliced
2 medium carrots, peeled and sliced diagonally
8 spring onions, shredded
75 g/3 oz fresh bamboo shoot
2 tablespoons pine nuts

**Batter:**
100 g/4 oz plain flour
2 eggs, well beaten
2 tablespoons water (approximately)

## AMERICAN

1 lb boo*
2 tablespoons sesame seed oil*
4 medium onions, peeled and finely chopped
2 teaspoons crushed garlic
2 teaspoons sesame seeds*
¾ cup thinly sliced liver
¼ cup vegetable oil
¾ cup sliced cod or other firm white fish fillets
1¾ cups ground beef
2 eggs, beaten
salt
freshly ground black pepper
3¾ cups beef stock
1 teaspoon msg*
½ lb cooked beef brisket or top round, cut into thin strips
1 medium cucumber, sliced diagonally
4 mushrooms, finely sliced
2 medium carrots, peeled and sliced diagonally
8 scallions, shredded
¾ cup fresh bamboo shoot
2 tablespoons pine nuts

**Batter:**
1 cup all-purpose flour
2 eggs, well beaten
2 tablespoons water (approximately)

## METHOD

Cook the boo in boiling water for 20 minutes, then drain and cut into small pieces. Heat the sesame seed oil in a frying pan (skillet), add the onion and fry gently until soft. Add the garlic and sesame seeds, then remove from the heat and mix with the boo.

To make the batter: Put the flour and eggs in a bowl and beat thoroughly until smooth. Add the water gradually, stirring constantly until the batter is smooth.

Dip the liver slices in the batter. Heat 1 tablespoon of the vegetable oil in the frying pan (skillet), add the liver and fry for 5 minutes. Remove from the pan with a slotted spoon, drain on kitchen paper towels and leave to cool. Meanwhile, dip the fish slices in the remaining batter. Heat another tablespoon of the oil in the pan, add the fish and fry for 5 minutes. Drain as for the liver.

Mix the minced (ground) beef and eggs together, then add salt and pepper to taste. Roll into 1 cm/½ inch balls. Heat the remaining vegetable oil in the frying pan (skillet). Add the meatballs and fry for about 5 minutes, turning frequently, until evenly browned. Remove from the pan with a slotted spoon, then drain on kitchen paper towels.

Put the stock in a pan with 1 teaspoon each of pepper and monosodium glutamate (msg). Bring to the boil, then lower the heat and simmer gently.

Meanwhile, arrange the ingredients in layers in individual Shin-Sol-Lo pots or a fondue pot. Put a layer of beef strips in the bottom, cover with boo mixture, then arrange the liver and fish slices on top in alternate layers.

Top with the cucumber, mushroom, carrot, spring onions (scallions), bamboo shoot and meatballs; arrange decoratively clockwise so that each third of the pan is filled in the same way.

Arrange the pine nuts around the funnel of the Shin-Sol-Lo pot or heap together in the centre of the fondue pot. Pour the stock gently over the ingredients, taking care not to disturb the arrangement.

If using Shin-Sol-Lo pots, put lighted charcoal into the centre, fan until the charcoal ignites, then heat for approximately 5 minutes. If using a fondue pot, bring gently to the boil over moderate heat. Serve hot.

SERVES 4 to 6

## Thak Tuigim Jang
### Deep-fried Chicken with Vegetables in Sweet Sauce

#### METRIC/IMPERIAL

450 g/1 lb boned chicken, cut into
    2.5 cm/1 inch cubes
vegetable oil for deep-frying
2 medium carrots, peeled and sliced
2 medium potatoes, peeled and cut into
    2.5 cm/1 inch cubes
½ small red pepper, cored, seeded and
    thinly sliced
½ small green pepper, cored, seeded
    and thinly sliced
1 medium onion, peeled and finely
    chopped
**Batter:**
100 g/4 oz plain flour
2 eggs, well beaten
2 tablespoons water (approximately)
**Sauce:**
2 tablespoons soy sauce
2 tablespoons water
1 tablespoon sugar
2 teaspoons crushed fresh root ginger*
2 teaspoons crushed garlic
2 tablespoons sake*
1 tablespoon sesame seed oil*
2 spring onions
½ teaspoon salt
½ teaspoon monosodium glutamate*

#### AMERICAN

1 lb boneless chicken, cut into 1 inch
    cubes
vegetable oil for deep-frying
2 medium carrots, peeled and sliced
2 medium potatoes, peeled and cut into
    1 inch cubes
½ small red pepper, cored, seeded and
    thinly sliced
½ small green pepper, cored, seeded
    and thinly sliced
1 medium onion, peeled and finely
    chopped
**Batter:**
1 cup all-purpose flour
2 eggs, well beaten
2 tablespoons water (approximately)
**Sauce:**
2 tablespoons soy sauce
2 tablespoons water
1 tablespoon sugar
2 teaspoons crushed fresh ginger root*
2 teaspoons crushed garlic
2 tablespoons sake*
1 tablespoon sesame seed oil*
2 scallions
½ teaspoon salt
½ teaspoon msg*

#### METHOD

First, make the batter: Put the flour and eggs in a bowl and beat thoroughly until smooth. Add the water gradually, stirring constantly until the batter is smooth.

Coat the chicken cubes in the batter. Heat the oil in a deep-fat fryer to 180°C/350°F, then add the chicken cubes and deep-fry until golden brown. Remove from the pan with a slotted spoon and drain on kitchen paper towels.

Blanch the carrots and potatoes in boiling water for 3 minutes, then drain and dry thoroughly. Deep-fry in the hot oil for 5 minutes, then remove from the pan with a slotted spoon and drain on kitchen paper towels.

To make the sauce: Put all the ingredients in a pan and mix well. Bring to the boil, then remove from the heat.

Coat the base of a large heavy frying pan (skillet) with oil. Heat gently, then add the chicken, carrots, potatoes, peppers and onion. Fry gently for about 1 minute, stirring constantly, then increase the heat and add the hot sauce. Cook for 1 minute, stirring and shaking the pan constantly over very high heat. Serve immediately.
SERVES 4

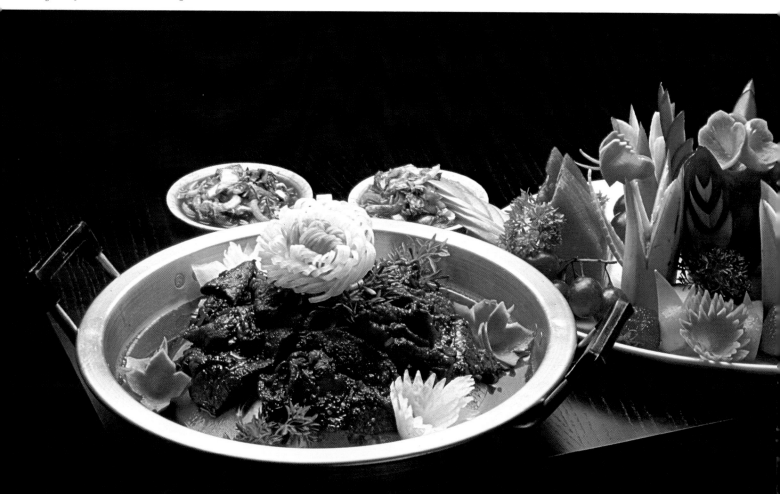

# Bulgogi
## Marinated Sliced Beef in Sweet Sauce

Bulgogi is Korea's most well-known dish. It is traditionally cooked and served in a special bulgogi pan, but it can equally well be made in a heavy frying pan (skillet).

Apart from the marinating, it is a very quick dish to make. If partially frozen beef is used, it will be easier to obtain very thin slices.

**Bulgogi, served with Kim Chee (see page 144); Decoratively cut fruit, often served as a dessert to complete a traditional Korean meal**

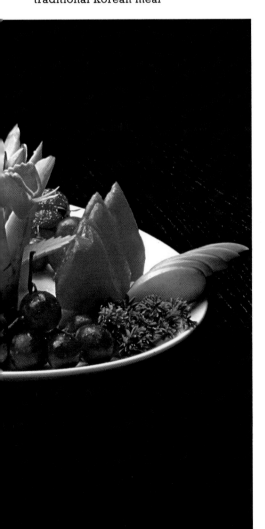

## METRIC/IMPERIAL

*750 g/1½ lb beef topside*
**Marinade:**
*1 small dessert apple, peeled, cored and grated*
*1 small hard pear, peeled, cored and grated*
*2 tablespoons chopped onion*
*4 tablespoons thinly sliced spring onions*
*4 tablespoons soy sauce*
*2 tablespoons sake\**
*120 ml/4 fl oz water*
*1 tablespoon chopped garlic*
*2 tablespoons sesame seed oil\**
*2 teaspoons sesame seeds\**
*1 teaspoon freshly ground black pepper*
*2 tablespoons sugar*
*1 teaspoon monosodium glutamate\**
**To serve:**
*carrot, boo\* and parsley (optional)*
*Kim chee (see page 145)*

## AMERICAN

*1½ lb beef top round*
**Marinade:**
*1 small dessert apple, peeled, cored and grated*
*1 small hard pear, peeled, cored and grated*
*2 tablespoons chopped onion*
*¼ cup thinly sliced scallions*
*¼ cup soy sauce*
*2 tablespoons sake\**
*½ cup water*
*1 tablespoon chopped garlic*
*2 tablespoons sesame seed oil\**
*2 teaspoons sesame seeds\**
*1 teaspoon freshly ground black pepper*
*2 tablespoons sugar*
*1 teaspoon msg\**
**To serve:**
*carrot, boo\* and parsley (optional)*
*Kim chee (see page 145)*

## METHOD

Slice the beef very thinly into 5 cm/2 inch squares. Place in a large bowl. Mix all the ingredients for the marinade together, then pour over the beef. Leave to marinate for at least 3 hours, preferably overnight.

Heat the pan until moderately hot. Add the beef and marinade and cook for 5 minutes or until the beef is tender, turning constantly.

Serve hot straight from the bulgogi pan, or transfer to a warmed serving dish if using a frying pan (skillet). Garnish, if liked, with flower shapes, cut from carrot and boo, and parsley. Serve with Kim chee.

SERVES 4

# Thak Jim
## Chicken in Soy Sauce with Ginger

### METRIC/IMPERIAL

*900 ml/1½ pints water*
*1 chicken, weighing 1.25 kg/2½–2¾ lb, cut into serving portions*
*1 medium green pepper, cored, seeded and thinly sliced*
*1 medium red pepper, cored, seeded and thinly sliced*
*2 carrots, peeled and thinly sliced*
*8 mushrooms, sliced*
**Sauce:**
*200 ml/⅓ pint soy sauce*
*450 ml/¾ pint water*
*4 spring onions*
*2 teaspoons crushed garlic*
*1 tablespoon sugar*
*2 teaspoons freshly ground black pepper*
*1 tablespoon crushed fresh root ginger\**
*½ teaspoon monosodium glutamate\**

### AMERICAN

*3¾ cups water*
*1 chicken, weighing 2½–2¾ lb, cut into serving portions*
*1 medium green pepper, cored, seeded and thinly sliced*
*1 medium red pepper, cored, seeded and thinly sliced*
*2 carrots, peeled and thinly sliced*
*8 mushrooms, sliced*
**Sauce:**
*1 cup soy sauce*
*2 cups water*
*4 scallions*
*2 teaspoons crushed garlic*
*1 tablespoon sugar*
*2 teaspoons freshly ground black pepper*
*1 tablespoon crushed fresh ginger root\**
*½ teaspoon msg\**

### METHOD

Bring the water to the boil in a large pan, add the chicken pieces and boil for 5 minutes.

Meanwhile, make the sauce: put all the ingredients in a pan, stir well, then bring to the boil.

Drain the chicken and add to the sauce with the peppers, carrots and mushrooms. Bring back to the boil. then lower the heat and simmer for 20 minutes or until the chicken is tender. Serve hot.
SERVES 4

**Yuk Kew; Shikumchee**

## Shikumchee
### Sweet Spinach with Garlic

For best results, always use the youngest and freshest spinach available.

METRIC/IMPERIAL

*750 g/1½ lb fresh spinach leaves*
*3 tablespoons soy sauce*
*1 tablespoon sesame seeds\**
*1 tablespoon sesame seed oil\**
*1 tablespoon crushed garlic*
*2 tablespoons chopped spring onions*
*2 teaspoons sugar*
*2 pinches of monosodium glutamate\**
*salt*

**To garnish:**
*carrot, boo\* and parsley (optional)*

AMERICAN

*1½ lb fresh spinach leaves*
*3 tablespoons soy sauce*
*1 tablespoon sesame seeds\**
*1 tablespoon sesame seed oil\**
*1 tablespoon crushed garlic*
*2 tablespoons chopped scallions*
*2 teaspoons sugar*
*2 pinches of msg\**
*salt*

**To garnish:**
*carrot, boo\* and parsley (optional)*

METHOD

Wash the spinach and discard the stalks. Bring a large pan of water to the boil, add the spinach and cook for exactly 3 minutes. Drain thoroughly, then chop roughly.

Place the spinach on a serving place and sprinkle the remaining ingredients on top. Garnish, if liked, with flower shapes, cut from carrot, boo and parsley. Serve hot.
SERVES 4

## Kal Bee Jim

### Beef Spareribs in Tangy Sauce with Chestnuts

METRIC/IMPERIAL

*750 g/1½ lb beef spareribs trimmed of*
*fat and cut into pieces 5 cm/2 inches*
*wide*
**Sauce:**
*4 tablespoons soy sauce*
*450 ml/¾ pint water*
*2 teaspoons sesame seed oil\**
*2 teaspoons sesame seeds\**
*1 tablespoon sugar*
*1 teaspoon freshly ground black*
*pepper*
*1 teaspoon crushed garlic*
*100 g/4 oz cooked chestnuts, finely*
*chopped*
*100 g/4 oz bamboo shoot*

AMERICAN

*1½ lb beef ribs or back ribs, trimmed of*
*fat and cut into pieces 2 inches wide*
**Sauce:**
*¼ cup soy sauce*
*2 cups water*
*2 teaspoons sesame seed oil\**
*2 teaspoons sesame seeds\**
*1 tablespoon sugar*
*1 teaspoon freshly ground black*
*pepper*
*1 teaspoon crushed garlic*
*8 large cooked chestnuts, finely*
*chopped*
*1 cup bamboo shoot*

METHOD

Parboil the beef for 5 minutes, then drain
and set aside.

To make the sauce: Put all the ingredients in a pan and stir well. Bring to
the boil, then add the beef and bring
back to the boil. Lower the heat and
simmer gently for 30 minutes or until the
beef is tender. Serve hot.
SERVES 4

## Yuk Kwe

### Spiced Raw Beef

This is the Korean version of Steak
Tartare. The egg yolk is broken at the
table and mixed with the beef, pear and
cucumber. Use either chopsticks or a
fork for mixing and eating. If partially
frozen beef is used, it will be easier to
obtain very thin slices.

METRIC/IMPERIAL

*450 g/1 lb beef fillet or topside*
*2 teaspoons sugar*
*2 teaspoons sesame seeds\**
*1 tablespoon sesame seed oil\**
*1 tablespoon crushed garlic*
*½ teaspoon monosodium glutamate\**
*salt*
*4 egg yolks (optional)*
**To garnish:**
*2 small hard pears, peeled, cored*
*and sliced into matchstick strips*
*12 diagonal slices of cucumber, cut into*
*matchstick strips*
*parsley sprigs*
*carrot (optional)*

AMERICAN

*1 lb fillet or beef top round*
*2 teaspoons sugar*
*2 teaspoons sesame seeds\**
*1 tablespoon sesame seed oil\**
*1 tablespoon crushed garlic*
*½ teaspoon msg\**
*salt*
*4 egg yolks (optional)*
**To garnish:**
*2 small hard pears, peeled, cored and*
*sliced into matchstick strips*
*12 diagonal slices of cucumber, cut into*
*matchstick strips*
*parsley sprigs*
*carrot (optional)*

METHOD

Cut the meat into very thin slices no more
than 3 mm/⅛ inch thick, then cut the slices
into matchstick strips. Place in a bowl
with the remaining ingredients, except
the egg yolks. Mix together, using the
hands (their warmth will thaw the meat),
then divide into 4 portions.

Divide the pear and cucumber strips
equally between 4 individual serving
plates, arranging them in separate piles.
Place the meat mixture on top. If using
egg yolks, mould the mixture into a neat
shape and put an egg yolk in each hollow.
Garnish with parsley sprigs and carrot
'flowers', if liked. Serve raw.
SERVES 4

## Chap Chee

### Spicy Vegetables

METRIC/IMPERIAL

*900 ml/1½ pints water*
*200 g/7 oz bean threads\**
*3 tablespoons vegetable oil*
*225 g/8 oz Chinese leaves, shredded*
*salt*
*1 large carrot, peeled and cut*
*diagonally into matchstick strips*
*100 g/4 oz fresh spinach leaves,*
*cooked and roughly chopped*
*8 medium Chinese dried mushrooms*
*soaked in warm water for 30*
*minutes, then drained (optional)*
**Sauce:**
*1 tablespoon sesame seed oil\**
*1 tablespoon soy sauce*
*2 teaspoons sugar*
*2 teaspoons sesame seeds\**
*½ teaspoon salt*
*½ teaspoon monosodium glutamate\**

AMERICAN

*3¾ cups water*
*3 small packages bean threads\**
*3 tablespoons vegetable oil*
*½ lb bok choy, shredded*
*salt*
*1 large carrot, peeled and cut*
*diagonally into matchstick strips*
*¼ lb fresh spinach leaves, cooked and*
*roughly chopped*
*8 medium Chinese dried mushrooms,\**
*soaked in warm water for 30*
*minutes, then drained (optional)*
**Sauce:**
*1 tablespoon sesame seed oil\**
*1 tablespoon soy sauce*
*2 teaspoons sugar*
*2 teaspoons sesame seeds\**
*½ teaspoon salt*
*½ teaspoon msg\**

METHOD

Bring the water to the boil in a pan, add
the bean threads and boil for 3 minutes.
Drain and set aside.

Heat 2 tablespoons of the oil in a pan.
When very hot, add the Chinese leaves
(bok choy) and salt to taste and fry for 2
minutes, tossing the leaves constantly.
Remove from the pan and set aside.

Heat the remaining oil in the pan. Add
the carrot and fry for 1 minute, stirring.
Return the Chinese leaves (bok choy) to
the pan, add the spinach and mushrooms
if using, and cook for a further 2 minutes,
shaking the pan constantly.

To make the sauce: Put all the ingredients in a pan and stir well. Bring to
the boil, then add to the vegetable mixture with the bean threads. Mix well and
heat through. Serve immediately.
SERVES 4

# Glossary

**Aburage** [JAPAN] Fried soybean cake.
**Agar-agar** [BURMA/CHINA/JAPAN/ MALAYSIA] Known as *kanten* in Japan. A kind of seaweed available in long white strands or powdered form. Use in very small quantities as a little will quickly set a large volume of liquid. It has almost no taste or colour. Powdered gelatine may be substituted, allowing 4 tablespoons gelatine to 25 g/1 oz agar-agar. Available from Oriental stores and some health food shops.
**Akamiso** [JAPAN] Soybean paste, reddish brown in colour.
**Azuki** [JAPAN] Red beans. Sweetened azuki beans are available in cans.

**Balachan** [MALAYSIA]
see **Terasi**.
**Bean curd** [CHINA/KOREA/ INDONESIA/MALAYSIA] Known as *tahu* or *taukwa* in Indonesia/Malaysia. Made of puréed and pressed soya beans, its texture is like soft cheese. Sold in cakes, 7.5 cm/3 inches square and 2.5 cm/1 inch thick. It will keep fresh for several days if stored in water in the refrigerator. Dried bean curd skin is also available, in packets of sheets or sticks: Soak in cold water overnight or in warm water for 1 hour before using. Available from Oriental stores and some health food shops.
**Beans, salted** [INDONESIA/MALAYSIA/ THAILAND] Known as *tao chiew* in Thailand, *tauco* in Indonesia/Malaysia. Black soya beans which have been steamed, spiced and preserved in salt Sold in cans and packets. Should be transferred to an airtight jar and stored in the refrigerator; will then keep for up to 1 year.
**Bean sauce** [CHINA] Also known as yellow bean sauce and brown or black bean sauce. Crushed yellow soya beans, mixed to a paste with flour, vinegar, spices and salt. Sold in jars and cans.
**Bean threads** [CHINA/JAPAN/KOREA/ THAILAND/VIETNAM]
see **Mung bean threads**.
**Belimbing wuluh** [MALAYSIA] A sour kind of fresh fruit. Common in South-East Asia, but unobtainable in Europe and U.S.A. Lemon, lime or rhubarb may be used as a substitute.
**Beni-shoga** [JAPAN] Red salt preserved ginger.

**Blacan** [MALAYSIA]
see **Terasi**.
**Boo** [BURMA/KOREA] A long white radish resembling a parsnip in appearance. It has a mild flavour and English radishes should not be used as a substitute. Available in high-class greengrocers or in areas where there are Chinese, Japanese and Korean inhabitants. If unobtainable, use tender white turnips as a substitute.
**Buah keras** [MALAYSIA]
see **Kemiri**.
**Bumbu** [MALAYSIA] A general term for any mixture of ingredients that gives a strong flavour to a dish. It can refer to the dry ingredients, or to the sauces that are made from them.
**Bun tâu** [VIETNAM]
see **Mung bean threads**.

**Cabé rawit** [MALAYSIA] Small, very hot chillis – red, green or sometimes white in colour.
**Candlenut** [MALAYSIA]
see **Kemiri**.
**Cellophane noodles** [CHINA/JAPAN/ KOREA/THAILAND/VIETNAM]
see **Mung bean threads**.
**Chinese parsley**
see **Cilantro**, see **Coriander**.
**Citronella**
see **Lemon grass**.
**Cloud ear** [CHINA]
see **Wood ear**.
**Coconut milk** [MALAYSIA/THAILAND/ VIETNAM] Known as *santen* in Indonesia and Malaysia. Best made from fresh coconuts: Grate the flesh of 1 coconut into a bowl, pour on 600 ml/1 pint/2½ cups boiling water, then leave to stand for about 30 minutes. Squeeze the flesh, then strain before using. This quantity will make a thick coconut milk, add more or less water as required. Desiccated (shredded) coconut can be used instead of fresh coconut: Use 350 g/12 oz/4 cups to 600 ml/1 pint/2½ cups boiling water. Use freshly made coconut milk within 24 hours. Canned coconut milk is also available.
**Coconut sugar** [THAILAND] Also known as palm sugar. Brown sugar may be substituted.
**Coriander** [ALL COUNTRIES] Also known as *pak chee* [Thailand], *ngô* [Vietnam], Chinese parsley and cilantro. Widely used in South-East Asian cooking

in the form of leaves, roots, stems, seeds and powder. In Vietnam, Laos and Kampuchea, only the fresh leaves and stems are used and are indispensable to these cuisines. The fresh leaves are usually chopped, the roots are washed and dried, then grated. The roots will keep in an airtight jar. Can easily be grown outdoors in summer. Parsley is often substituted for fresh coriander although it does not impart the same flavour. Available at Oriental and Continental specialist stores.
**Creamed coconut** [BURMA/MALAYSIA/ THAILAND] Sold in packets, tubs, slabs and cakes. More concentrated than coconut milk. Cut up roughly before using, then heat gently with water added until melted, stirring frequently. Use as coconut milk.
**Culantro** [VIETNAM] Also known as *ngo tay*. A member of the coriander family. Each stem has 1 elongated leaf which grows in a dark green cluster.

**Daikon** [JAPAN] A long white radish. Sometimes referred to as the 'workhorse' of the Japanese diet, it is a basic vegetable in Japanese cooking. Use both raw and cooked.
**Daun jeruk purut** [MALAYSIA] The leaf of a fruit similar to a lime.
**Daun kunyit** [MALAYSIA] Turmeric leaf.
**Dried mushrooms** [CHINA/JAPAN/ KOREA/THAILAND/VIETNAM]
see **Mushrooms, dried**.

**Ebi** [MALAYSIA] Tiny uncooked dried shrimps.

**Fiddlehead ferns** [MALAYSIA]
see **Paku**.
**Fish paste** [KAMPUCHEA] A thick paste made from fermented fish or shrimps and salt. Used in small quantities as a relish. Kampuchean fish paste is made from whole preserved anchovies which are strained when required. Available from Oriental stores.
**Fish sauce** [KAMPUCHEA/LAOS/ THAILAND/VIETNAM] Known as *nam pla* in Thailand, *nuoc cham* or *nuoc mam* in Kampuchea, Laos and Vietnam. As important to these schools of cooking as salt is in the West. Prepared from fresh anchovies and salt which are layered in wooden barrels and left to ferment. The

liquid that is drained off initially is light and clear and considered to be the best quality; the two subsequent extractions are darker and of a poorer quality. Available from Oriental stores.

**Five spice powder** [CHINA/MALAYSIA] A reddish-brown aromatic powder, made from a combination of ground spices – anise, fennel, cloves, cinnamon and Szechuan pepper. These spices are also sold as 'five spices', ready-mixed but whole. Will keep indefinitely in an airtight container.

**Galingale** [MALAYSIA/THAILAND/ VIETNAM] Known as *laos* in Malaysia, *kha* in Thailand. It is the root of a plant resembling ginger, creamy white in colour, with a delicate flavour. Used fresh, but only dried galingale is obtainable in the West. Soak in hot water for 1 hour before using in cooking, then remove before serving. Galingale (*laos*) powder is also available.

**Ginger** [ALL COUNTRIES] Fresh root ginger, sometimes referred to as 'green ginger'. Peel before using, then slice, crush or chop finely. To keep fresh: Peel, then wash and place in a jar, cover with pale dry sherry, seal and store in the refrigerator. Ground ginger is not an acceptable substitute, but dried root ginger may be used, in which case the quantity should be decreased as it is sharper in taste.

**Glutinous (sweet) rice** [KAMPUCHEA/LAOS/JAPAN/ MALAYSIA/THAILAND/VIETNAM] Known as *mochigome* in Japan. Also sometimes referred to as 'sticky rice'. Short-grain rice that becomes very sticky when cooked. Used in stuffings, cakes and puddings. In Laos it is used in place of long-grain rice and served with all meals.

**Glutinous (sweet) rice flour** [KAMPUCHEA/LAOS/MALAYSIA/ JAPAN/THAILAND/VIETNAM] Known as *mochiko* in Japan. Made from ground glutinous (sweet) rice. There is no substitute. Obtainable from Chinese supermarkets.

**Gobo** [JAPAN] Edible burdock roots.

**Goma** [JAPAN]
see **Sesame seeds**.

**Goma abura** [JAPAN]
see **Sesame seed oil**.

**Goma jio** [JAPAN] Salted sesame seeds. Dry fry 1 tablespoon black sesame seeds in a hot frying pan (skillet) until they 'jump', shaking the pan constantly. Transfer to a bowl, then sprinkle with

2 teaspoons salt.

**Gula jawa** [MALAYSIA] Also known as *gula malaka*. Brown palm sugar, sold in thin blocks. Demerara or Muscovado sugar may be used as a substitute.

**Gyoza skins** [JAPAN] Round in shape. *Wun tun* (wonton) skins may be used as a substitute.

**Hakusai** [JAPAN]
see **Napa**.

**Harusame** [JAPAN] Soya bean noodles. Can be used instead of mung bean threads if these are unobtainable.

**Hijiki** [JAPAN] Brown algae seaweed.

**Hoi sin (hosin) sauce** [CHINA] Also known as Chinese barbecue sauce. Made from soya beans, flour, sugar, spices and red food colouring. Available in jars or cans from Chinese supermarkets, it will keep for several months in the refrigerator.

**Horapa** [THAILAND] A member of the *ocimum* family, like sweet basil. Use fresh rather than dried. Sweet basil may be used as a substitute.

**Jelly mushrooms** [THAILAND]
see **Wood ear**.

**Kapi** [THAILAND]
see **Terasi**.

**Kasu** [JAPAN] Rice wine lees. Sold in 2.25 kg/5 lb blocks in Asian stores.

**Katsuobushi** [JAPAN]
Dried bonito fish. Used in making Dashi (basic stock).

**Kecap** [INDONESIA/MALAYSIA] Soy sauce. It is darker and sweeter than Chinese dark soy sauce and quite different from Chinese light soy sauce which is very salty.

**Kemiri** [MALAYSIA] Also known as *buah keras* and candlenuts. Used in many South-East Asian dishes. Pale yellow nuts, roughly the same size as chestnuts. They are usually shelled before being exported and the kernels break into fragments. If '2 kemiri' are specified in a recipe, this means the equivalent of 2 whole nuts.

**Kha** [THAILAND]
see **Galingale**.

**Kochujang** [KOREA] Hot bean mash paprika paste. Nearest equivalent is mashed onions and chilli powder fried in oil. Available in cans from Oriental stores.

**Kombu** [JAPAN] Tangle or kelp seaweed. Used in making Dashi (basic stock).

**Konnyaku** [JAPAN] Tuber root cake.

**Laksa** [MALAYSIA]
see **Rice vermicelli**.

**Laos** [MALAYSIA],
see **Galingale**.

**Lemon grass** [BURMA/MALAYSIA/ THAILAND/ VIETNAM] Known as *serai* or *sereh* in Malaysia, *takrai* in Thailand. Also known as *citronella*. Fresh lemon grass is available from Oriental stores. The lower third of the stalk, the bulb-like portion, is the part to use when a recipe specifies 'chopped or sliced lemon grass'. Alternatively, the whole stalk may be bruised and added during cooking, but then it should be removed before serving. Dried lemon grass is a good substitute: Soak in hot water for about 2 hours before using, then remove from the dish before serving. (1 tablespoon dried lemon grass is roughly equivalent to 1 stalk fresh.) Powdered lemon grass is also available.

**Lentil flour** [BURMA] Made from ground or pounded lentils. Can be made at home using an electric blender or pestle and mortar.

**Lime leaves** [THAILAND/VIETNAM] Fresh lime leaves are preferred, but virtually unobtainable in the West. Dried lime leaves are available from Oriental stores.

**Lombok** [MALAYSIA] Chilli. *Lombok merah* are red, *lombok hijau* are green, *lombok rawit* are the hottest and are available in dried form in the West.

**Makrut** [THAILAND] An ugly-looking citrus fruit with very strongly flavoured peel and leaves. The peel is ground with other ingredients in curry pastes and the leaves are used in soup. Lemon leaves can be used as a substitute.

**Matcha** [JAPAN] Powdered green tea used for the traditional Japanese tea ceremony. This tea is made from the most tender tea leaves of the first spring picking, and is processed by a very expensive, tedious method.

**Mint** [THAILAND]
see **Saranae**.

**Mirin** [JAPAN] Sweetened *sake* (rice wine) used in cooking and for seasoning. If unavailable, substitute dry sherry and sugar in the proportion of 4 tablespoons (¼ cup) sherry to 1½ tablespoons sugar.

**Miso** [JAPAN]
see **Soy bean paste**.

**Mochigome** [JAPAN]
see **Glutinous (sweet) rice**.

**Mochiko** [JAPAN],
see **Glutinous (sweet) rice flour**.

**Monosodium glutamate (msg)**
[CHINA/JAPAN/KOREA/THAILAND]
Known as *oji-no-moto* in Korea, *veh t'sin* in China. A chemical compound sometimes known as 'taste essence'. It is used to bring out the natural flavours in food, and is entirely optional in all recipes where it is specified. It is widely used in restaurants, but should be used sparingly at home: ¼-½ teaspoon is ample in any recipe. Obtainable from most Oriental stores.

**Mung beans** [KOREA/VIETNAM] Dried mung beans are very small and green in colour. Dried split peas may be used as a substitute, although mung beans are usually available at good health food shops. When their green husks have been removed, dried mung beans are yellow in colour.

**Mung bean threads** [CHINA/JAPAN/KOREA/THAILAND/VIETNAM] Known as *saifun* in Japan, *wun sen* in Thailand, *bun tâu* in Vietnam. Also known as Chinese bean threads or transparent (cellophane) noodles. They are very fine dried noodles made from mung bean flour. Sold in packets. Soak in water for about 10 minutes before using.

**Mushrooms, dried** [CHINA/JAPAN/KOREA/THAILAND/VIETNAM] Known as dried *shiitake* in Japan. Chinese and Japanese dried mushrooms (lentinus edodes) are sold in plastic bags in Oriental stores. They are very fragrant, and will keep almost indefinitely in an airtight jar. They have an entirely different flavour from their fresh counterparts. Soak in warm water for 30 minutes before using. Ordinary mushrooms do not make a good substitute.

**Mushrooms, dried jelly** [THAILAND]
see **Wood ear.**

**Nam pla** [THAILAND]
see **Fish sauce.**
Napa [JAPAN] This is *hakusai* or Chinese cabbage sometimes referred to as celery cabbage. Not to be confused with Chinese leaves (bok choy). Napa has very delicate leaves and is used both raw and cooked. Bok choy can be used as a substitute.
**Ngapi** [BURMA]
see **Terasi.**
**Ngô** [VIETNAM]
see **Coriander**.
**Ngô tay** [VIETNAM]
see **Culantro**.
**Nori** [JAPAN] Dried seaweed. Often toasted, then shredded and used as a garnish.

**Nuoc cham/Nuoc mam** [KAMPUCHEA/LAOS/VIETNAM]
see **Fish sauce.**

**Oyster sauce** [CHINA] A thickish brown sauce with a rich flavour. Made from oysters and soy sauce. It keeps indefinitely in the refrigerator.

**Pak chee** [THAILAND]
see **Coriander.**
**Paku** [MALAYSIA] Also known as *pakis*. Young edible fern shoots, called 'fiddlehead ferns' in North America. Young curly kale may be used as a substitute.
**Panko** [JAPAN] Coarse breadcrumbs.
**Prawns, dried** [THAILAND] Sold in packets in Chinese supermarkets. Best kind are bright pink in colour because they are the freshest. Rinse before use to remove dirt and excess salt.

**Radish, white Chinese** [BURMA/KOREA]
see **Boo.**
**Rice flour** [BURMA/INDIA/MALAYSIA] Made from ground rice. Can be made at home using an electric blender, coffee mill or pestle and mortar.
**Rice papers, dried** [VIETNAM] Known as *banh trang*. A thin, brittle, disc-like pancake (crêpe). Used in many ways to make spring rolls and as a wrapper for a variety of foods. Must be moistened with water or egg to make them flexible before using. Mostly imported from Thailand and available at Oriental stores.
**Rice powder** [MALAYSIA] Known as *tepung beras*. Extremely fine powdered rice. When specified in a recipe it must be assumed that rice flour may not be used.
**Rice vermicelli** [MALAYSIA/THAILAND/VIETNAM] Known as *laksa* in Malaysia, rice sticks or rice noodles in North America. These are noodles made from rice flour which come in various sizes. In soups, the very thin string-like variety called *bun*, are used. The different sizes can be interchanged in recipes if it is difficult to obtain the exact type specified.
**Rice wine** [CHINA/JAPAN/KOREA/MALAYSIA]
see **Sake.**
**Rijsttafel** [MALAYSIA] Rice table. The name given by the Dutch to a variety of Indonesian dishes that are all served together.
**Rock sugar** [VIETNAM] Known as rock candy in North America. It is crystallized sugar, amber in colour, which is used to give a glaze to certain dishes. 1 lump

rock sugar is equivalent to 1 tablespoon granulated sugar.

**Saifun** [JAPAN]
see **Mung bean threads.**
**Sake** [JAPAN/KOREA] Rice wine. Dry sherry makes an acceptable substitute. Sold in Oriental stores.
**Salam** [MALAYSIA] The leaves of this plant are used extensively in Malaysian cooking. Bay leaves can be used as a substitute.
**Salt fish, dried** [BURMA] Sword fish is the commonest fish used. Rinse well to remove excess salt before using. Available at Oriental stores.
**Sambal ulek** [INDONESIA] Used as an accompaniment and in cooking. Made by crushing fresh red chillis with a little salt: Remove the seeds from the chillis, chop finely then crush with salt using a pestle and mortar. Three chillis will make about 1 tablespoon sambal ulek. Also available ready-prepared in small jars from Oriental stores and some delicatessens.
**Sansho** [JAPAN] *Zanthoxylum pieratum*. Fresh leaves of this bush are used for fragrance and garnish. Powdered sansho, is also available.
**Santen** [MALAYSIA]
see **Coconut milk.**
**Saranae** [THAILAND] Mint. Always use spearmint (*Mentha spicata*) in preference to other types of mint for Thai recipes.
**Saté** [MALAYSIA] Also known as *satay*. A general name for any kind of meat, poultry or fish that is grilled (broiled) on a skewer.
**Serai/Sereh** [MALAYSIA]
see **Lemon grass.**
**Sesame seeds** [BURMA/JAPAN/KOREA/VIETNAM] Known as *goma* in Japan. There are 2 types – white (*kurogoma*) and black (*shirogoma*). Can be used raw or toasted. To toast sesame seeds, dry fry in a hot frying pan (skillet) until they 'jump', shaking the pan constantly.
**Sesame seed oil**
[CHINA/JAPAN/KOREA/THAILAND/VIETNAM] Known as *goma abura* in Japan. A strongly flavoured seasoning oil made from roasted sesame seeds. Used for its fragrance and the flavour it imparts to other foods. Sold in bottles. Keeps indefinitely.
**Shichimi** [JAPAN] A mixture of 7 spices, ground to a spicy hot powder. Not to be confused with Five Spice Powder. Used on noodles and other cooked dishes.
**Shiitake, dried** [JAPAN]
see **Mushrooms, dried.**

**Shiitake, fresh** [JAPAN] Japanese mushrooms, which have an entirely different, more delicate flavour than their dried counterparts. Vitamin-packed and exalted 'the elixir of life' in many Asian countries. Ordinary mushrooms do not make a good substitute.

**Shirataki** [JAPAN] Yam noodles. Sold in cans. Mung bean threads may be substituted.

**Shiromiso** [JAPAN] White soybean paste.

**Shoyu** [JAPAN] Light soy sauce prepared from fermented cooked soya beans, wheat, malt and salt.
Do not substitute Chinese or other *soy* sauces, their flavour is completely different and will spoil Japanese dishes.

**Shrimp-flavoured soy sauce** [BURMA] Also known as fish sauce. It gives a fishy taste to dishes. Ordinary soy sauce can be used as a substitute. Available from Chinese stores.

**Shrimp paste** [BURMA] Made from salted dried shrimps. Greyish pink in colour. Anchovies mixed with a little vinegar may be used as a substitute, but this is not very satisfactory. Available in jars from Chinese stores.

**Shrimps, dried** [BURMA] Available whole, pounded or powdered, from Oriental stores.

**Somen** [JAPAN] Very thin thread-like wheat vermicelli.

**Soy bean paste** [CHINA/JAPAN/KOREA] Known as *miso* in Japan. A basic seasoning made from cooked soya beans, malt and salt. Sold in plastic packs at Oriental stores and some health food shops.

**Split pea flour** [BURMA] Made from ground or pounded split peas. Can be made at home using an electric blender or pestle and mortar.

**Su** [JAPAN] Rice vinegar, distilled from white rice. It has a very sweet aromatic quality and is much milder than cider vinegar. If unobtainable, substitute distilled white vinegar and mix with water. Seasoned rice vinegars, with sugar and monosodium glutamate added, are also available.

**Szechuan preserved vegetable** [CHINA] A root vegetable pickled in salt and chilli, which is therefore very hot and salty to the taste. Sold in cans, it should be transferred to an airtight jar once opened, then it will keep for several months in the refrigerator.

**Tahu/Taukwa** [INDONESIA/MALAYSIA] see **Bean curd.**

**Takrai** [THAILAND] see **Lemon grass.**

**Tamarind** [BURMA/INDIA/MALAYSIA/ THAILAND/VIETNAM] Also known as *asam* or *assem*. An acid-flavoured fruit resembling a bean pod. Sold as dried tamarind pulp in blocks and is dark brown in colour. The dried tamarind pulp must be made into tamarind water before using: Soak about 25 g/1 oz tamarind pulp in 300 ml/½ pint 1¼ cups water for 5 to 10 minutes, then squeeze, strain and use the water. The longer the tamarind is left to soak, the stronger the flavour. The amount of tamarind pulp and water can be adjusted according to the thickness required; the thicker the water, the more sour it tastes. Lime, lemon or mango juice or vinegar may be used as substitutes but the flavour of the finished dish will not be the same. Tamarind paste is also available, packaged in plastic bags. It should be refrigerated once opened, in which case it will keep indefinitely. Both tamarind pulp and tamarind paste are available at Oriental stores.

**Tao chiew** [THAILAND] see **Beans, salted.**

**Tauco** [INDONESIA/MALAYSIA] see **Beans, salted.**

**Tepung Beras** [MALAYSIA] see **Rice powder.**

**Terasi** [MALAYSIA] Also known as *balachan/blacan* (Malaysia), *kapi* (Thailand) and *ngapi* (Burma). A kind of pungent shrimp paste, used in very small quantities. Depending on the recipe in which it is used, it can be crushed with spices to make a paste which is then sautéed in oil. Alternatively, it may be grilled (broiled) or fried first, then added to other ingredients.

**Tofu** [JAPAN] Soybean cake.

**Tonkatsu sauce** [JAPAN] A commercially prepared thick brown sauce made from fruit and vegetables combined with spices and seasonings. Soy sauce or ketchup may be used as substitutes.

**Transparent noodles** [CHINA/JAPAN/ KOREA/THAILAND/VIETNAM] see **Mung bean threads.**

**Tree ear** [CHINA/THAILAND/ VIETNAM] see **Wood ear.**

**Tung chai** [THAILAND] Tiensin preserved vegetables. Obtainable from Chinese supermarkets.

**Udon** [JAPAN] A thick, broad noodle made from flour and water (without eggs).

**Wakame** [JAPAN] Lobe leaf seaweed. Traditionally, the heavy vein is removed. The vein can be eaten, but it is rather chewy.

**Wasabi** [JAPAN] A green horseradish grated from the root of the Eutrema Wasabi. Use green horseradish powder which is very pungent and hot for convenience, as fresh wasabi is both difficult to obtain and very expensive. Dry mustard mixed to a paste with a little water may be used as a substitute.

**Water chestnut** [CHINA/JAPAN] A walnut-sized bulb with brown skin; the inside flesh is white and crisp. Canned water chesnuts are ready-peeled and will keep for about 1 month in the refrigerator.

**Wood ear** [CHINA/THAILAND/ VIETNAM] Known as tree ear in North America, cloud ear in China, jelly mushrooms in Thailand. A dried tree fungus. Use only in small quantities. Soak in warm water for about 20 minutes before using, until they become glutinous and crinkly. The dried fungi will keep indefinitely. Available at Chinese supermarkets.

**Wun sen** [THAILAND] see **Mung bean threads.**

**Wun tun skins** [KOREA/MALAYSIA] Known as wonton skins in North America. Paper-thin squares or circles of dough. Can be made at home, or bought ready-rolled and trimmed at Chinese supermarkets. Store in the refrigerator or freezer.

# Index

## ACKNOWLEDGEMENTS

Food photography by Robert Golden
Food prepared by Caroline Ellwood
Japanese food prepared by Susumu Okado
Photographic stylist: Antonia Gaunt

The publishers would like to thank the following individuals and organisations for their kind permission to reproduce the location photographs in this book:
Alan Hutchinson 66; Sonia Halliday Photographs (Jane Taylor) 84; Korean Embassy 142-3; Roland Michaud 142-3; Vision International (Paolo Koch) 85; Zefa (Bitsch) 38-9, (Schmidt) 7, (Starfoto) 53, (Steinhaus) 122-3.

The publishers would also like to express their gratitude to the following companies for the loan of accessories for photography: Ajimura Japanese Restaurant, 27 Endell St WC2; Collet's Chinese Gallery & Bookshop, 40 Great Russell St WC1; Craftsmen Potters Shop, William Blake House, Marshall St W1; Frida, 111 Long Acre WC2; Ikeda Japanese Restaurant, 30 Brook St W1; Mitsukiku, 15 Old Brompton Road SW7; New Neal Street Shop, 23 Neal St WC2; Nice Irma's Floating Carpet, 46 Goodge St W1; Paul Wu Ltd, 64 Long Acre WC2.